WHERE ELK ROAM

Conservation and Biopolitics of Our National Elk Herd

BRUCE L. SMITH, PHD

Bruce Smith

LP

LYONS PRESS
Guilford, Connecticut
An imprint of Globe Pequot Press

ALSO BY BRUCE L. SMITH

Imperfect Pasture: A Century of Change at the National Elk Refuge

Wildlife on the Wind: A Field Biologist's Journey and an Indian Reservation's Renewal

Lyons Press is an imprint of Globe Pequot Press.

Text design: Sheryl P. Kober
Layout: Kirsten Livingston
Project editor: Kristen Mellitt

Map on p. 23 by Daniel Lloyd © Morris Book Publishing, LLC

Library of Congress Cataloging-in-Publication Data is available on file.

ISBN 978-0-7627-7074-8

Printed in the United States of America

10 9 8 7 6 5 4 3 2 1

CONTENTS

INTRODUCTION

CERTAIN SPECIES OF ANIMALS CAPTURE OUR IMAGINATION. They possess aesthetic, spiritual, cultural, utilitarian, or economic values to humans who have looked upon them with wonder or to plunder. Archaeological evidence suggests this is true from the dawning of humankind. Tarantulas and crocodiles, great white sharks and great whales, Andean condors and bald eagles, African elephants and Bengal tigers—like magnets, they repel, attract, or captivate us. On the North American continent, one such species is the elk, or wapiti.

I recall first learning of elk from the *National Geographic* documentary, *Grizzly*. Scientists John and Frank Craighead were filmed in Yellowstone National Park studying another of North America's icons, the grizzly bear. Sharing the grand stage of the world's first national park were herds of elk, regal beasts with dark manes, sweeping antlers, and sculpted bodies three or four times the size of the white-tailed deer in Michigan where I grew up. Amid steaming geysers, snowcapped peaks, and silver-tipped grizzlies, the elk made an indelible impression on this 1960s adolescent.

As one of the world's largest and most social deer species, elk are of immense interest to wildlife enthusiasts. As bulls tend harems, their eerie bugling and clashing of antlers provide millions of visitors to Western national parks an autumn show that rivals sights on the African veldt. For eleven million big-game hunters in the United States, deer and elk are the most popular quarry. Recovered from a low of fifty thousand at the turn of the twentieth century to about one million in North America today, elk are hunted in twenty-six states and Canadian provinces. So treasured are elk for viewing, sport, and table fare that populations have been reestablished in Arkansas, Kentucky, North Carolina, Tennessee, Wisconsin, and Ontario during the past twenty-five years. Additional resettlements are being considered elsewhere.

It's no accident that elk are found largely in Western wildlands. Unlike its ubiquitous cousin the white-tailed deer, the elk is less well suited to places where man wields a heavy hand on the land. Elk need room to roam. Only two hundred years ago, elk were the most widely distributed of the continent's deer. Millions ranged from Atlantic to Pacific coasts, from Alaska to Mexico. Then a mélange of human exploitation, competition, and habitat fragmentation ravaged their numbers and shrank their range. Had America not discovered an ecological conscience, elk and most other large mammals may well have vanished a century ago. Instead, wildlife conservation on a national scale ripened as one of America's most significant and exported inventions.

When President Theodore Roosevelt proclaimed Pelican Island the first national wildlife refuge in 1903, he launched an unparalleled addition to the U.S.'s conservation lands. More than a century later, a system of national wildlife refuges—553 and counting—enriches every state. Each refuge is filled with wondrous plant and animal diversity, a tapestry of nature's handiwork. Each plays a role in preserving breeding range, wintering grounds, migratory pathways, and endangered species. Nothing elsewhere in the world rivals this 150-million-acre archipelago of protected habitats. These lands where wildlife receives priority are Americans' lands too. Over forty million of us visit a refuge annually. There we find recreational and educational opportunities and inspiration from nature at work.

Among the first was the National Elk Refuge, established in 1912 in a northwest Wyoming valley called Jackson Hole. This modest safe haven, together with Yellowstone, the world's first national park, became the nucleus for the rescue and restoration of elk. Perhaps the largest in the nation, the Jackson elk herd remains emblematic of an American triumph in conservation.

So it's ironic that the Jackson herd's well-being now appears vulnerable to its own success. For some twenty-five thousand elk scattered north to south through western Wyoming, the very winter feeding programs that originally helped save elk now foster increasingly pernicious problems. Elk packed into feedgrounds damage plant communities, indirectly impacting other animal species. But it's their own welfare that is at risk from diseases that might spread among the elk like colds in a daycare center. Chronic wasting disease (CWD), a newly emerged brain disorder that's fatal to elk and other deer species, is marching ever closer to thousands of Wyoming elk. Once it arrives, no one can be sure of the outcome for the animals and those who value them.

Scarcely an issue or challenge confronting elk—and therefore elk managers—is not faced in Jackson Hole, but a century-old paradigm of feeding more animals than winter habitat can support is unique to western Wyoming's elk management. Among the questions explored in the following pages: Is winter feeding warranted despite the ecological disorder it fosters? Should persistent diseases at feedgrounds be confronted as symptoms of human intervention or as unavoidable by-products of an unchangeable socioeconomic system? Can hunting in a national park and wildlife refuge be justified to afford economic rewards to local communities?

My perspective on these issues is shaped by my twenty-two years of experience and research as the National Elk Refuge biologist, but perhaps more importantly by my passion for wildlife and wild places. My purpose is to bring greater clarity to perhaps the most complex wildlife management situation on the continent.

CHAPTER I

Mad Elk

"But I don't want to go among mad people," Alice remarked.
"Oh, you can't help that," said the Cat. "We're all mad here. I'm mad.
You're mad."
"How do you know I'm mad?" said Alice.
"You must be," said the Cat, "or you wouldn't have come here."
　　—LEWIS CARROLL, 1865, *ALICE'S ADVENTURES IN WONDERLAND*

FEBRUARY 2004

The hayrack's steel runners clatter over frozen ruts from the previous days' feeding. Dressed in barn coat, leather chaps, and hay-tinged, crumpled Stetson, driver Royce calls to the team, "Chub, Coaley." The coal-black pair of Percherons—nearly two tons of chiseled horseflesh—speed up with a lurch, nearly sending three of us tumbling from our perch atop three-deep stacked bales of hay. The closest of eight hundred elk skitter away, momentarily alarmed at the sudden flurry of the sleigh, or perhaps the unfamiliar human voices chattering above the mewing and coos of the herd.

We pass a gnarled clump of russet willows a stone's throw from the Gros Ventre River. Flanked by dark, forested hillsides to the south and by sage-studded foothills and gray, lavender, and paprika cliffs to the north, the river winds westward toward Jackson Hole. Beyond where the Gros Ventre pours into the Snake, the Tetons jut nearly fourteen thousand feet skyward, bold and austere in their March cloak of snow. It's a scene worthy of Thomas Moran's, Conrad Schwiering's, and Ansel Adams' considerable talents.

Rick, the other half of Royce's feed team, swings a hay hatchet, popping bales open and rolling sheaves of sweet-smelling grass to opposite sides of the creaking sleigh. Elk bustle behind, chirping and trotting, inhaling the morning meal.

"This is good," I say softly. Royce eases back the leather reins. The elk look with interest at the hayrack strewn with passengers, then file just yards from us toward the trailing twin lines of hay.

"Okay, let's find a younger cow," I remind everyone.

In a huddle of bodies to the right, I spot a prime target. Tawny brown sides contrast sharply with her chocolate head, belly, lower legs, and flowing rust-tinged mane. The vestige of a tail—smaller than a mule deer's—blends perfectly into a pale orange rump patch. But it's her taut hide, youthful face, and the smart manner of carrying herself that attract my attention as she strides past several larger cows and two calves. This energetic animal, well short of her prime, promises years of useful data about where and how she spends her seasons.

As anticipation prickles my neck, my mind drifts off like elk calls on the breeze. As a boy hunting rabbits in Michigan, I had never imagined that my life could lead here: living in this mountain paradise, as the National Elk Refuge biologist, conserving the premier elk herd in North America with catch-and-release hunting a stock tool of my trade. Now, barely two weeks from retirement, this cow might be the last of these magnificent beasts I'll ever handle. But her future and that of the herd remains unclear, even uncertain. *Have I done enough?*

Steve and Doug, wildlife biologists for the State of Wyoming, glance at me, then in the direction of my gaze. "You got one?" Doug asks.

"Yeah," I answer, regaining the moment. I pluck a dart from the plastic case tucked in the chest pocket of my coveralls. Slipping the bolt back, I chamber the dart—a three-inch aluminum cylinder tipped with a sturdy inch-and-a-half-long needle. I loaded this one and three others at six-thirty this morning in Jackson, an hour before our drive to the trailhead and fourteen-mile snowmobile run to the Patrol Cabin feedground.

After locking the bolt, I rest my left forearm and rifle on my left knee, then find her in the scope.

"Which one?" Doug asks.

I nudge the rifle barrel forward. "That slick cow with the reddish mane. There. She just looked at us."

Little does she know that her day's about to turn like none before. By chance and chance alone, she'll become a marker of the Gros Ventre elk's fortunes.

"Whoa-a-a," Royce shushes when the sleigh nudges forward with a jerk. The horses settle. Now all eyes flit from me to the reddish-maned elk, drifting among two dozen others.

I scoot my butt across the bale to gain a more relaxed rest for the rifle. Just then she stops, and the traffic between us clears out. The scope's crosshairs find the big rump muscles. With instinct from past repetitions, I raise the intended point of impact five inches to compensate for the dart's drop at thirty-five yards.

Crack! sounds the .22 cartridge, and a flurry of hooves prattle across packed snow. In moments, eight hundred bewildered elk, detecting nothing further awry, return to munching hay or threading toward the sleigh's mother lode.

"Time?" I ask.

"Ten, forty-six, fifty-seven," Doug replies.

All five of us watch the silver cylinder bob in her hip as the cow stretches backward and sniffs at the intrusion. Unable to reach it, she looks intently at us, then dissolves into the throng.

I tug back the sleeve from my wristwatch. It's now a hair past ten fifty. She should go down in another five minutes. "Let's circle right so we can keep an eye on her," I call.

"Hey Chub, hey Coaley," Royce prods. The team steps out, and elk part like skiffs in the path of a Lake Superior ore boat. Amid the staccato jostling of others, she appears frozen in her tracks with nose tipped up.

Two minutes more and I see the first signs. Her ears droop; her hips buckle and recover. Then she lists in slow motion to her left. Just before tumbling over, she recovers, juts her nose skyward, and squats back on her haunches. The elk around her dance nervously away.

Rick chuckles, "Looks like she's going to sit like a dog."

Then she drops in a heap to the ground.

"Twelve minutes," Doug announces.

That's a bit longer than average, but an average is made up of bigger and smaller numbers, I muse. How much of the drug blew back, how much found the bloodstream and wasn't bound up in fat, and other annoying vagaries—all influence drug induction. I'd seen elk go down in two minutes with chance IV injections. A few took longer than this one.

Royce prods the horses.

"Hey, Royce. Let's just wait here until she's fully under. Another couple minutes and she'll be more manageable."

As the sleigh halts ten yards behind her, Rick, Steve, Doug, and I climb off. I slip the elastic strap of a neoprene blindfold over her ears. Then in unison, we tuck her legs and roll her onto her brisket so her breathing won't be impaired by the weight of her ruminant stomach. Its soupy contents may weigh sixty pounds or more.

We fasten a radio collar around her neck and check its performance with my telemetry receiver, garnish her left ear with a coded metal ear tag, and assess her body condition. Rolling down her lower lip, I find she has all eight permanent incisors.

"Minor wear on the crowns of the premolars," I tell Doug, who has been recording the details on a clipboard-held form. "I'd say about four years old. What do you think?" and I scoot out of the way so he can look.

At the backpack, I unwrap and twist a sixteen-gauge hypodermic needle onto a ten-cubic-centimeter plastic syringe. "Just straighten her neck and rest her head on your knee, Rick."

Approaching an immobilized elk on the Patrol Cabin feedground
(Mark Gocke, Wyoming Game and Fish Department)

Kneeling at her side, I press my fingers into her neck and feel for the cord-like jugular hidden beneath hide and her glossy flow of mane. Palpating, I feel the blood pool and angle the needle forward to slip it through the skin and into the bloodstream. After the syringe has filled, I empty the ten milliliters of burgundy liquid into a labeled glass Vacutainer and pack it away. Finally, I fetch a vial of naltrexone and draw 1.3 milliliters from the inverted glass vial. This will reverse the effects of the potent narcotic that immobilized her muscles and sedated her.

"This will take just two minutes. As soon as I've injected her, you can pull off the blindfold," I advise Rick.

Steve and Rick have kept her upright, Steve straddling her back, Rick supporting her head and neck. "If she only knew how well she'd been treated," I tell them.

But maybe she does. We talk softly, cognizant that on some level in her state of anesthesia her ear twitches show she's aware of us. An occasional jerk of her leg muscles suggests some signals are crossing the synapses. But without the reversal drug, she'd be unable to function for several hours.

Doug jots the time as I poke the needle into her rump. I drop the syringe into the sharps container, and stuff the drug kit and telemetry receiver into my backpack. While the others retreat to the sled, I hesitate and turn back to elk #528. We call her Des, Doug's offering as tribute to the office manager in his Pinedale office. I crouch beside her and brush my hand from the silky mane back to the warm rise and fall of her flank. After capturing over four hundred elk, some two or three times to replace failing radios, I'm still awed by this. *How remarkable to place my hands on this wild beast.* Nearly five hundred pounds of living animal, with melon-size heart, and lungs and diaphragm several times the size of my own. Each breath expands her barrel-like chest to nourish muscles and organs with oxygen-enriched blood, some of which I now carry in glass to test for disease and to see if the miracle of new elk life grows in her uterus.

Her ears begin to turret. Then her head comes up. *Time to go.* In a minute forty seconds, #528 is back on her feet. She looks curiously at us for several pensive seconds, then bolts away in search of hay.

Fifteen months earlier, in December 2002, I boarded my return flight from Madison, Wisconsin. A woman in her fifties, with a pile of sculpted hair atop her head, took the seat next to mine. After the DC10 was airborne, we struck up a conversation.

"Do you live in Madison?" she asked.

"No. I was here on business," I replied. "And you?"

"Yes, my husband and I live on the outskirts. I'm on my way to Minnesota to visit my grandchildren." She radiated the joy of someone visiting small children for whom she had no responsibilities.

"That's nice, that you are close enough to visit them with a short flight. Do they live in the Twin Cities?"

"Oh, no. They like the country where there's lots of open space and wildlife. I suppose my daughter got that from me. I was raised on a farm."

"Like you, I was raised in the country. I think that had a lot to do with me becoming a wildlife biologist."

"Oh, was your meeting in Madison about wildlife?" she asked with genuine curiosity.

"Yes. A group of state and federal scientists and veterinarians were discussing a disease that's threatening deer and elk in North America. It's of real concern here in Wisconsin."

"In Wisconsin?"

"Yes, your Department of Natural Resources is trying to stop its spread. They're giving out extra hunting permits to reduce deer numbers, and testing the animals for the disease. It's called chronic wasting disease, or CWD for short."

"Oh, I've been reading about that in the papers. And it's been on TV. I can't tell you how those reports upset me. Is the disease really as bad as it sounds?"

Never could I have imagined that my conservation career would take this turn—working with one of the world's premier wildlife populations, but watching as a dreadful disease crept closer. As CWD spread, the situation had every ingredient for epidemic media coverage: the potential for disaster, a charismatic victim, conflicting government interests, and plenty of people speculating contradictory outcomes. It left a bewildered public unsure what to think. But neither the specter of dying animals nor growing unease was going away. One upshot was my assignment in Madison, and other CWD meetings to follow.

"I'm afraid so. It kills deer, and also elk, the animals that I work with mostly. Once they're infected, death is certain."

"How did this happen?"

"You may have heard of the mad cow disease problem that England suffered in the 1990s."

"Oh yes, where hundreds of sick cows were killed by the British government?"

"That's right. Actually it was more like two hundred thousand cattle.[1] It was an economic disaster for their livestock industry—lots of dead cows and horrible press."

"I never understood why it was called mad cow."

"The technical name is bovine spongiform encephalopathy, or BSE. It's a disease that slowly destroys the brain, giving it a spongy appearance under a microscope. Mad cow refers to one of the symptoms. Diseased animals lose their motor skills. They crash into things, fall down, and basically lose their wits. Eventually they waste away and die from degeneration of their central nervous system."

"How horrible!" She leaned closer and continued in a hushed voice. "I remember seeing those pathetic animals lying on the ground kicking. They were pushing and picking them up in the buckets of big tractors. So why did they get it? Didn't sheep have something to do with it?"

"That's right," I said and explained what I knew about mad cow disease. It's one of a family of creepy brain disorders that have been described as making Ebola look like chicken pox. The group is referred to as transmissible spongiform encephalopathies, or TSEs. They affect species as varied as cattle, deer, mink, monkeys, and sheep. Scientists once thought that each species had its own unique strain, but now we know that in some cases it can be transmitted between species.

These are not your garden-variety diseases. They aren't caused by bacteria, or viruses, or larger parasites attacking the body, with the immune system in response rushing to the scene to kill or deactivate the invader. Instead, TSEs are caused by a rogue form of an animal's own tissue, brain proteins called prions. When these aberrant prions invade an animal, they can cause healthy brain proteins to deform. Because prions don't contain DNA, animal immune systems don't recognize them as foreign. So the invading prions go unmolested as they alter normal brain proteins. The result is equivalent to death of brain tissue. Eventual death of the animal may take months.

"Oh, my God. And then other animals get it."

I realized that I'd been on a roll, fired up by three days of meetings with other equally concerned scientists and veterinarians about how CWD's emergence may play out. "I'm sorry if I've disturbed you with the details of this."

"Oh, no. It's really very interesting . . . but it's also very upsetting. I don't think many people know much about it, except for the killing and burning of all those cows."

"You said you were raised on a farm. May I ask, did your family raise cattle?"

"Dairy cows."

"Now I see why you have a special interest in this."

"Something like this would've put our farm out of business. Just like that," she said with a sweep of her arm. "But it's not in the U.S., right?"

"No, there's no evidence of it here. And the U.S. has banned importation of suspect animal products from Britain and other European countries that also have cases of mad cow."

"Like what kinds of products?"

"Well, this gets back to your question about sheep. The history of TSEs begins in Europe in the 1700s. That's when shepherds described a disease in sheep we now call scrapie."

"Scrapie. I've heard of that."

I explained that scrapie is like mad cow disease. As brain tissue is damaged, the sheep lose coordination. They are often seen leaning against walls or fences for balance, as if they are trying to scrape something off their sides. When sheep are slaughtered, waste tissues, including brain and spinal cord, are sometimes processed into cattle feed.

It's believed that cattle originally developed their own form of TSE from scrapie-infected sheep. Then to make matters worse, the same practice of processing nervous system tissue into livestock feeds—done in the interest of increasing animal weight gains—has been repeated with slaughtered cattle. For years Britain exported BSE-infected feeds all over the world, likely leading to cases in a number of other countries.

She looked as horrified as I had been when I first learned of the practice of giving herbivores feed made from slaughtered animals. A silence ensued as she gathered her thoughts. "And what about people? Can we get the disease too?"

"Some people did. That's, of course, what caused the greatest alarm in Britain. So far, about 150 people have died from the human form of the disease, called Creutzfeldt-Jakob, probably from eating infected beef products."

"Deadly burgers."

"Maybe, but more likely products in which leftovers are ground and disguised as things like sausages and tube steaks."

"Tube steaks?" she questioned.

"Hot dogs," I replied, and we both chuckled. "And then there's our wildlife."

"That's why you were in Madison."

"Yes, to try to figure out what wildlife managers can do to limit the spread of chronic wasting disease—the prion disease spreading to deer and elk in more and more places."

A chime sounded in the cabin as the FASTEN SEAT BELT sign illuminated. Then over the PA system, "This is your captain, we are beginning our descent to Minneapolis–St. Paul International Airport. . . ."

"So what did your group decide?" she asked after plucking a cell phone from her bag.

I described why a major focus is on concentrations of animals. When wildlife or livestock are crowded, they more readily spread diseases. Game-farmed animals are confined by fences, often at higher densities than the habitat can support. So farmers must feed them, and if one gets sick, others crowded at feedsites might also.

"Like when my kids were in school and brought home every sickness known to mankind."

"Exactly. Plus, game-farmed animals are moved from farm to farm for new breeding stock or to start new farms."

"And the diseases go with them?"

"Yup."

"So why don't they test them, you know, so sick ones aren't moved?"

"Unfortunately, there isn't a useful live animal test for CWD. They're infected for months, sometimes years, before they show signs of the disease. By the time they're symptomatic, they're doomed to death. Worse yet, they can infect others until they die."

"So more just keep getting sick? Until . . . ?" The anxiety in her voice was poignant.

"I've gone on enough about this," I said, realizing the conversation was driven as much by my worries about CWD as by her questions.

"No, don't apologize. It's just that I can't help feeling terrible for those poor animals. But what I don't understand is that wild deer aren't confined, so why do they have such a problem with it?"

I explained that diseases are sometimes like roadside bombs. Their victims are often innocent passersby. If a game farm was infected, the disease could spread to wildlife outside the fence. Although wild deer don't have nearly the prevalence of CWD as confined animals, high densities in the wild can facilitate its spread.[2]

"I know my neighbors put out corn before deer season, you know, to attract the deer. So, that could help spread CWD?"

"It certainly could. The principle of concentrating animals at feedsites is the same. And that's a big concern in western Wyoming where elk are fed in close quarters every winter."

"They feed elk?"

"Yes. About twenty-three thousand."

"I had no idea. So you have lots of risk for passing diseases there."

"The elk where I work in Jackson Hole appear safe so far. But elk, mule deer, and white-tailed deer farther east in Wyoming have CWD. And it's moving closer every year to where those large herds of elk are fed."

"You really must be worried about what might happen."

"Yes, I am." The jet banked sharply, and through the window humanity loomed—the Twin Cities. As the wings leveled and flight attendants made their last trash run, I realized I'd been talking to this woman for almost an hour without knowing her name.

"It's been a pleasure talking to you," I smiled. "My name is Bruce."

"And I'm Marie," she said. "Thank you. I learned so much."

"I enjoyed it. It's always a pleasure talking to someone who's really interested."

"One more thing: I remember hearing that people might be able to get this disease from deer, the way they got mad cow in England. My husband still hunts. We like to eat the venison. Are we being foolish?"

"We don't know if people can contract CWD by eating game meat. There are no documented cases of it. But states are urging precautions when dressing out animals, like boning out meat. This is a disease that we don't know a lot about, so I suggest that your husband follow those precautions. I know what you mean ... I eat game meat too."

"Well thanks, and I wish you luck with your work. I hope my husband and I can travel to Yellowstone and Jackson Hole someday to see your elk."

On a blustery February evening in 2004, an audience of more than two hundred packed the Grand Room of Jackson's Snow King Resort. The topic of the three-hour forum: How might chronic wasting disease affect Jackson Hole's elk and deer? Following presentations by Drs. Terry Kreeger and Ron Dean (Wyoming Game and Fish Department) and Dr. Tom Roffe (U.S. Fish and Wildlife Service) about the disease's effects and spread across Wyoming and the nation, my speaking assignment focused on where and how CWD might find its way into Jackson Hole.

A map of northwest Wyoming flooded the screen behind the lectern. On it colored polygons identified Grand Teton National Park, the National Elk Refuge, the Gros Ventre watershed, and areas to the east and south where the Wind River and Green River drainages border the Jackson elk herd. Like measles, hundreds of red dots speckled the map. "The dots represent locations where the twenty-five elk captured and collared on Gros Ventre feedgrounds were radio-tracked in summer and fall of 2002 and 2003," I explained.

The Gros Ventre drainage supports some 3,500 elk in winter. Two-thirds use the Patrol Cabin and two other elk feedgrounds where I captured and radio-collared Des and twenty-four others so far. Together with elk from the National Elk Refuge and several hundred scattered farther north, they comprise the fifteen-thousand-strong Jackson elk herd, the largest in the world at the time.

"The Jackson elk herd is considered to be a 'non-leaky' herd," I told the audience. "By Wyoming Game and Fish Department's definition, that means there should be less than 10 percent interchange with adjacent herds. But what's interesting is that a third of those elk captured in the Gros Ventre left the herd unit and spent summer and fall in either the Green River drainage or went east over the Continental Divide to the

Wind River. Here's what's significant about that: The most recent cases of CWD in deer are about eighty miles east of the Continental Divide. Now we find that Gros Ventre elk are crossing the mountains and mingling with deer and elk in the Wind River basin. That puts them even closer to known CWD-infected deer, possibly within sixty miles, and within the same river basin."[3]

I paused to let this sink in. "Because the elk we tracked returned to Gros Ventre feedgrounds each winter, if one becomes infected, it could provide CWD a gateway to western Wyoming's twenty-three feedgrounds. We can no longer afford to wait. Given the unique and insidious nature of this disease agent, it will be impossible to roll back the clock once CWD is in our midst."

After a measured applause, a man in a black ten-gallon hat rose from a seat several rows from the front. I had expected a question from him because he and I had sparred before—something I considered just a difference of perspective. As a hunting outfitter, he was partial to elk. A ten-day elk hunt ran three thousand dollars or more per person—successful or not. Of course, successful hunters were good advertising, and he and a contingent of others saw more elk as good for business. More elk meant the state would offer more permits for sale. More permits meant more clients, more successful hunts, and more future clients. In his position, I'd probably be likewise inclined, as were other business owners and hunters, and certain politicians hoping to placate their most vocal constituents.

On the other hand, winter feeding and the conditions it spawned might jeopardize the product. It might risk the health and welfare of the elk themselves. From my scientist's viewpoint, ecological concerns trumped socioeconomics. I'd let the policy makers deal with the politics. As a biologist, I'd do right by the public by doing right by the elk.

"So you're telling us that CWD is going to end up on the feedgrounds and kill hundreds and hundreds of elk?" Black Hat asked.

"I can't predict the future. Do I know with certainty that CWD will infect elk on western Wyoming's elk feedgrounds? I don't," I responded, then paused. "But can anyone here be sure that it won't?"

CHAPTER 2

A New Land

The elk herd is the greatest single thing about the valley. Its history is that of the valley and to a very real extent so is its fate.
—JACKSON NOVELIST DONALD HOUGH, 1943, SNOW ABOVE TOWN

When I landed in Jackson, I had a modest understanding of the valley's (and the elk herd's) history and conservation issues. I was primed only with what I'd gleaned during the four previous years while working on the sunrise side of the Continental Divide. I fretted that working at the National Elk Refuge (NER) would prove unchallenging. My mind and heart lingered three hours east, trapped in the Wind River country and the clear-cut mission of helping the Shoshone and Arapaho peoples restore their wildlife heritage. I'd interviewed tribal elders to reconstruct wildlife's history, evaluated habitat conditions, conducted the first-ever inventories of wildlife species, and crafted a comprehensive plan to secure their future.[1]

Foremost I wanted to see a game code adopted, something leaders of both tribes and I had labored to achieve. Following news media outreach, educating schoolchildren, and tense general council meetings with tribal members, we'd come so close. Yet on the day my pickup trailered the last U-haul load of belongings from Lander, Wyoming, to Jackson Hole, unregulated hunting remained in place. Resolution of the hunting issue was left to federal courts and Washington, D.C. bureaucrats—a scary thought. No, leaving my previous job was not what I'd wanted or planned—not in June 1982. But, my position was terminated; my cord to the Wind River cut. It was Jackson or unemployment, at least with the USFWS.

And so I began my new assignment with awkward introspection. The NER had a seventy-year conservation record. Its elk herd was secure and prolific, so large it was fed in winter—something about which I had uncertain feelings. Would I be satisfied with no wildlife legacy to recover? No apparent constituency seeking my help? No clear occupational endpoint where success could be claimed? Could the NER's long-established mission fill the void of the Wind River badlands slipping from my rearview mirror?

Celebrities like Elvis, Madonna, and Bono require one name alone. Likewise, the Rocky Mountain resorts of Aspen, Sun Valley, and Jackson Hole stand on their own, preceded by their reputations for stunning vistas, powder skiing, trophy cabins, and jet-setters. But Jackson Hole is singularly identifiable for another reason. If a place can be considered synonymous with an animal, then Jackson Hole is interchangeable with elk. What other county with a performing arts center, three ski resorts, oodles of art galleries, and four-star restaurants can brag more elk than people in its midst?

The Jackson herd is arguably the best-known, most thoroughly studied and glamorized population of elk in existence. The jagged peaks of the Teton Range, jutting seven thousand feet skyward above the Jackson Hole valley's western flank, provide an inspiring backdrop worthy of its famed elk. The "Hole," as trappers referred to it in the early 1800s, is a high mountain valley bisected by the Snake River. The Gros Ventre Mountains on the east and the soaring plateaus of Yellowstone National Park to the north complete a grand horseshoe framing Jackson Hole. Geographic isolation, brutal winters, a short growing season, no gold, and relatively late exploration by such legendary figures as John Colter, Davey Jackson, and Osborne Russell delayed exploitation of northwest Wyoming's wildlife years after surrounding areas had been "shot out."

There my career would become so closely identified with elk, that at speaking engagements I'd be introduced as an elk biologist, rather than a wildlife biologist. This despite the fact that the NER was home to forty-eight species of mammals, 175 species of birds, plus various amphibians, reptiles, and fish. Yet the elk were squarely the focus. So it's only right that I provide some background on this species that absorbed me and virtually shaped the next twenty-two years of my life. Like decoding the condition of a community, a nation, or a people, retracing a species' past is necessary to understand its present situation.

The history of the deer family (Cervidae) is written in stone. Extensive fossil records trace cervid origins to subtropical southern Asia. Fossil evidence suggests that *Cervus elaphus*—the scientific name of North American elk, Siberian wapiti, and European red deer—radiated throughout Eurasia five hundred thousand years or more ago. Although elk may have crossed the Bering Land Bridge nearly that long ago, fossils definitively of the genus *Cervus* are rare in North America. More likely, *Cervus elaphus*, the elk or *wapiti* (the animal's American Indian name in the Shawnee language), arrived during the late Pleistocene, just forty thousand years ago. This coincides with the Wisconsin glaciation, the continent's fourth and final major glacial advance. Coincident with human use and preservation of their remains at archaeological sites, fossil evidence of wapiti in North America became plentiful only within the past ten thousand years.[2, 3, 4]

Geologic Time Table				
Age	**Divisions**			
Era	Epoch	Glaciations	Years from start to present (in millions)	Major events concerning *Cervus elapus*
Cenozoic	Recent (Holocene)		0.01	Colonization throughout North America
	Pleistocene	Wisconsin	0.06	Probable arrival in North America
		Illinoian	0.13	
		Kansan	0.39	
		Nebraskan	0.79	
		Pre-Nebraskan	1.8	
	Pliocene		5.1	Cervid radiation and ecological differentiation, including *Cervus*
	Miocene		24.6	First true cervids

The Pleistocene was not a continuously ice-bound, 1.8-million-year span. Rather, warm interludes of glacial retreat punctuated the four major glacial advances, and briefer periods of warming, called interstadials, further arrested the ice. During these glacial "time-outs," the Cordilleran ice sheet covering the Rocky Mountains and the Laurentide ice sheet to the east receded, opening an ice-free, north–south, migratory corridor to terrestrial fauna east of the Rockies. Once wapiti reached Alaska from Asia, they eventually spread southward and coast to coast throughout suitable habitats of North America, like molecules filling a vacuum. By the early Holocene epoch, beginning ten thousand years ago, archaeological sites from northern British Columbia east to southern Ontario and across the mid-continent region held fossilized remains of elk.[3, 4]

Like other newcomers to lower North America (grizzly bears, wild sheep, Paleoindians, and dozens of other Eurasian species), elk grazed only briefly alongside the rich Pleistocene fauna of North American specialists—wooly mammoths, giant peccaries, camels, and many primitive species of horses. Elk did well because the competition collapsed. The retreat of the continental glaciers, appearance of modern grasslands, and extinctions of grazing competitors and many megafaunal predators (such as gargantuan American lions, dire wolves, and saber-toothed cats) probably contributed to the expanding distribution of wapiti at the beginning of the Holocene. Wildlife scientist Dr. Valerius Geist summarizes the New World success of the species this way: "Elk are the most highly evolved subspecies of red deer, able to cope with open landscapes, coarse-fibered forage and cold climates. They are not only more highly adapted to plains life and seasonal climates than any other Old World deer alive, they are the only member of that subfamily ever to set foot in the Americas."[5]

By the late Holocene (four thousand to five hundred years before present day), elk had colonized most of the continental United States as far south as Georgia and northern Mexico. In 1535 Jacques Cartier was possibly the first Euro-American to write about the elk in North America. He wrote of "great stores of Stags, Deere, and Beares . . ." as he ascended the St. Lawrence River as far as Montréal. Various writers noted that elk were numerous in New York State, the Carolinas, and Virginia during the mid-1600s. In 1748 they were hunted where Philadelphia now stands. They were numerous in the Great Lakes region in 1764, but by 1837 elk had almost entirely disappeared from the vicinity of Chicago.

The Swiss nature artist Rudolph Kurz reported on the decline of elk herds in the eastern United States in 1851. "According to Audubon and Bachmann, *Elaphus canadensis* [several writers of the 1800s used this name] is met with nowadays in regions east of the Mississippi only in small herds that range in a narrow strip in the Allegheny Mountains. Solitary herds of elk are still found also in West Virginia."[3, 6]

How many elk once roamed the deciduous forests, prairies, and swamps of the eastern United States is pure speculation. All were extirpated during the 1800s. Those east of Saskatchewan fared no better in Canada. By 1850 elk disappeared from Vermont, Massachusetts, New York, Maryland, North and South Carolina, Louisiana, Tennessee, Kentucky, Ohio, Indiana, and Arkansas. Another twenty-five years, and Pennsylvania, Virginia, West Virginia, Iowa, and Missouri were devoid. By 1900 the bugling of wapiti faded from their remaining strongholds in Michigan and Wisconsin. A handful may have persisted in Minnesota until 1908.[3]

The exploitation of North American wildlife began two-and-a-half centuries ago when French, English, and Russian settlers in the New World tendered furs as a medium of exchange. Trappers sought their fortune by satisfying the demand for furs in Europe and the American colonies. Beaver were especially vulnerable and over the next 150 years were nearly trapped to extinction in Canada and the eastern United States.[7]

Elk remained abundant west of the Mississippi until western settlement burgeoned following the Civil War. Although subsistence hunting by white settlers altered distributions of elk and other game animals, it diminished their populations only moderately. But as more Western towns and cities sprang up and the Industrial Revolution boosted leisure time, outdoor recreation—including recreational trophy hunting—became an increasingly popular pastime. Railroad travel became cheaper and faster, giving city folk access to formerly remote areas.[7, 8]

At the same time, market hunting began to flourish, accelerating the slaughter of bison for their hides and prime cuts, passenger pigeons for meat, and egrets, ibises, and swans for plumes and quills. War was declared on large predators to protect livestock interests, and because they

Market hunting circa 1900
(B. D. Sheffield Collection, Grand Teton National Park)

were viewed as competitors with hunters for deer, elk, and other game. As bison herds faded, and until almost the close of the century, a good hunter could still make a fair living selling deer, mountain sheep, and elk to rail-road construction crews and in mining camps.[8] Allied with market hunt-ers were the railroad interests, which profited from shipping meat and hides to Eastern tanners, millners, and meat suppliers. Market hunting and support ventures were accepted elements of the nineteenth-century economy, backed by strong support in Congress and state legislatures. Finally, much of the killing was encouraged by the U.S. government to reduce grazing competition with livestock, to feed the Indian-fighting army, and to purposefully starve out the Indian. Most of the carnage took place between 1870 and 1890.[8, 9] It's a sad legacy that glorified frontier accounts often downplay or overlook.

By the 1890s the great herds of pronghorn and twenty-five to fifty million bison were all but gone. Grizzly bears, wolves, mountain lions, mountain sheep, and elk were banished to scattered wilderness strong-holds. Where any protective laws existed at all, poaching and eluding game wardens were widespread pastimes. The extirpation of all big game south of Canada seemed inevitable.

The wildlife conservation movement began as a resistance to powerful political and social forces that were squandering the nation's heritage without regard for the future. During the 1870s–1890s, states and territories adopted regulations limiting numbers of certain wild animals a hunter could kill each year. Some states established hunting seasons, in response to appeals from recreational hunters, and prohibited bison hunting. Eventually an embryonic framework of game management emerged.

It could be argued that the establishment of Yellowstone National Park in 1872 was the first seed of wildlife conservation in North America. In future years a handful of early conservationists, including Teddy Roosevelt, John Muir, and Gifford Pinchot, fostered the reservation of wildlands as national forests and parks, along with regulation of their recreational and commercial use. However, another three decades passed after Yellowstone's establishment before the first national wildlife refuge was created and the U.S. Forest Service and National Park Service were born.

With few safe havens from exploitation, only fledgling controls on hunting, and sparse enforcement staffs, states were hard-pressed to curb wildlife's slide toward oblivion. As elk were progressively exterminated over much of their broad former range (of all the world's living large land mammals, *Cervus elaphus* has experienced the greatest loss of its historic range[10]), the Rocky Mountains gave refuge to remnant herds. This prompted the misconception that elk required high mountain wilderness. In reality, elk survived where they could. Amid a Euro-American onslaught—fed by the 1862 Homestead Act, completion of the transcontinental railway, subjugation of the Plains Indian tribes, and the lure of the West's bountiful resources, including gold—elk were squeezed into scattered islands of Western wilderness. By 1900 millions had been reduced to just fifty thousand elk.[11]

The greatest of their island retreats lay in and around Yellowstone National Park. Now dubbed the Greater Yellowstone Ecosystem (GYE)—an eighteen-million-acre wildland presently comprised of Yellowstone and Grand Teton National Parks, two national wildlife refuges, portions of seven national forests, and other federal, state, and private lands—this inhospitable fastness was settled late in the West's history. In the mountains around Yellowstone, elk herds found an abundance of forage and security during summer. But as fall snowstorms blanketed the high country, the elk drifted out of the mountains and fanned across foothills, valleys, and semiarid plains as much as two hundred miles from their summer ranges. Those lowlands provided relatively snow-free grazing. There was no reason for elk and other ungulates to linger in excess of the range's capacity in snowbound Jackson Hole. Periodic severe winters ensured large numbers did not persist there yearlong.[12, 13]

As the open valleys and lowlands of Idaho, Montana, and Wyoming were increasingly farmed and ranched, and communities and transportation routes sprang up, herd migratory patterns were cut short or eliminated. The elk found old travel routes blocked by fences, traditional wintering grounds studded with homes, and forage usurped by domestic sheep and cattle. Several reports contend that in prehistoric times substantial numbers of elk, from what was called the southern Yellowstone herd (as opposed to elk that occupied the northern and eastern portions of the park), passed through the Jackson Hole and Gros Ventre valleys each fall en route to wintering areas in the Green River basin, Little Colorado Desert, and Red Desert of southwest Wyoming. But in leaving the mountains, they soon ran an ever-tightening gauntlet of human exploitation.[12, 13, 14, 15, 16]

The wanton killing of elk for their upper canine teeth began about 1904 in Jackson Hole. The tuskers, as they were called, were blood brothers of the buffalo tongue hunters, mercenaries who killed buffalo for only that epicurean delicacy. Thousands of elk were slaughtered for their teeth, which at peak prices brought ten dollars a pair. Mounted on gold watch fobs, elk canines or "tusks" were ironically the official badge of membership in the Benevolent and Protective Order of Elks, whose members numbered in the millions. Although outlawed by the Wyoming legislature in 1907, tuskers illegally operated into the 1920s. Hard work on the part of law enforcement people and even some vigilante efforts by local settlers finally rid the valley of this gruesome trade and the unsavory reputation it earned local communities.

By 1911 the elk of Jackson Hole and southern Yellowstone Park were imperiled. With migrations to the desert all but wiped out, and with the Jackson valley's forage cut and stockpiled to feed cattle and horses, elk were faced with raiding haystacks or starving to death. As it turned out,

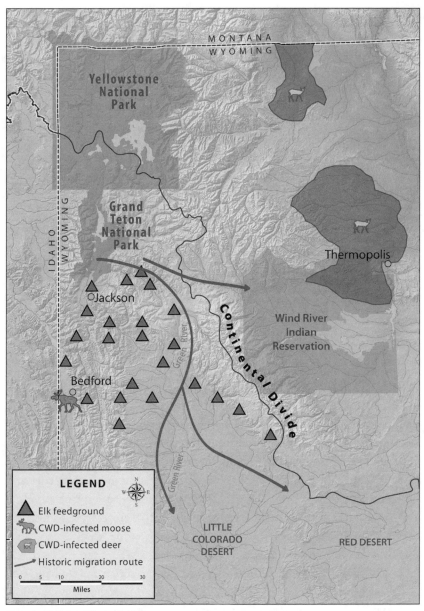

Yellowstone
National
Park

MONTANA
WYOMING

Grand
Teton
National
Park

IDAHO
WYOMING

Thermopolis

○Jackson

Wind River
Indian
Reservation

Green River

Continental Divide

Bedford

Green River

LEGEND

▲ Elk feedground

CWD-infected moose

CWD-infected deer

Historic migration route

0   5   10   20   30
Miles

LITTLE
COLORADO
DESERT

RED DESERT

(Map produced by the Greater Yellowstone Coalition)

they did a good deal of both during the severe winters of 1882, 1886, 1891, 1909, 1910, and 1911.[13, 16, 17] In the worst of winters, it was said you could "walk for miles on the strewn carcasses of dead elk."[18]

Paneled haystack and dead elk circa 1900
(Stephen Leek Collection, American Heritage Center, University of Wyoming)

As elk-human conflicts reached crisis level, efforts were launched to save the elk. In 1895 Wyoming prohibited the sale of game meat and required nonresidents of Wyoming to purchase hunting licenses (mostly to discourage hunting by American Indians, who were not considered residents). Albert T. Nelson was appointed the first state game warden in 1898, followed by Daniel C. Nowlin in 1902. Both resided in Jackson Hole. Wyoming established the Teton Game Preserve in 1905, covering much of what is today the Teton Wilderness Area between Jackson Hole and Yellowstone Park. To bolster elk numbers, the preserve was closed to elk hunting until 1947.

Protection produced crowding on those lands where the elk were tolerated in the Jackson valley. Despite ongoing competition for land and forage, most residents of Jackson Hole wanted to maintain the elk population, even while elsewhere frontiersmen solved similar conflicts by killing the elk. Reporting on this paradox, scientist Edward Preble—who was tasked by the U.S. Biological Survey (forerunner of the U.S. Fish and Wildlife Service) to investigate the plight of the elk of Jackson Hole—noted that elk augmented the local economy. Many Jackson Hole settlers earned a

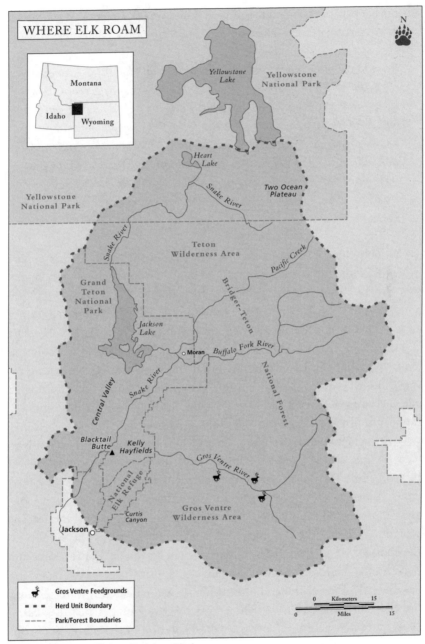

WHERE ELK ROAM

Montana

Idaho   Wyoming

Yellowstone
Lake

Yellowstone
National Park

Yellowstone
National Park

Heart
Lake

Two Ocean
Plateau

Snake River

Teton
Wilderness Area

Pacific Creek

Grand
Teton
National
Park

Bridger-Teton

Jackson
Lake

Moran

Buffalo Fork River

Snake River

National Forest

Central Valley

Snake River

Blacktail
Butte

Kelly
Hayfields

Gros Ventre River

National
Elk Refuge

Curtis
Canyon

Gros Ventre
Wilderness Area

Jackson

N

Gros Ventre Feedgrounds

Herd Unit Boundary

Park/Forest Boundaries

Kilometers   15

Miles   15

Present geographic range and features of the Jackson elk herd substantial part of their livelihood by guiding wealthy clients on elk hunts. In his 1911 report to Congress on the condition of the elk, Preble wrote:

> *Some of the most intelligent residents of Jackson Hole have estimated the value of the elk to the region is equal to the revenue derived from stock raising, which is the principal industry . . . and that without them the region under present conditions would not support nearly so large a population as it now does. Whatever the opinion of individuals on this point, it is evident that elk have played a very important part in the development of the region. Probably a majority of the more successful residents owe their start to the presence of these animals.*[19]

Nonetheless, problems for the elk herd continued. In his report Edward Preble advocated establishment of "a winter refuge, where the feed can be preserved by excluding stock during the summer. . . ." He noted that in 1906, the state game warden D. C. Nowlin suggested setting aside such a refuge for elk and other game in the Gros Ventre valley east of Jackson Hole. In 1909 the Wyoming legislature passed a resolution requesting that the U.S. Congress grant the state a tract comprising six townships of public land in the Gros Ventre valley for a winter game refuge, including acquiring the several claims occupied by livestock ranchers. Opposition by local residents killed the proposal.[20]

During 1909 and 1910, the State of Wyoming used public funds to feed hungry elk and reduce conflicts with private ranch operations in Jackson Hole. No local fees were exacted to support it, yet valley residents gained economic benefits. At Wyoming's request, the U.S. Congress appropriated twenty thousand dollars for an emergency winter feeding program in 1911. The hay handouts served only to focus the severity of the shortage of adequate winter range, as elk crowded onto feedsites and depleted natural forage on adjacent lands.

By 1911 Preble found that sentiments had changed toward a refuge for elk. He advocated establishing one or more refuges in the Jackson Hole and Gros Ventre valleys as the best solution to the problem of conserving the Jackson elk herd. Preble estimated that six hundred tons of hay could be harvested and used to feed elk on the land claims then occupied by settlers in the Upper Gros Ventre. In combination with natural forage, he believed that more elk could be supported there than in the Jackson valley. Consequently, fewer elk would migrate to Jackson Hole where most conflicts with homesteaders occurred.

After further debate and arm-twisting, the present site of the NER in the Jackson Hole valley was chosen as the single location for an elk reserve. An act of Congress established the refuge on August 10, 1912. With a fifty-thousand-dollar congressional appropriation, the Biological Survey purchased 1,760 acres of privately owned ranchland. Combined with one thousand acres of adjacent public domain, this became the nucleus of the NER. With hay purchased from leftover funds, the federal government continued feeding thousands of elk. As a stopgap to alleviate starvation and to separate elk from haystacks and people, winter feeding was a noble and practical endeavor.

But artificially supporting the elk herd was likely not viewed as a long-term solution a century ago. The NER's establishing legislation set aside lands "for the establishment of a winter game (elk) reserve in the State of Wyoming, lying south of the Yellowstone Park. . . ." Subsequent acts and executive orders broadened the purposes of the refuge to include the conservation of habitat for all big game animals and birds. These legal directives made no mention of feeding elk. Instead, by default, feeding elk became policy out of repeated practice.[21]

By 1912 elk were extirpated from nearly 90 percent of their former range, and Yellowstone National Park and the NER became the sources for continent-wide reintroductions of thousands of elk.[5] Elk were sent by truck and rail as far south as Mexico, north to Alberta, east to New York and West Virginia, and west to Washington. Reintroductions to at least thirty-seven states continued for half a century. These translocations—which began in 1892 and accelerated after 1911—restored this magnificent and valued species across large areas of its range, but were also intended to reduce overcrowding in the NER and Yellowstone Park. Yet under the most favorable conditions, trapping removals represented only a fraction of the annual increase. Requests for live elk waned once former habitats were restocked.[22]

In sum, the provisioning of hay in Jackson Hole simultaneously attracted elk, intercepted dwindling migrations, and concentrated foraging in localized areas near feedgrounds. Fences, urbanization, hunting, poaching, harassment, and artificial food all conspired to end elk migrations out of Jackson Hole. By 1917 the spectacle of thousands of elk coursing southward from the mountains to southwest Wyoming was over.[14, 15, 16] The winter distribution of the southern Yellowstone herd, now known as the Jackson elk herd, was reduced to the Jackson Hole, Gros Ventre, and Buffalo Fork valleys. The herd memory of snow-free desert pastures to the south was forever lost.

By June 1982, when I arrived, a series of land acquisitions and exchanges—largely transacted during the Dust Bowl/Great Depression years of the 1930s—had grown the refuge to twenty-four thousand acres. Even across this acreage the congregation of elk in winter was extraordinary. Most were confined to the southern 40 percent of the refuge—flat grasslands, marsh, and sagelands. Steeper uplands, where deeper snow hampered elk grazing, comprised the northern 60 percent.

Two other federal biologists had preceded me. The U.S. Biological Survey sent Olaus Murie to Jackson Hole in 1927 to "investigate the elk problem." As Murie himself relates it, "there were two reliable topics of discussion during Jackson Hole's long winters, the proposed establishment and subsequent expansion of Grand Teton National Park, and the problem with the elk." Over the next eighteen years, Murie conducted research on elk biology, diseases, and ecology. His work culminated in his landmark 1951 book, *The Elk of North America*.[23] He was a "tolerated maverick" in the Biological Survey because he disagreed with the agency's policy of eradicating predators in the late 1920s and early 1930s. He viewed wolves, coyotes, and other carnivores as integral components of functioning ecosystems, a philosophy shared by few Jackson Hole residents at that time. Following his retirement from government employment in 1945, Murie served as president of the Wilderness Society and a director of the Izaak Walton League of America, and received many conservation accolades. Although he did not live to see the federal Wilderness Act passed in 1964, its enactment was attributable in part to Murie's convictions and tireless work.

Olaus's wife, Mardy, outlived her husband by forty years. She became a renowned conservationist in her own right and a revered advocate of wildland protection. Her eloquent writings and passionate dedication to land protection—particularly preservation of the Arctic National Wildlife Refuge where she and Olaus had traveled by dogsled as newlyweds early in the twentieth century—led President Clinton to award her the Presidential Medal of Freedom in 1998.

The NER was without a biologist from 1945 until 1968. That's when the Denver Wildlife Research Center—the research arm of the USFWS—stationed Russell "Buzz" Robbins at the refuge. His work centered on refinement of the winter elk feeding program and studying its effects on elk reproduction. Buzz's efforts contributed to the mechanization of feeding the seven to eight thousand elk on the refuge.

When he left Jackson Hole in November 1981 to manage the Arctic National Wildlife Refuge, some of Buzz's studies remained uncompleted. Someone was needed to finalize and publish that important work. The USFWS's Denver Regional Office, which supervised the NER and all other refuges and field offices in the eight-state Central Mountains and Plains Region, added a wildlife biologist position to the refuge staff. By virtue of timing, and perhaps my accomplishments at the Wind River Indian Reservation, I was chosen to fill the big biological boots of my two predecessors.

Chapter 3

Trials and Telemetry

The aim of science is to discover and illuminate truth.
—Rachel Carson, 1962, *Silent Spring*

"There. Behind that spindly sagebrush with the forked top." Marjean pointed to a hint of rust piercing the gray-green brush.

"Okay, I see it," I acknowledged. "I'll follow you."

Our stooped advance didn't conceal our intrusion on the calf's world, but somehow made us feel less conspicuous, less threatening. Along one side of the fenced pasture, the ten cow elk—six closely followed by new babies—jostled nervously. One barked a startling, sharp protest. No matter how often I heard it, I was always impressed by the volume and resonance of that singular alarm.

Now within feet of the immobile mound pressed against the dewy earth, Marjean whispered, "You catch this one."

Marjean had been a biological technician for Buzz Robbins. Following his departure, she had overseen his field studies and two other assistants until I arrived in June 1982. She was a soft-spoken but confident biologist. She'd already handled nineteen calves born this spring to the female elk partitioned in the six five-acre pastures. This was her fourth year as field tech on the feeding trials. She was an old hand at this. I was the newbie.

I refocused on the calf whose first day of life would begin very differently from the three to four thousand calves to be born this spring throughout Jackson Hole. When our research of female nutrition and survival of their offspring ended in early August, we'd free the calf and its anxious mother along with the others. But now we needed to impose

28

on its first hours of life for just five minutes—long enough to log its vital statistics as the newest member of the study.

I felt a prickle of anticipation, knowing that I was moments from touching, briefly possessing, a live elk. Like a child cradling his or her first puppy, I was about to experience a minor miracle.

With several quick steps and a pounce, I clutched the trembling body in my hands. One throaty bleat later, we had stuffed the calf in an onion sack and suspended it from a spring scale. The quivering red hand on the round dial read thirty-five pounds—average for a newborn elk. That weight, our research would reveal, gave this calf an 88 percent chance of surviving until August. Newborns weighing less than twenty-nine pounds survived only 67 percent of the time.[1] As with most other species of mammals, including humans, low birth weights translate to poorer survival.

Withdrawing the sack, we checked the sex—male—then his general body condition, and finally his teeth. Of the eight incisiform teeth—six incisors flanked by a pair of incisor-shaped lower canines—only the middle pair had poked through protective pink gums. Likewise the upper canines, which were so prized by members of the Benevolent and Protective Order of Elks earlier in the century, had not erupted. That would take another four or five days. I pressed the upper dental pad that would toothlessly oppose the lower incisors throughout the calf's life. The calf reflexively sucked my finger.

I grinned at Marjean. "Looks like he's hungry."

After spray-painting the backs of the calf's ears with a distinctive color combination, I laid him where I had found him. He stretched his head low against the grass and flattened his ears. The highest point along his back measured just eight inches above the ground. His ribs rose and fell beneath my hands with steady, shallow breaths, as moist black nostrils flared slightly with each exhalation. He seemed totally vulnerable.

Only his mother's nutrition, watchfulness, and wisdom stood between life and death. Beyond the confines of the wired enclosure, her previous and future calves were born among Jackson Hole's carnivores. In future days on strengthened legs, he may burst from hiding at an intruder's approach. For now, motionlessness was his only defense. Remain still. Remain safe where sunlight filters through sheltering sage and dapples your spotted coat.

Marjean and I backed away, slipped through the gate in Pasture 6, and watched a large cow press forward from the knotted group. She stretched

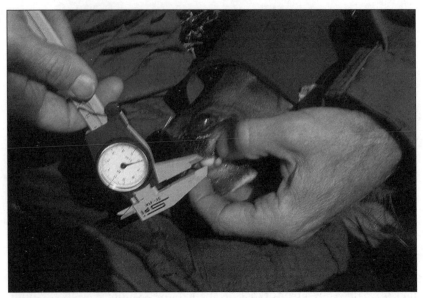

Measuring newly erupted incisors of an elk calf
(Alan Strassler, US Fish and Wildlife Service)

her neck and scented the air. She stomped a front foot, then returned to the others.

"That must be mom," Marjean observed.

The numerals on her white neckband would thereafter bond her in our database to the calf's red right and yellow left ears. Our daily observations of nursing behavior and maternal grooming would confirm she was the dam. Over the next two months of confinement, we'd monitor the calf's well-being from a platform-mounted blind. Should he become one of the study's 20 percent that fell ill to disease, malnutrition, or other neonatal demise, we would retrieve his body for diagnostic tests. But this one survived.

In the refuge headquarters built of logs felled nearby in 1942, I sat in a squeaky chair hunched over a 1950s gray metal desk. Mine was the only work space in the basement, next to the room where coal was stored—a place where mice scuttled and radon seeped. It was quiet down here. Real quiet. Only the occasional creak of footsteps on the floor overhead interrupted my scratching of pencil on paper. Beneath flickering fluorescent light, I boldly began charting what would become the next twenty-two years of my life. Confidence is what one begins with before completely understanding the situation.

Inevitably, all useful science bears its fruit in some sterile environment, like my basement office. Without methodical analysis and the production of written results, knowledge resides only in the mind and file cabinets of scientists, where it has little opportunity to do good. As I punched the numbers on my programmable calculator in 1983, I sought to elucidate the salient findings of Buzz's field research. Finalizing these nutritional feeding trials—popularly called "the pen studies" by refuge staff—was one of three priority projects refuge manager John Wilbrecht had assigned to me. The others—finishing an ongoing study of elk migrations and assessing impacts of winter recreational use on wildlife adjacent to the refuge—would augment my duties of managing the winter feeding program, initiating an interagency bison management plan, monitoring all wildlife species on the refuge, evaluating and updating the refuge's habitat evaluation procedures, and coordinating graduate students' research. My new job might lack the novelty of working at the Wind River Indian Reservation, but it would be anything but boring.

Buzz designed the earliest round of feeding trials, conducted during 1971–73, to test the suitability of pelleted alfalfa hay as supplemental winter feed for refuge elk. For decades the elk were fed long hay to both deter their wanderings onto adjacent ranchlands and to supplement the standing forage that grew on the refuge. Some hay was harvested from irrigated refuge fields, the remainder purchased from growers in the Jackson valley. Drivers dispensed the hay to the wintering elk from horse-drawn sleds over a feeding period averaging two-and-a-half months. In 1958 tractors replaced horses, permitting the feeding sites to be located farther from the storage barns. This better dispersed the elk across refuge lands, enhancing their use of standing forage and promoting more sanitary and healthful feedground conditions.

Then in 1966 refuge manager Don Redfearn changed policy to leave all forage that grew on the refuge uncut. All supplemental feed came from off-refuge sources. Redfearn's intent was simple—allow the elk to feed themselves, and limit human intervention that bordered on animal husbandry. This bonus standing forage deferred the need to supplement elk diets.

From 1952 to 1972, the majority of hay came from the Kelly Hayfields, locally known as Mormon Row (for the religious affiliation of the residents who settled there). In 1950 Public Law 787 expanded Grand Teton National Park (GTNP), swallowing the Hayfields and vast lands to the north and west. This federal "land grab" was contentious and largely opposed by locals. Nonetheless, the park was tripled in size to 310,000 acres. The Kelly Hayfields became national park lands, where hay production was deemed an unfitting land use. At the urging of the U.S. Fish and Wildlife Service and backed by the state of Wyoming, the Park Service signed a twenty-year agreement in 1952 that permitted continued farming of hay to feed refuge elk. Refuge staff now farmed the Hayfields.[2]

As expiration of the twenty-year agreement neared, refuge manager Redfearn posed the following questions: (1) What will be the future source of supplemental feed? Replacing three thousand tons of hay annually was no minor matter. (2) What operational improvements can be made to promote better use of the winter range and reduce dependence on winter feeding?

During the 1960s Redfearn contacted hay producers throughout Jackson Hole to assess the market. Ranchers complained that hay supplies were tight—barely sufficient to feed their livestock. Prospects for any improvement were dim because of ongoing hayland conversion to residential development. Elsewhere in western Wyoming, Redfearn found even less sympathy for Uncle Sam's predicament. State purchases for their own elk feedgrounds consumed most surplus hay. Neither livestock operators nor the Wyoming Game and Fish Department were thrilled about federal government competition.

"Purchasing three thousand tons of western Wyoming hay will be politically inexpedient," is how Redfearn explained it to his Denver bosses. Alternative sources lay 150 or more miles away in central Wyoming or Idaho—a prospect diminished by steep transportation costs.

Discussions with agricultural scientists turned to alternative feed types. The choices were hay processed into cake, cubes, or pellets. Some obvious advantages of compacted feeds included (1) reduced bulk that would in turn reduce transportation costs, (2) reduced loss of feed to wind and trampling, and (3) the opportunity to automate feeding and more widely distribute thousands of elk. The latter advantage promised savings in labor costs as well as reduced disease transmission among the elk.[3]

Hay cubes and cake were less easily handled and dispensed than pelleted hay, and also in short supply. Redfearn and Robbins focused on pellets produced for livestock feed. Although mixed grass and grass/alfalfa long hay—what the elk were fed for decades—were suitable feedstuffs, pure alfalfa compressed into two-inch-long by three-quarter-inch-diameter round pellets was nutritionally superior. Increased protein content and digestibility of pure alfalfa yielded more absorbed nutrients per pound of feed. Theoretically, smaller rations would satisfy the nutritional requirements of elk, providing yet another cost saving over long hay. These advantages became the basis for testing pelleted hay on dozens of elk confined to four fifty-acre refuge pastures during 1971–1973.

Throughout the studies, Redfearn and Robbins heard a chorus of naysayers decrying the heresy of feeding elk anything but long hay. All that would prevent elk from suffering digestive disorders, some suggested, would be their refusal to eat compressed feed. But after briefly sniffing and rolling the pellets across the snow, elk learned they were yummy. That elk should eat hay shaped like pellets is no more surprising than astronauts sucking food from a tube. My analyses of the data showed that mixed groups of cow, calf, and bull elk achieved the same performance (little to no weight loss over winter) when provided 20 to 40 percent less pelleted hay (six to eight pounds per animal per day) than the ten pounds of long hay fed daily to control groups.[3]

On refuge feedgrounds, Buzz monitored competition from 1972 to 1974. Again the results were encouraging. He observed five times fewer aggressive interactions among elk provided pellets as among those fed long hay. More competition over long hay likely arose for logistical reasons. As in the past, two to three sled trips and considerable handling time were needed to feed the daily ration of baled hay to each herd of 1,500 to 2,000 elk, as opposed to a single trip and just twenty minutes to dispense alfalfa pellets. So beginning in 1975, 100 percent of refuge elk were fed pelleted hay. This winter feeding protocol, with adaptive fine-tuning, has continued to the present. Subsequent feeding trials from 1978 to 1982 focused on refining the maintenance ration required by cow elk.[1,3]

In public meetings across Wyoming, state employees disparaged the refuge's decision to test and then feed pelleted alfalfa to Jackson Hole's elk (Wyoming has fed only long hay at twenty-two state-operated elk feedgrounds). At its Sybille research facilities in southeast Wyoming, the Wyoming Game and Fish Department initiated similar studies to test alfalfa pellets on elk. The outcome validated Buzz's findings, confirming that lower rations of pelleted hay than long hay could maintain elk weights. Both studies also demonstrated that confined elk did not develop digestive disorders on diets of pelleted hay.

But the obvious question, and one fundamental to western Wyoming elk management, is why feed wild elk at all? Especially out there in sparsely populated Wyoming where vast tracts of vegetation remain unmowed. In Teton County, where 97 percent of lands are national forests, parks, refuges, or state-managed lands, isn't the practice peculiar, even unwarranted?

A technical review I published in 2001 reported that just 3 percent of all wild elk in the United States and Canada—just thirty-one thousand out of one million—were fed by state and federal agencies. Wyoming was an early and ardent proponent of feeding, first pitching hay to elk in 1909 at the refuge's future location. By 1981 sixteen thousand elk were fed each winter at twenty-two state feedgrounds—dotting creek bottoms and ridgelines from the Gros Ventre River south beyond the towns of Pinedale and Big Piney—plus thousands more at the National Elk Refuge. Born of a conscious desire to maintain historic elk numbers even as migrations to distant winter ranges faded, many of these feedgrounds were established as concessions to the livestock industry—to mitigate competition between elk and livestock and to curb disease transmission (subjects discussed in later chapters). Thus, 75 percent of those thirty-one thousand fed elk gather on western Wyoming feedgrounds, whereas 97 percent of North America's elk rustle wheatgrass rather than relying on wapiti welfare. Managing elk by feeding them is an anomaly.[4]

By mutual agreement between Wyoming and the USFWS, an average 7,400 elk have wintered on the NER for the past century. But as early as the 1940s, Olaus Murie warned that maintaining such large numbers threatened the health of refuge vegetation and the elk themselves.[5, 6, 7] As we shall see, ecological concerns were trumped long ago by the economic gains derived from elk. This became the "political reality" of Jackson Hole's elk management—a phrase that came to irritate me like fingernails scratching a blackboard.

Although all three refuge managers for whom I worked conceded that winter feeding should be minimized, even ended, the beat went on. And so our elk feeding trials during 1978–1982 served a useful purpose: to tailor the feeding program to meet metabolic requirements, not simply to satisfy elk appetites for tasty alfalfa. Limiting the amount of feeding would reduce the taxpayers' bill, but more importantly it might limit habitat and disease consequences from crowding elk.

As elk were released at the conclusion of feeding trials, Buzz Robbins and I adorned seventy-six adult females with radio collars. Randomly selected from among the 190 females that "participated" in the research, these animals formed the nucleus of a seven-year study of seasonal distribution, migrations, and survival of the Jackson elk. Another four females and seventeen adult males were radio-collared from the free-ranging herd. Through 1984 I monitored the wanderings of the forty-eight survivors from this sample of ninety-seven. This was the second of my assigned priority projects.

The author radio-tracking from atop a feed trailer
(US Fish and Wildlife Service)

Locating the animals was a straightforward business from December through March, when 97 percent wintered on the NER. Like taking classroom attendance, each transmitter's unique radio frequency "beeped" each elk's presence through a radio receiver. To plot the weekly locations of elk after they left the refuge, my summer field technicians and I triangulated radio signals from three high points surrounding Grand Teton National Park's central valley. Simultaneously, we tuned in the signals of each radio collar and recorded a handheld antenna's compass bearings to each. Later we'd draw the azimuths on topographic maps. The pencil lines originated at our three locations and intersected, presumably, where each elk had been. A mathematical formula spewed out the error probability of each location.

These weekly "telemetry sessions" provided a window into the lives of these elk. We learned that #45, for example, spent summers in an area of Grand Teton's central valley called The Potholes. Its topography was pocked with glacial kettles, several of which sustained seasonal or perennial ponds. These depressions formed when huge blocks of ice detached from retreating glaciers and melted over eleven thousand years ago. The ponds and varied topographic aspects surrounding the kettles provided reliable summer water and grazing favored by elk.

Elk #45 migrated from the NER between the second week of April and last week of May. Annual weather conditions, which influenced snowmelt and regreening of her favorite grasses, seemed to dictate when The Potholes could satisfy the increasing demands of her growing fetus. During the last week of May and first two weeks of June, pale-spotted, ginger calves suddenly littered The Potholes and other Jackson Hole calving areas. Evolutionary trial and error has compressed birthing to coincide with this period of rising nutrition of forage plants, though a handful of deliveries strung into early July. This synchronization ensured that dams could produce sufficient milk for their newborns as they recovered from pregnancy. Born too early, a calf may suffer malnutrition or the perils of late-spring storms. Born too late, a calf may not grow large enough to withstand the rigors of winter.

Unlike #45, most gravid females that dropped their calves in The Potholes did not remain there during summer and fall, but left after a week or two. Some migrated as far as forty miles north to the high meadows of Yellowstone National Park. Radio relocations showed us where each elk spent the summer, and provided road maps of migrations to and from summer range.

In the 1960s, Glenn Cole, a National Park Service research biologist, had delineated three major summer ranges of the Jackson elk: Grand Teton National Park, the Gros Ventre drainage, and the Teton Wilderness–southern Yellowstone National Park.[8] Jackson's elk managers referred to these as herd segments—relatively distinct subherds that intermingled in winter. How discrete they were in summer and fall was anyone's guess.

Buzz Robbins and I tested Cole's deductions, which he had deciphered from aerial observations and from the tracks of migrating elk left in the snow. Before Cole, in the 1950s, Wyoming state biologist Chester Anderson had mapped elk numbers and distributions from repeated ground counts and from aircraft.[9] And before him, Olaus Murie had chronicled their seasonal secrets while living among the elk during the 1930s and '40s.[10] With the enhanced technology of radiotelemetry, we sought to verify, refine, and update our predecessors' work. Like an embryonic river fed by tributaries of evidence, science's authority grows more certain with each passing study. From this pursuit of what Rachel Carson termed truth, we derive the most likely explanations for natural phenomena.

Over half of our radioed animals spent summers in roadless tracts where ground triangulation was impractical. Tracking them required aircraft: two-seat Super Cubs and four-seat Cessnas. While pilots flew the aircraft, I managed the VHF (very high frequency band) telemetry equipment, plotted locations on lapfuls of maps, and recorded the associated habitat of each elk. Depending on weather conditions (especially air turbulence), and how widely the animals were scattered, we could locate eight to ten animals per hour. After three to four hours of beeping, circling, and jostling, I was ready for terra firma. My pilot and I were ready sooner if the occasional backseat passenger lost his breakfast an hour into the flight.

Still, I looked forward to each mission. There was always something new to see: a herd of two hundred elk lounging on a remnant snowfield on Wildcat Peak, a colony of white pelicans nesting on a Yellowstone Lake island, a grizzly bear and cubs foraging in talus for army cutworm moths, and the ever-changing scenery of the high country's mosaic of streams, peaks, meadows, and forests.

"You do not know the wilderness until you have flown over it. You may have had an inkling, traveling by foot or horse, but only from a plane can you realize the crazy, wild, wonderful jumble of it," Montana's Pulitzer Prize–winning author A. B. Guthrie wrote.[11] These words rang true with me.

As our study wore on, we learned most elk were faithful to their summer haunts. For example, adult female #65 spent all four summers on Barlow Peak and Chicken Ridge in Yellowstone Park. In fact, ten of eleven radioed elk that summered in Yellowstone returned to the same drainage or mountain complex each year. Furthermore, I determined that Yellowstone and the Teton Wilderness Area should be viewed as harboring discrete subherds of elk. At this coarse scale, fidelity to each of the four herd segments was a remarkable 98 percent among elk monitored for two or more years. Thus, elk numbers in no herd segment prospered from dispersal of elk from the other segments. Population increase was chiefly a result of reproduction and survival. Theoretically, this knowledge simplified the elk managers' task of designing hunting seasons to equitably harvest elk from all four herd segments.[12]

Progress of the Jackson herd's fall migration was a fascinating and valuable aspect of the research. This grand procession of thundering hooves is a visual drama surpassed in the New World only by arctic caribou. Each autumn's performance plays out against a backdrop of the snow-cloaked Tetons jutting skyward through cloudbanks layered against the range's evergreen ridges. Below, the migrants emerge from the Snake River's slumbering cottonwood galleries. Groups ranging from handfuls to hundreds surge across Jackson Hole's sage-studded stage. Some have already traveled fifty miles, as the raven glides, from Yellowstone's soaring Two Ocean Plateau. Across the Yellowstone–Jackson highway, they trail clods of mud and snow. Some charge straight east, curl around the backside of Blacktail Butte, then swing south through the tawny grasses of Kelly Hayfields. They set their sights on the cottonwood and willow security of the Gros Ventre River and the refuge's Gros Ventre Hills beyond. Only reports of hunters' rifles may blunt their resolve, scattering them three miles eastward to national forest woodlands.

Other bands ascend Blacktail's thickly treed ravines and ridges in search of shelter. Content to complete the journey another day, they are relatively secure one thousand feet above the surrounding plain. They may seek the elk refuge after nightfall, or gather in hundreds until the next snowstorm exhorts them on. Still others trail through sprouted subdivisions farther south, where fences and barking dogs replace sportsmen clad in fluorescent orange. But this pathway too, must ultimately negotiate the NER's own treacherous hunting grounds. Only when each matriarch-led convoy reaches the marshes and grasslands of the southern refuge is their journey complete. Here they are safe from the hunters, their passage rewarded by a banquet of forage. (Since 2007 the entire refuge has been open to hunting.)

These general patterns of migration were already known. But the specific timing and interaction of elk migrating from various summer ranges were not. As migration toward winter ranges began in late October, I increased the frequency of telemetry sessions to three times weekly. These early efforts established that elk departed all summer ranges at about the same time. Thereafter the procession varied with distance between summer and winter ranges and the pathways the elk traveled.

At numerous meetings I reported our findings and how migration patterns during 1978–1985 affected elk harvests. Still, there never seemed to be time to fully analyze the data, until mounting consternation drove me to convert my kitchen table into an office away from the office. In 1994 I finally published the results.[12] Future studies during the 1990s, with larger numbers of radioed animals, more precisely explained why elk migrated when they did and how migration patterns influenced their survival.

The third project John Wilbrecht assigned me created heartburn for NER managers as well as Bridger-Teton National Forest, Grand Teton National Park, and Wyoming Game and Fish Department officials. In 1958 these agencies founded the Jackson Hole Cooperative Elk Studies Group (JHCESG). The group was born to cooperatively identify, fund, and conduct studies to benefit elk conservation and management. An annual meeting provided agency representatives a forum to share information and problem-solve. A technical committee, comprised of a wildlife biologist from each agency, did most of the heavy lifting, including my third priority project—curbing unregulated winter recreation adjacent to the refuge's east boundary.

These were Bridger-Teton National Forest lands recognized since 1918 as critical to wintering big game, when the Forest Service withdrew about four thousand acres from livestock grazing to reserve forage for wintering elk, mule deer, and bighorn sheep. The Bridger-Teton constructed a road through the refuge in the 1940s to access timber stands near Curtis Canyon. In 1984 Congress established the Gros Ventre Wilderness Area. This 318,000-acre wildland adjoined the refuge's sixteen-mile-long east boundary, with one exception: Lands in the Curtis Canyon–Sheep Creek area were webbed with logging roads and therefore excluded from wilderness designation. In 1982 the access road through the refuge, just fifteen minutes from the town of Jackson, remained open year-round. John Wilbrecht directed me to work with the JHCESG's technical committee to study what impact foot and vehicle traffic were having on big game.

Two years of monitoring produced a convincing case for managing human use of Curtis Canyon. Snowmobilers, skiers, and chained-up pickups commonly displaced elk and deer, sometimes at distances up to

Curtis Canyon winter range east of the National Elk Refuge lies mid-ground beneath Sleeping Indian Mountain
(Bruce Smith)

half a mile away. On occasion photographers approached bighorns too closely, precipitating harried escapes across cliffs. In the worst-case scenario, elk stampeded from the forest slopes and onto the refuge below. The offended animals, with tongues dangling and puffing clouds of vapor, were clearly stressed in the depths of winter. Our agencies strived to keep elk scattered across available winter ranges because displacing elk onto the overstocked refuge accelerated forage depletion and the onset of winter feeding.

Options we considered included a partial area closure, closure to only certain types of activities, and complete winter closure of the national forest lands and the refuge's access road. Two groups would be pivotal in gaining acceptance of any restrictions: the backcountry ski club and the Jackson Hole Snow Devils snowmobile club. Both groups resisted curtailment of their winter pastimes, but the skiers were especially invested in the area. They had built a cabin many years prior in the Gros Ventre backcountry—high above where big game wintered in Curtis Canyon. A tradition of overnight excursions to the Goodwin Lake cabin for powder sluicing was well established.

The preferred alternative in Bridger-Teton National Forest's environmental assessment (EA) was to close Curtis Canyon Road and adjacent lands from December 1 to May 1 each year. All four government agencies concurred. Jackson Hole residents overwhelmingly favored restrictions— a clear signal that wildlife ranked high among the community's priorities. Without this support, the proposed closure would have been doomed. But when the proposal hit the streets, the EA provoked dozens of letters to the forest supervisor and to editors of both Jackson newspapers. The sharpest comments came from backcountry skiers who felt their impact on wildlife did not justify being shut out. "Besides, the Forest Service," one argued, "had turned a blind eye to the Goodwin Lake cabin when drawing the Gros Ventre Wilderness Area's boundary," ostensibly grandfathering its use. In response, the Forest Service's 1985 decision conceded to skiers a designated access to the cabin. The ski route largely avoided big game by sticking to areas of deep snow.

The December–May closure, with its ski access exemption, remains a successful public policy compromise. During the decade after the plan's implementation, an average 976 elk were counted annually from aircraft east of the refuge compared to 465 before 1985. Our goals of reducing wildlife harassment and displacement were achieved, supporting my contention that 90 percent of wildlife management is people management.

The fulfillment of these three projects during my early years inspired me to remain at the NER. The study of migrations and survival of the Jackson elk, in particular, became a springboard to greater challenges in the years ahead.

CHAPTER 4

Wapiti Welfare

One of the most critical situations the wildlife manager has to face is a public demand to feed elk on an overstocked range.
—OLAUS MURIE, 1951, *THE ELK OF NORTH AMERICA*

FEBRUARY 1982

The Kenworth rumbles and pitches across a snow-covered plain called Poverty Flats. This broad alluvial fan, centrally situated on the National Elk Refuge, was so named by the homesteaders who tried to scratch a living from its rocky ground. The thirsty soils—I considered anything less than two inches in diameter good dirt—sucked irrigation water from hand-dug ditches before most arrived at tilled fields. Each acre seemed to grow rocks far better than vegetables, grains, or hay. Hand-gathered windrows of cobble still stand testament to the toil of settlers who farmed the land early in the twentieth century.

Despite its six-foot-diameter pneumatic tires, the Kenworth reacts with lurching indignation to the rough terrain where the elk are fed. And when laboring in deep snow, it bounces in a spine-compressing rhythm—my closest encounter with rodeo competition. Once it loses forward momentum, the bright yellow behemoth bogs down in its own ruts even in six-wheel drive. Once stuck, it's *really* stuck. I recall one day when Pape's Pumpkin (so named by the refuge mechanic, Roger Pape, who modified this cast-off military transport) settled frame-deep in wet snow like an overgrown gourd. After an hour of Olympic shoveling with driver Bob Rowley, I watched as a bulldozer and chained-up grader worked in tandem to free the Kenworth. Instead of breakfast, we served brunch to 1,500 befuddled elk.

Kenworth feedtruck
(US Fish and Wildlife Service)

Bob remained partial to the Kenworth—the only feedtruck of its kind at the refuge, or anywhere else for that matter. The other two feeding rigs were steel-tracked bulldozers that towed twelve-ton capacity trailers (upgraded nowadays to fancy, rubber-tracked, heated-cab Cat Challengers). Compared to the bulldozers, the Kenworth's cab was perched high above the ground. Like the bridge of a battleship, it provided Bob (an ex-Navy man) a commanding view of the surrounding terrain and the elk herd to be counted.

In my first winter as refuge biologist, on my maiden voyage aboard the Kenworth, I'm still naïve to the Pumpkin's idiosyncrasies. I'm simply captivated by the setting's novelty. Sunlight slips over the eleven-thousand-foot Sleeping Indian, that headdressed hulk resembling its namesake. Reclining on the west flank of the Gros Ventre Mountains, the "Indian" guards the refuge's eastern border. To the west, dawn's rosy glow creeps from the summit snowfields of the Teton Range's peaks—Moran, Teewinot, Owen, and Les Trois Tetons. In the foreground a swarm of two thousand animals charges to meet us and weaves past the lumbering transport. In the side mirror, I watch them swirl and reverse direction, now pursuing us en masse. One outlier bucks and kicks her hind feet while arching her neck to one side, then the other. Some say that animals don't feel joy. They're either cynics or have spent too little time among nature's creations.

As we reach a clean stretch of landscape, Bob nudges a red-knobbed lever rearward. From one of the four steel-plated bins holding a combined twenty tons of pelleted alfalfa, breakfast is now being served. A glance in the side mirror confirms a green swath spewing from a rear bin's opened gate. Hundreds of elk brake to taste this initial stream of pellets. Others continue to follow, scattering along the feedline in our wake. After dispensing six serpentine lines, each a quarter mile long, we stop to gauge our work.

Clambering atop the still-full front bins, I announce, "Left rear bin is empty. The right rear has just a ton left." Then the counting begins.

To provide a proper ration, several factors must be taken into account. First, the feeder counts, or rather estimates, the number of elk at his feedground. Elk are fed at four locations each morning, but with eight thousand elk roaming the refuge, that doesn't mean there are two thousand at each location. Interchange between feedgrounds, spaced about a mile and a half apart, can grow or shrink numbers from day to day. Fortunately, elk distribute themselves neatly across the feedlines, making counting a thousand or two less problematic than might seem possible. At least, once you get the hang of it.

Elk spread on National Elk Refuge feedlines
(Jim Griffin, US Fish and Wildlife Service)

Over time I learned to partition the columns of feeding elk into groups of one hundred. After counting them all, I repeated the process twice more to validate the result. It's a little like slicing a pie into equal-size pieces of one hundred calories each. Of course, counting elk is easier. Calories are invisible; the elk are pleasingly apparent.

Bob, the contrarian, would josh coworkers, "I don't count elk that way. I count all the legs and divide by four."

Why not the ears and divide by two?

With the elk counted, and the doled tonnage determined, Bob punches in the numbers to calculate how much feed he's dispensed per elk. An adequate ration averages seven to eight pounds—more in severely cold or windy weather, less when conditions moderate. Excessive crowd-ing or aggression signals that more breakfast needs serving for the pre-vailing conditions.

Ask someone who's even vaguely familiar with the NER, "What does the refuge do?" You will likely hear, "That's where they feed the elk."

Winter feeding is the most noteworthy, scrutinized, and controversial of the refuge's functions. The dilemma is not that sufficient habitat wasn't set aside in Jackson Hole. We did pretty well. A twenty-five-thousand-acre national wildlife refuge, two premier national parks, and expansive national forest lands cover 97 percent of Teton County's 4,222 square miles, approaching the area of Connecticut in size. However, this is high-elevation country that's mostly snowbound half the year. The decision was made—and reaffirmed repeatedly—to maintain more elk than the available winter range could support. Each year my biologist counterparts at Wyoming Game and Fish Department and I monitored refuge conditions and recommended to our supervisors when feeding should begin. While I was there, December 6 and February 27 were the earliest and latest starting dates. I analyzed a host of variables and found that 96 percent of the variation in the starting date of feeding was explained by two factors: snow accumulations in December and the number of elk on the refuge.[1] More snow and more elk meant less forage available per elk. Consequently, we supplemented their diets with alfalfa sooner.

I fed elk during my last ten years at the NER, but coordinated the feeding program and monitored the elk herd's health throughout my tenure. Once feeding began, I met each morning with refuge staff who would operate the Kenworth (which fed two herds daily) and two trailer-towing bulldozers that day. We discussed the previous day's feeding and any adjustments that might be needed. We reviewed how many elk were in each of the herds and whether we needed to move some from one location (Nowlin, for example) to another (maybe Poverty Flats). Yes, the elk were so habituated to meals on wheels that we could lure them to areas of our choice. Like the Pied Piper of Hamelin's fife that summoned both rodents and children, a rumbling diesel's stack chummed throngs of elk.

We began each feed season by doling elk a ration of three or four pounds each and nudged it to a full ration after ten days. The purpose was to allow the elk's rumen microflora—the community of bacteria and protozoans that inhabit the first two chambers of the four-part stomach—to adjust to a new food. These symbionts, which do the digestive heavy lifting for the elk, rapidly reproduce. They churn out more of the microbes that digest what the elk are currently eating and fewer of those varieties not presently needed. This adjustment can take several days, so an elk subsisting on native grasses, sedges, and other cured plants in January could develop digestive disorders if abruptly fed a bellyful of rich, green alfalfa. The "phase-in" period allows the microflora to adapt. A similar "phase-out" period occurs in late March, as elk begin grazing the refuge's first new growth—food more digestible and nutritious than alfalfa hay.

Elk are among the most social of the deer species. However, the unnatural crowding of so many animals into so little space spawns some unavoidable competition that takes several forms. Most commonly one animal challenges another to displace it from its position on a feedline. Confrontations range from threat posturing with laid-back ears to an outright charge. Closely matched elk sometimes rear onto hind legs, heads heaved eight feet in the air, and assail their opponents with flailing forelegs. Bouts last only seconds but are exciting competitions of showmanship. Once dominance is established, sometimes requiring multiple rounds of sparring, both parties retreat to the alfalfa.

Most aggression is harmless, a show of strength and assertion of social rank, but bulls gore others from time to time. These blows usually damage only egos and the nap of fur coats, although at times a sinister wound might be inflicted. Fatal wounds are exceptionally rare. Those we observed resulted when a bull ran headlong into a feedline, dropped his head to gulp pellets, and his protruding brow tines pierced the skull of an unwitting animal feeding opposite him. The outcome was instantaneous.

Once all feedlines were laid—a twenty-minute routine—elk dined shoulder to shoulder with remarkable calm. Once the alfalfa was spread, I'd park my rig some thirty yards away. From my perch atop the trailer, I could soak it all in. The sounds of elk permeated the morning: snow crunching beneath hooves; molars crushing food; calves and cows mewing to keep in touch with one another; the occasional clacking of antlers as two satiated bulls leisurely sparred. More elk than most people see in a lifetime breakfasted around me.

Like horses and cows, elk can munch and swallow their food while seldom raising their heads. The goal is to economically fill the stomach. Most of the chewing will occur later when resting elk regurgitate and thoroughly grind the rumen's contents. Rumination contributes to energy conservation, as elk burn fewer calories ruminating while bedded than masticating food while foraging.

Some elk take the process of energy conservation to an extreme. I've watched an elk—usually an older (and wiser?) cow—dash to a feedline, then drop to her front knees and dine from this comical, butt-inclined stance. One propelled herself along a feedline with her hind legs while vacuuming pellets into her mouth as she skidded forward on her chest. I saw others simply lay beside feedlines and leisurely slurp anything within reach that was green.

The winter feeding program reduced conflicts with ranching interests and rescued Jackson Hole's besieged elk at the turn of the twentieth century. But it was never intended as a long-term solution to the ongoing assaults on elk and their habitats.

Early refuge managers emphasized land acquisition and habitat enhancement to sustain the herd even while they continued feeding. Since 1912 the draft horses and diesels remained stabled and silent during just one in ten winters. In the nine years of no feeding, low snowfall in surrounding areas meant fewer elk came to the refuge. I'd have enjoyed observing elk in an "open winter," but in my twenty-two years, one never came, nor has one since. Extra elk and now a burgeoning bison herd simply depleted the refuge's forage regardless of the weather conditions.

The bison began as a private herd of twenty animals, fenced on lands owned by John D. Rockefeller in the Jackson Hole Wildlife Park. In 1950 Rockefeller transferred those lands and the fenced bison to Grand Teton National Park. Park Service officials fed the animals in winter, though on occasion some escaped, were rounded up, and returned to the enclosure east of the town of Moran. After the herd (down to eleven animals) escaped from the enclosure in 1968, Grand Teton National Park elected to remove the bison enclosure and allow the bison to range freely. After a decade of roaming the park and increasing very slowly, the herd discovered the NER alfalfa feedlines. When I arrived in 1982, there were but fifty-five. Yet each lumbering buffalo consumed as much forage as two-and-a-half elk. By 2004 the herd topped one thousand.[2] Added to seven to eight thousand elk, bison overwhelmed what groceries the refuge grew (see Appendix A).

Cost alone is a significant drawback of feeding the elk. During my tenure, the annual cost averaged $335,000, or $45 per elk each winter (in 2004 dollars). The sum covered the purchase of about 2,400 tons of pelleted alfalfa, salaries of feedtruck drivers, and fuel. The bison herd, which could not be excluded from the feedlines, cost two to three times per animal more than the elk to feed. What this didn't include were the indirect expenses for equipment depreciation, administration, maintenance, and biological monitoring. The total bill for the program—including capital outlays for feed storage sheds, feed trucks and trailers, associated feed handling equipment, and equipment replacement costs—would be staggering, especially considering that none of these expenditures are required for 97 percent of North American elk (animals that are not fed at all).[3] Beyond the economics are the ecological liabilities of winter feeding, which I'll discuss at length in later chapters.

People, in general, viscerally relate to the notion of feeding wildlife. It is a step early humans took many times in the process of domesticating cats, dogs, horses, cattle, goats, and others. And like many wild species, elk readily habituate to handouts of tasty food. A 1994 survey of Idaho citizens (one of the five states that feed elk in winter) found that 93 percent of hunters and 79 percent of nonhunters supported their state government spending money to feed big game animals.[4] However, habituating elk to following feed wagons, rather than rustling for wheatgrass, troubles some observers. As one wildlife manager I interviewed in Oregon (where about 2,500 elk are fed out of a statewide population of 120,000) observed, "Once you control the food of the critter, you control the critter."[3]

Jackson's elk became conditioned first to horse-drawn hayracks and then to diesel-powered behemoths, and the presence of people on both. Day after day watching thousands of elk crowd my rumbling feedtruck

Bull bison with elk in background
(Bruce Smith)

to gobble hay pellets, I couldn't help asking, "When is wildlife no longer truly wild?" Beyond western Wyoming's elk, this is a pivotal question in a world rapidly losing its wildness both from the direct plunder of biodiversity and from human disruption of natural systems.[5]

What makes places wild is that nature, and not humans, define the landscape and its workings, including its wild residents. In *The End of Nature*, Bill McKibben argued, "Nature's independence *is* its meaning; without it there is nothing but us." When we deprive wildlife of its independence from us, *that* is fatal to its essence.[6]

We are too recently removed from our hunter-gatherer roots to not feel at least the occasional tug of wild, pristine places—at least most of us. This, I believe, is why most Americans favor protection over drilling in the Arctic National Wildlife Refuge, a place trodden by only a few hundred visitors each year. To a vast majority, untamed caribou herds and untrammeled lands are more important than a year's worth of oil. We *imagine* ourselves in wild Alaska, even if we may never go there.

Aldo Leopold addressed our need to maintain wild things by invoking the prospective loss of grizzly bears south of Canada. "There seems to be a tacit assumption that if grizzlies survive in Canada and Alaska, that is good enough. It is not good enough for me. . . . Relegating grizzlies to Alaska is about like relegating happiness to heaven; one may never get there."[7]

The abiding choice to draw elk to winter feedgrounds symbolizes one way that the dewilding of wildlife for human convenience gains acceptance through our policy-making. Terry Lonner, a former research scientist for the Montana Department of Fish, Wildlife, and Parks, framed our relationship to elk this way: "There are three kinds of elk: wild-wild, mild-wild, and defiled-wild." In a witty dialogue, Lonner explained to a rapt conference audience what he meant: "Wild-wild" elk are those that remain free-roaming. They rely on humans only to preserve unfettered access to sufficient wildlands where nature governs their lives. "Mild-wild" elk are those where man has assumed some control—by curtailing their migratory tendencies or cultivating their numbers via animal husbandry practices. These include the 3 percent of North American elk that government agencies have relegated to welfare wards on winter feedgrounds. "Defiled-wild" refers to the practice of game-farming elk for commercial goods.

North American wildlife conservation—hailed as the greatest model of effective conservation worldwide—rests on the bedrock philosophy that wildlife is a public resource. In creating something called the Public Trust Doctrine, an 1842 U.S. Supreme Court case ruled that wildlife cannot be owned by people but instead is held in trust by government for the benefit of all citizens. This landmark principle has guided American wildlife policy for over 169 years. As collective proprietors of America's wildlife heritage, all citizens are empowered as advocates of its well-being and enjoyment. In recent years, however, privatization and commercialization have created profound legal and philosophical dilemmas with regard to the public trust of wildlife. A recent essay in the *Wildlife Professional,* a publication of The Wildlife Society (the leading scientific association of wildlife professionals with nine thousand members worldwide), stated the consequences this way: "The current status of the Public Trust Doctrine puts public rights, property law, and the very notion of 'the commons' at loggerheads with private property rights and the quest for profit derived from wildlife, whether personal, corporate, or even communal."[8]

Game farms—or in more romantic parlance, game ranches—have proliferated over the past twenty-five years in North America. They are principally stocked with elk, white-tailed deer, and exotic cervids such as fallow deer. The owners sell lean meat to consumers, antlers largely to Oriental markets as aphrodisiacs and medicines, and guaranteed trophy heads to those who can afford the pricey hunting fees. Because most are stocked in excess of habitat carrying capacity, farms supplement elk diets with processed feeds and mineral blocks to promote body and antler growth, which further concentrates animals in these fenced compounds, increasing potential for disease transmission.

They still look like wild elk, but they've been reduced to livestock status—their breeding and longevity dictated by market conditions. Indeed, their commerce is governed by state and federal departments of agriculture, rather than their conservation by wildlife management agencies.

I spent some time visiting game ranches in South Africa and Namibia in 1992. Because of my work with diseases of the "mild-wild" Jackson elk, I was invited to speak at the Third International Wildlife Ranching Symposium in Pretoria.[9] While elk on the dole at the NER are light-years removed from farmed animals (one could at most make the case that they are "farmed elk granted summer vacations," as refuge manager Barry Reiswig once mocked), and they remain in the public trust as an integral fiber in the ecological fabric of public lands, that experience in Africa gave me some insight into another side of game farming.

Game ranchers of Africa certainly profit from their enterprise, just as many did raising livestock, or some still do in mixed livestock-wildlife operations. Excess animals are culled and sold for the retail market, while breeding stock are traded or sold to other ranchers. What makes ranching African game an attractive alternative to livestock is that wildlife enthusiasts pay for the privilege of observing and photographing wildlife, often while lodging and dining at ranch accommodations. This "ecotourism" has spilled from Africa's national parks and game reserves into private ranches that cater to clients' needs. Sale of hunting experiences often supplements income from nonconsumptive wildlife recreation.

In most African countries, where people compete with wildlife to maintain a meager standard of living and wildlife increasingly are driven into scattered enclaves, large landowners play an important role in conservation. With professional managers, and often in consultation with resource agencies, wildlife ranches provide habitat secure from land exploitation and poaching that are rendering perpetuation of wildlife increasingly problematic continent-wide.

In Namibia, for example, I found adjacent landowners joining forces. They removed adjoining fences to form large nature conservancies. With more room to roam and access to habitat features on one neighbor's property that were scarce on another's, larger populations of more species were sustained. If they met government standards for size, habitat characteristics, and sound management, some ranches acquired endangered species, such as rhinos, from overstocked reserves. With species conservation and private enterprise as partnered priorities, I find confinement of wildlife more palatable.

In North America, no such higher calling of game farming exists. Game-proof fencing impedes wildlife migrations and deprives public populations of habitat. Exotic species of farmed cervids threaten "genetic pollution" when escapees join wild herds of elk and deer. Foremost, escapees, and even contact through fences, represent potential disease vectors to susceptible wild populations.[10, 11]

The Wildlife Society and the Rocky Mountain Elk Foundation view North American game farming as an unacceptable threat to wild, free-ranging wildlife. Both organizations also agree that feeding of wild elk and other big game animals should be avoided. The RMEF will actively support winter feeding only when a state or provincial agency determines that an emergency exists and solicits RMEF support for a "short-term emergency" operation. The Wildlife Society has encouraged phasing-out feeding of wild ungulates, by both government agencies and the general public, and reducing populations to levels that are sustainable by habitat.[12, 13] Given that game farming benefits neither the general public nor its wildlife, and winter feeding is unsupported by scientific evidence as advantageous to the long-term well-being of the resource, these are sensible policy positions.

Unfortunately, game farms have spread across North America like wildfire. In 1997 there were nearly 1,800 game farms in Canada raising 46,000 elk and red deer. Another 110,000 elk were privately owned on hundreds of U.S. farms. Hundreds of game farms hold tens of thousands more exotic and native cervids across North America.[14] Out of distaste for "canned hunts" and the ecological hazards of game farms, the citizens of Montana passed Initiative 143 in 2000. It prohibited any new game farms and outlawed commercial hunts and transferring title of existing farms. Wyoming's legislature prohibited game farming two decades earlier. Other states have entertained similar legislation over ecological concerns.

In concluding their essay on the Public Trust Doctrine, John Organ and Shane Mahoney pose the following questions: "In future decades, will citizens continue to have free access to enjoy wildlife in traditional as well as emerging pursuits? Will governments preserve biodiversity for future generations? Will wildlife remain wild?"[8]

To protect wildlife's essence, its independence from us, requires guarding against policies that incrementally move in that direction. The best safeguard is an informed public's understanding of what's at risk and accordingly assuming their shared responsibility for it.

CHAPTER 5

When Elk Die

If biological principles are to be utilized in game management, biological laws must be allowed to function. One of these laws is selection.

—OLAUS MURIE, 1951, *THE ELK OF NORTH AMERICA*

One of the yardsticks of the NER feeding program's success was elk survival during winter. Thus, one of my responsibilities was to measure winter mortality—a task of my predecessors as well. Beyond reporting the total number of elk found dead on feedgrounds each winter, in 1940 Olaus Murie began classifying mortalities as calves, cows, spike bulls, and branch-antlered bulls. And besides canvassing only feedgrounds, in 1968 Buzz Robbins began hunting down carcasses concealed in outlying areas of the refuge.

In 1982 I expanded these protocols by collecting teeth of the unfortunate. Like annular rings on cross-sections of trees, elk teeth can tell us their ages. Each year a layer of cementum—a substance anchoring teeth in jaw sockets—is laid down on the root. After decalcifying the tooth and removing a slice with a microtome, a cross-section is mounted on a microscope slide. Metachromatic staining of the section highlights its concentric rings for counting. In the case of elk and most other ungulates, the teeth of choice are the middle pair of incisors. In the second year of life, these are the first deciduous teeth to be replaced by permanents. So the number of rings counted, plus one, equals an elk's age.

Not all elk that perished required aging by their teeth. Both calves and yearlings—about 37 percent of each winter's loss—were readily aged by their two-year schedule of deciduous tooth replacement.

Each May I mailed that winter's harvest of teeth to Tom Moore at the Wyoming Game and Fish Department Lab in Laramie, Wyoming. I always looked forward to sharing Tom's report with refuge staff, some of whom were unconvinced that playing elk dentist was worth the effort but nonetheless were curious just how long some elk might live. Each year several females died in their twenties. That's old for elk from a heavily hunted herd. But as time went by and new age records were set, the quest to break thirty kept everyone's interest. Finally, a cow who could no longer gum pellets surrendered. Her stubby incisors bore thirty rings, making her a ripe thirty-one years old. This may still be the oldest wild elk on record. Over twenty-two winters of aging dead elk, females older than calves averaged eleven years old, while males averaged seven years old. In both elk and humans, we males flame out faster.

Besides recording age and general body condition (good, fair, or emaciated), we broke open femurs to evaluate the appearance and consistency of bone marrow, an important fat depot. We categorized the marrow as white and solid (lots of stored fat), pink and soft, or red/orange and gelatinous (fat depleted due to malnutrition from disease or injury or other fault).

A bull elk with severe scabies
(Bruce Smith)

We also assessed the severity of scabies, a parasitic affliction of elk. The tiny scab mite, *Psoroptes cervinus,* is endemic in northwest Wyoming, but rare elsewhere in North American elk.[1,2] Each winter a small percentage of adult males (about 5 percent) and one or two aged females exhibited the clinical signs of alopecia (hair loss) and exudative dermatitis (moist, dark scabs that layer the skin in sheets). The hair loss began at the withers and spread fore and aft with increasing severity of the parasite load. In the worst of cases, half an elk's hair coat was lost. Parasitologist Dr. Bill Samuel of Alberta documented 1,500 mites *per square inch* on the hide of one ill-fated bull.[1]

Bulls with scabies were among the largest antlered males. Their elegant headgear rendered their plight all the more obvious to photographers, hunters, and those who simply loved elk. Obviously irritated by the persistent feeding of mites, they shook their heads miserably and scraped mats of hair-encrusted scabs from their necks, backs, and flanks using their antlers and hind feet. Snowfall blanketed the well-insulated bodies of healthy herdmates, but on balding bulls snow melted quickly, chilled naked skin, and produced hypothermia. Public concern fed my own sympathy for these pitiful sufferers, as well as my scientific interest in the relationships between antler size, scabies, and survival of male elk. Antlers are, after all, such an obvious manifestation of male vigor, and therefore pivotal in the advancement of genetic material. At the NER, I had a unique opportunity to correlate antler size with environmental conditions. So what factors, I wondered, might be at play here—winter feeding, weather conditions, population size, or others?

When the first antlers dropped about March 1, feedtruck drivers collected them daily on and near feedgrounds. This prevented the dagger-like tines from puncturing pneumatic trailer tires, and discouraged thieves from copping antlers after dark and sending the elk into a frenzy. Refuge lands were closed to unauthorized public entry to protect elk and other wildlife. But some folks couldn't resist the lure of "found money." Some calcified currency developed legs, and later sold for the price of filet mignon per pound.

In late April, after feeding had ended and the elk had scattered, local Boy Scout troops gathered the bulk of shed antlers. A hundred or more Cub Scouts, Boy Scouts, and Scout leaders descended on the refuge to comb the flats and hills. Refuge staff supervised the operation, which one described as "herding ants." For me, the day was occasion for nature education as

Scouts with collected elk antlers
(Bruce Smith)

finds of rodent bones, badger and coyote skulls, and sometimes a dead bird of prey kindled far-ranging discussions with Scouts. Above all, the jubilant look on the face of a ten-year-old packing armfuls of antlers was priceless.

After they'd been gathered, weighed, and bundled, nine to ten thousand pounds of antlers were auctioned the third Saturday of May on the Jackson Town Square. This annual event can only be described as Jacksonesque. Lively bidding among artisans, Asian buyers from the medicinal market, and individuals seeking souvenirs lasted the morning. The annual take averaged $60,000–$80,000, with a record $112,000 earned in 1997. The Scouts donated 80 percent to the refuge for feeding equipment and habitat programs and kept the remainder for their efforts. Beats car washes and bake sales!

Unfortunately, these shed antlers were of no value to my research. What I needed besides antlers were the age and health of their owners. Like an evil opportunist, my ready sources were winter's victims. For five years my assistant of ten years, Roxane Rogers, and I sawed the skull plates with attached antlers from each bull that perished. We compared weight and dimensions of each set with age and physical condition of the animals.

Well established is the correlation between antler size and age, and I found that Jackson elk produced successively larger and more complex antlers each year, until the age of ten. Of the 5 percent of those measured that lived beyond age ten, antler weight, number of points, and beam circumference all declined. But all seven-year-old elk, for example, did not sport equally elaborate racks. The question of why some individuals grew larger antlers than others had a less than obvious answer.[2]

Over the five years of study, I found that winter feeding did not play a significant role. Bull elk that died on the refuge—thus giving me a chance to age them and measure their racks—did not grow larger antlers following winters when elk were fed more days or higher rations. Rather, elk grew larger antlers, for their age, following winters with above-normal temperatures in March and April—the months in which both new vegetation growth and antler growth began. Antler growth is highly sensitive to nutrition, and spring green-up is more nutritious and digestible than even alfalfa pellets. Early green-up during these warm springs apparently boosted antler growth.

Taking a cue from Tim Clutton-Brock and his colleagues' findings in red deer, I also discovered a secondary explanation of the antlers that bulls amassed. Calves were in part predestined to a life blessed or cursed by large or small antlers. Males carried by their mothers during winters with warmer temperatures during their birth year were favored by larger antlers later in life.[2,3] Only by inquiring about environmental conditions during calves' gestation could this conclusion be deduced. Now, who would not wonder if a warming global climate will boost future antler size?

Ultimately, these things are more important to elk than to scientists. Lifetime reproductive success—the cumulative opportunities for breeding and passing on one's genes—is correlated with both body size and antler mass.[3,4] Size matters in gathering, defending, and breeding harems of females. Whereas females contribute their genes to future generations by successfully nurturing their offspring, male elk employ the shotgun approach of fertilizing as many eggs as possible. Bulls with robust bodies, massive antlers, and dashing courtship behavior find favor with numerous mates. Genetic immortality is theirs.

Bull elk on the National Elk Refuge
(Bruce Smith)

Of 1,216 Boone and Crockett Club record elk trophies catalogued over the years, the Jackson herd produced just sixteen of those. The herd is large and presumably genetically diverse, so why didn't more Jackson bulls grow record racks than elk not treated to catered meals if humongous antlers are a reflection of nutrition and animal health?

As secondary sex traits, antlers selectively advance the genetic material of males. Larger bulls with larger antlers seem to get most of the girls. However, there is clearly a limit to the size of the headgear an elk can brandish. Even the outsize antlers of *Megaloceros giganteus*—the extinct Irish elk whose antlers topped out at eighty-eight pounds—did not grow unrestrained. Large antlers are costly to produce and costly to carry. To successfully attract mates, antlers need only marginally surpass the next suitor's. The conclusion is blithely embodied in a quip by Abe Lincoln. Someone once asked the great man how long a man's legs should be. He replied, "Just long enough to reach the ground."

Our study also considered the relationship of scabies to antler size and survival of male elk. Scabies contributed to the death of twenty to thirty of 1,100 bulls on the NER each winter. Afflicted males were of peak breeding age, averaging seven years old. Another fifty bulls showed signs of the disease but survived and recovered in spring.[5,6]

The research shed light on a popular misconception that bull elk developed scabies because they were poorly fed. However, two or three months before feeding had begun, afflicted bulls arrived already showing the hair loss pattern and dark gray appearance (from skin lesions) characteristic of scabies. Some actually improved in condition once they arrived at the NER. No longer rutting and lovesick, they devoted long hours to feeding on the refuge's lush forage.[2]

Males with scabies grew significantly larger antlers than those without the disease. This suggested that afflicted bulls had directed more energy to this secondary growth priority, a circumstance inconsistent with undernourishment at the end of winter when antler growth began. Some animals that grew superior antlers during April through August developed scabies during the breeding season. Large, harem-tending males lost up to 20 percent of body weight during the breeding season, and some of these were likely predisposed to scabies by their physiological decline during the fall rut. This was most evident in GTNP where high bull-to-cow ratios amplified breeding competition. At the NER the most severely infested bulls groomed excessively, damaging body insulation, sapping energy, and compromising immune response to the feeding of mites—an ugly downward spiral. Not all the largest-antlered bulls developed scabies—a mystery that needs further study—but elk crowded shoulder-to-shoulder on feedlines enabled scab mites to gain new hosts, thereby perpetuating the disease in the herd. Scabies, I learned, was one of the by-products of the compromising conditions of refuge life.[2,6]

About 120 of the average 7,400 elk on the NER died each winter. This 1.6 percent mortality rate was remarkably low considering refuge elk suffered scabies and several other diseases that seldom afflict most elk in North America. Blood tests of elk captured in corral traps showed high exposure rates to several bacterial and viral diseases.[7]

We might expect that provisioning pelleted hay would compensate for the less healthful environs of feedgrounds, where a carpet of feces fouled soils and spring snowmelt. While feeding certainly prolonged lives of some compromised animals—those with chronic infections, worn-out teeth, or only three legs—and increased winter survival of calves by 20 percent over those not on feedgrounds, it also predisposed animals to diseases.[6, 8]

When environmental resistance to survival was most severe, the infirm and inferior checked out. Refuge scavengers were the beneficiaries. The "cleanup crew" could transform a five-hundred-pound adult into skeleton and skin within forty-eight hours, a calf even quicker. The scavengers were rightly welcomed and protected by refuge policy, engrossing tourists and removing both pathogens and their culture media from the environment.

Witnessing their trade was not for the faint-hearted. Ravens sometimes commenced before an unfortunate had expired. I watched several pluck out the eyes as helpless, prone elk flopped their heads from side to side. Coyotes began dining as soon as a moribund animal lapsed into powerless resignation. Beginning at the anus, where flailing limbs and head could not defend, they began the feast. Although I recoiled at the sight of this spectacle, I found that shock quickly numbed an elk's agony. Coyotes simply hastened suffering souls past death's doorstep.

During my first winter I discovered the pluck of certain coyotes, fifty to seventy-five of which converged on the refuge to dine on elk carrion in winter. Riding with Bob Rowley in the Kenworth, I pointed to a circling flock of ravens above several coyotes far beyond the elk herd we had just fed. I needed to investigate, assuming an elk had met its end.

Bob eased us toward the edge of Flat Creek marsh, where beneath a blanket of snow, murky spring holes and soggy ground were lurking death traps for the Great Pumpkin.

As the Kenworth shuddered to a stop, Bob announced, "This is it."

"You want to come along?"

"And leave my nice warm cab?" Bob quipped as he filled a cup from a steaming thermos of coffee.

"See you shortly." And I headed out with a single-bit ax in hand and a day pack slung over one shoulder.

Word travels fast on the refuge. The number of coyotes I had estimated earlier I now could see had swelled. Ravens are pros at spotting moribund animals and tip off the coyotes, who watch them like signposts. But it's a symbiotic relationship, with both opportunists aiding the other. As coyotes arrive, they dominate the action, ripping open the tough elk hide that raven beaks struggle to pierce. Eagles—both bald and golden—and magpies quickly join the feast, bracketing the ravens in the pecking order. The avian scavengers exploit strategic openings, or await less risky dining after sated coyotes retire. All feed together, but all watch their backs.

This day's experience was unusual and indicated a vigorous coyote population. Their numbers in the Jackson valley fluctuated with rodent populations, canine disease, and other less tangible factors. In future years I would find that far fewer coyotes feasted on elk carcasses.

As I approached, the more timid animals peeled off, either in search of alternate fare or to wait me out at a distance. I expected all of them to scatter, having spent enough time around coyotes to know they are cowards around people. By the time I was four or five yards from the carcass—now reduced to skeleton, scraps of hide, and shredded flesh on the upper neck—twenty-eight coyotes had scurried away. But one remained. Defiantly, this rather small but resolute animal faced me, his head held low, hair on the ridge of his back erect, and teeth bared through a blood-soaked muzzle. I halted, perplexed, even anxious. *Coyotes don't threaten people. Could he be rabid, or suffering from some other mind-altering disease?*

I stepped closer, shouted, and waved the ax. He dodged backward, too alert and agile to be gravely ill. Disconcertingly, he resumed his menacing stance. I glanced back toward the Kenworth where Bob must have been enjoying this over a second cup of Folgers.

The standoff continued for a minute more. Growing impatient, I reasoned, *He's just a twenty-five-pound coyote, for goodness sake. And I have data to collect.*

With a wave of the ax, I charged. "Eeeeaaaah!"

He turned tail and skulked away, though not without a final, defiant, growling turn of the head. He joined an audience of brethren lying passively in the snow, his stature perhaps now enhanced like a warrior counting coup. He was unquestionably the brashest coyote I encountered in my years at the refuge, and testament to his species' tenacity.

Coyote on elk carcass
(Bruce Smith)

From the adjacent town and highway, sick, moribund, and stone-cold elk were visible for all to see. For the paying public there were close-up views—these from a refuge contractor's horse-drawn sleighs that toured customers through the elk. This "death on display" remains utterly unique to elk packed onto feedgrounds. But I found that disease and, more generally, animals dead from anything besides acute lead poisoning, were unacceptable to certain vocal citizens. It was during my second winter in Jackson that I got my first true taste of the politics of reconciling mortality within this cherished elk herd.

The winter of 1983–84 was the most severe of my tenure. As I mentioned previously, snow accumulations in December largely dictated when refuge feeding began. As forage became buried by snow—and particularly when thaw-freeze cycles caused crusting—elk expended extra energy to keep their engines burning. At the close of December, my state counterpart, Garvis Roby, and I recommended that supplemental feeding begin on January 4—three weeks earlier than average.

As I monitored the behavior and feeding of elk, everything seemed to progress as well as the year before—with one exception. There were fewer elk than anticipated. A written agreement between the USFWS and Wyoming specified that the refuge should winter a maximum of 7,500 elk. The remainder of the Jackson herd wintered in the Gros Ventre and Buffalo Fork river valleys. In 1978 numbers on the NER reached 8,400. In response, elk managers instituted liberal hunting regulations that were successful in reducing elk numbers, arguably too successful. As elk numbers declined, Wyoming elk managers slashed hunting opportunities, offering far fewer permits and closing seasons in most of Jackson Hole's eleven hunting units one to four weeks earlier in 1983 than in earlier years. Preliminary data showed over a thousand fewer elk were harvested than in previous years, and Garvis and I expected more than the previous winter's total of 5,800 elk on the NER. As the feedtrucks rolled on January 4, they were greeted by barely 4,500 head. *So where were the elk?*

During the third and fourth weeks of January 1984, fifteen calves were found dead, a startling spike from just four that had died thus far that winter. Apart from bulls with scabies (forty-two having died by the end of December), calves are most sensitive to severe weather and tough foraging conditions. By now the refuge was blanketed by two feet of heavy snow and we were feeding eight-pound rations each day.

Refuge manager John Wilbrecht and the Wyoming Game and Fish Department regional supervisor, Tom Toman, agreed we should contact the Wyoming Game and Fish Department's wildlife veterinarian in Laramie for assistance. I called Tom Thorne, whom I'd met during my work at the Wind River Indian Reservation. From John and from correspondence in the refuge files, I knew that Tom was an outspoken opponent of the refuge's conversion to pelleted hay. So I made the call with some reticence.

"Tom, we've lost a number of elk calves quite suddenly at the refuge. I'd like your thoughts on what the reason might be."

I described the snow conditions and our feeding protocols, and told him that most of the calves that had died were found on the feedgrounds. All had little fat in their bone marrow. This, he advised me, was not unusual. At the expense of fat storage, calves direct most energy toward muscle, organ, and skeletal growth—an evolved priority to achieve maximum body size by winter.

"What kind of elk numbers do you have on the refuge?" he asked.

"Less than five thousand, but there are lots more just east of us on Forest Service lands. Your guys counted 1,200 from helicopter on the twelfth," I said.

Tom acknowledged that this was shaping up to be a tough winter throughout the state. Record snows and cold had stranded hundreds of pronghorn behind fences and even in towns across southern Wyoming.

Then he said, "I can't offer much advice without examining some animals."

"Can you come up to Jackson and do just that?" Neither I nor anyone at the local Game and Fish office had the training to perform animal necropsies, the animal equivalent of human post-mortems.

"I'm pretty tied up the next week or so," he said. "I suggest you bring one or two calves to Ken Griggs. He's a good hand. He helped pregnancy-test elk in the refuge research pens in the past."

I knew of Dr. Griggs, a Jackson veterinarian. Marjean Heisler, who had since left the refuge for the Peace Corps, had mentioned that Dr. Griggs necropsied several calves born to elk in the refuge feeding trials. So I informed Wilbrecht of Thorne's suggestion, and he concurred. When two more calves died on the twenty-first, I called Dr. Griggs and he offered to examine them after clinic hours. So began a chain of events I could not have anticipated.

After we unloaded the calves onto a concrete-floored bay at his veterinary practice in south Jackson, he opened the thoracic and abdominal cavities of the first one, then sliced and probed the internal systems: cardiopulmonary, digestive, urinary, etc. The idea was to find anything unusual that contributed to the animal's death.

"Lungworms," Ken said, glancing up from the "pluck" of lungs, trachea, and heart he'd laid next to the carcass. The lungs and bronchi were packed with threadlike nematode worms. They looked like twisted bundles of vermicelli.

I knew lungworms were a major contributor to pneumonia among western bighorn sheep. Epizootics had all but eliminated populations on some overcrowded ranges. I recalled seeing bighorns in respiratory distress at adjacent Whiskey Mountain when I was working at the Wind River Indian Reservation. They stood stock still with necks extended as they hoarsely coughed and hacked.

"That's got to compromise their breathing," I said, aghast at the number of parasites clogging the animal's airway. I winced at the image of an Italian dinner I had planned for the evening.

Ken agreed, but added, "That's not why this one died."

From the red and gray mottled lungs he redirected the scalpel toward the heart, an organ the size of a beefsteak tomato.

"See," he pointed. "The pericardial fat is used up."

The crown of the organ was ringed with a clear, gelatinous collar. Before being catabolized for energy, the collar would have been a creamy white. This is one place even calves store fat.

Ken offered a solemn verdict, as his surgical scissors slit another section of intestine. "This one starved to death."

The words struck hard. Yet when we opened the basketball-size rumen, it contained a pungent green mass that could only be alfalfa hay. All natural forages were now largely dormant, cured tan in the absence of chlorophyll. Ken discounted the stomach contents, pointing to the spare ingesta of the intestines. "See how little is being digested? This animal hasn't been getting enough to eat."

After a pause I asked, "Do you have a scale I can borrow? I'd just like to weigh the stomach contents for my notes."

With latex-gloved hands, I scooped the green mash into a plastic bag. The scale registered twenty-eight pounds—near capacity of an elk calf's rumen. The second calf was in a similarly declining condition. It was thin, its heart fat depleted, and the lower GI tract was not filled with digesting food; only the absence of *Dictyocaulus* lungworms was different. Again I weighed as much of the stomach contents as I could scoop and scrape from the finger-like papillae lining the walls of the pale gray sack. Nine-and-one-half pounds, the scale read.

During his exam Ken collected and placed several sections of lung and intestine in plastic bags and formalin-filled jars. Later he would package the tissues for shipment to the Wyoming State Veterinary Lab for diagnostic tests, he said. Final diagnosis would await a pathologist's report. Until then, Ken's conclusions of "malnutrition and starvation" were only preliminary.

"How long before you'll get the results?" I asked as I helped him reload the eviscerated carcasses into my pickup bed.

"A week or two," he replied.

As I painfully watched calf losses continue, I tried to beat the coyotes to other necropsy specimens. With John Wilbrecht's approval, I brought two more corpses for Ken to examine the next week. As in all scientific endeavor, the more samples, the better chance of establishing an explanatory pattern and isolating a smoking gun.

John had called the USFWS National Wildlife Health Center in Madison, Wisconsin. He'd informed Dr. Milton Friend, the center's director, of the situation shortly after I called Tom Thorne. But the center's purpose was not to chase around the country investigating elk deaths. Endangered species, migratory birds, and emerging or catastrophic wildlife disease outbreaks were its priorities. Not that the lab's staff wouldn't assist with disease evaluation of a resident state species if requested. It's just that elk, being abundant and generally thrifty, simply didn't warrant their oversight—especially since Wyoming Game and Fish Department had a staff veterinarian. A soon-to-emerge uproar in Jackson Hole would change all that.

During early February, mortality of calves accelerated. John and I decided that I should fly to Madison, where I spent three days learning field necropsy, tissue collection, and preservation techniques. Road-killed whitetails provided perfect surrogates for elk. When I returned to Jackson, a shipment of necropsy supplies and packaging materials from the lab awaited me.

In late February the first shock wave struck. A Jackson Hole newspaper article declared that elk were being starved on the NER. Ken Griggs made this assertion based on the four animals he'd examined. We'd paid him to conduct the necropsies, yet he contacted the media before providing his clients the results. Wilbrecht, a mild-mannered, silver-haired man who had been refuge manager for seven years, was livid. "That's it!" he announced. "No more business for Griggs."

Predictably, the refuge phones began ringing. Among the first were reporters from Jackson's competing weekly newspapers, the *Jackson Hole Guide* and *Jackson Hole News*. What was our side of the story? Why weren't we feeding the elk enough? Was there a problem with pelleted hay? And so the articles continued for the next three months—point–counterpoint, each newspaper trying to outdo the other. "Starvation may be decimating refuge elk," "Experts debate cause of elk deaths at refuge," and "Residents want action to save dwindling elk herd," the headlines read. Any sensationalism the news reports and editorials overlooked was strictly accidental. The letters to the editor were even more incendiary.

Over the next three weeks, my phone calls to discuss the situation with Ken Griggs went unreturned. Stymied by this evasion, I went to his office. When he appeared and asked what I wanted, I said, "To talk directly, not through the newspapers."

He reluctantly agreed, but our meeting proved of little value. He was unapologetic for releasing his post-mortem results to the media, convinced that the feeding program was a disaster.

After mid-March, mortality abruptly abated. By then Ken Griggs had fostered what became known as Concerned Citizens for the Elk (CCE), a loose-knit consortium determined to straighten out the refuge. Among the group leaders, Albert Feuz, a soft-spoken man around seventy, was recruited for his cattle ranching background and experience feeding refuge elk from 1936 to 1944. Aided by the news media, the CCE whipped into a frenzy some local hunters, outfitters, and business owners, and organized a public forum the evening of May 1.

For many of the three hundred who attended, the 7:00 p.m. meeting began an hour or so earlier in the bar adjoining the Virginian Motel's conference room. Although we were requested to attend, no agenda indicated what was expected of Garvis Roby, Tom Toman, John Wilbrecht, and me. I would attend other heated meetings in the future, but none would compare to this one in the town that the Chamber of Commerce bills as "The Last of the Best of the Old West." Indeed, Jackson still boasted wooden boardwalks, western storefronts (although few are original), two playhouses, the World Famous Cowboy Bar with saddles for bar stools, and rodeo grounds within shouting distance of the Town Square. The atmosphere of that evening's gathering was reminiscent of frontier days, minus the gunplay.

Ken Griggs opened the proceedings by reaffirming that the four calves he examined had died of malnutrition and starvation. "My opinion is that not one healthy elk should die of starvation on a federally funded feedground," he announced. His comments were brief but were an indictment of the refuge staff's failure to take care of the elk.

Several others rose to certify Griggs's condemnation of the refuge's indefensible starvation of elk. "The refuge should be feeding long hay, not pellets," one chided.

Albert Feuz's concern was not that the pellets were killing the elk, but that the older elk kept the calves from getting their share. To that point, someone insisted, "The refuge needs to build 'creeps' for the calves."

Creeps—short for "creep feeders"—are hay bunks surrounded by pole fencing. The perimeter fencing would exclude adult elk but calves could crawl under, advocates contend. Many in attendance were too new to the valley or had forgotten that the refuge tried that device in the early 1970s. The experiment's upshot was that dominant bulls staked out the feeders. When calves and cows approached, bulls swung their heads and hideously gored other animals. So ugly was the experience that refuge staff burned the death traps. Creep feeders were a solution looking for a problem.

The prominent brow tines of an elk, feeding on alfalfa pellets
(Bruce Smith)

The refuge's mechanized program of feeding pelleted alfalfa had ten years of success. Routine observations by refuge staff showed that calves readily competed for pellets. The inordinate loss of calves this winter was perplexing and distressing to everyone. I wondered, *How had Olaus Murie dealt with the loss of eight hundred elk calves in 1943?*

As the meeting progressed, the crowd grew more rowdy. When John Wilbrecht was called upon to defend the feeding program, he pointed out that the USFWS managed the refuge not as a feedlot, but as a winter range for thousands of elk. We supplemented the animals when dwindling forage supplies dictated, but the purpose of wildlife management was not to save every last animal. John's stoic efforts failed miserably based on the catcalls.

Tom Toman offered to address the decline in Jackson elk numbers. Tom wisely confessed that elk hunting had been overdone in recent years and would be remedied. The local state Game and Fish commissioner, who was a crowd favorite, quickly praised Tom and other state wildlife professionals. "If the federal government was as responsive as the state, we'd really get something done."

A great cheer erupted from the audience. The feds were left the obvious culprits. This led to discussion of a citizens' advisory committee—an oversight group to keep tabs on the refuge. In a letter to the editor in the previous week's *Jackson Hole News*, Albert Feuz had proposed that citizens accompany refuge officials to count dead elk. "If the refuge will not allow a citizens' committee to help make a count, I can only wonder about the numbers they wish to cover up."

The accusation that we were hiding how many elk had died wasn't just one skeptic's opinion; a local pilot and several cohorts had made low-level flights over the refuge looking for clandestine "burial sites of dead elk." Not only was the charge unfounded, it scapegoated the unfortunate loss of animals and the underlying issue that Tom Toman had raised.

As the meeting wound down and the crowd filed out, two local hunting outfitters stationed at the room's exit solicited signatures. Their petition called for the transfer of the refuge manager and refuge biologist. Trapped behind a crush of eager John Hancocks, John and I waited as names filled the pages. We declined when invited to add ours to the list.

As elk vacated the refuge in May, I drafted an informational release. It served two purposes: to provide a historical perspective on elk feeding and mortality, and to offer an explanation of the current winter's elk losses, which I felt were due to a convergence of contributing circumstances.

The hunting season on the adjacent Bridger-Teton National Forest closed on November 4, a full month earlier than in past years. Previously, pursuit by hunters had driven elk onto the refuge far sooner than weather conditions dictated. The early closure proved successful as hundreds of elk remained on forest lands, thereby reserving refuge forage for later in winter. However, precipitation in December—nearly always snow in Jackson Hole—was 50 percent above normal in 1983. December's subnormal temperatures concluded with an eight-day stretch registering twenty-two to thirty-five degrees below zero. All wildlife were stressed.

In the high country beyond the refuge, elk battled deep snow conditions and bitter cold through mid-January. Then the snow settled during a major thaw and froze hard during the return of cold, enabling elk to travel on the snow's crust. Feedground counts increased by four hundred elk between January 26 and February 15.

State game warden Doug Crawford focused the issue. "This year has been worse than normal," the *Jackson Hole Guide* quoted him in mid-January in an article titled "Errant elk moving into new neighborhoods this winter." He explained, "I think what happened is that a lot of them got caught in the middle of their migrations by the early snowfall and are just now finding their way down to the winter range."

The *Guide*'s story detailed that 120 of those errant elk took up residence in southeast Jackson at the mouth of Cache Creek canyon. As so often happened with neighborhood deer, hay handouts from some residents began habituating the elk to backyards.

As winter progressed, I advised the media that a combination of factors were contributing to elk losses on the NER. Beyond the refuge and Jackson's neighborhoods, elk filled their stomachs with whatever vegetation they could find, like the pine needles I found in the stomach of a calf I necropsied in February. As newcomers reached refuge feedgrounds in late January and February, they gorged on alfalfa. With their rumen flora depleted or conditioned to poor forage, their capacity to digest rich alfalfa was compromised. It wasn't that they didn't consume enough alfalfa pellets; stomach contents of the six calves necropsied by Ken Griggs and me averaged twenty pounds. Their intestines contained so little ingesta because their stomachs simply couldn't digest the food.

The refuge had been feeding for over three weeks when calf losses spiked during late January. Losses peaked in February and rapidly abated by mid-March. Yet winter feeding continued through April 20, almost three weeks later than average. As I saw it, the remaining seven hundred elk calves on the refuge should have continued dying if the feed program was to blame. But that didn't happen. Instead, I believe that severely weakened and malnourished late arrivals were victims of a perfect storm.

Wildlife losses were not limited to Jackson Hole. Eighty miles southeast on the Wind River Indian Reservation, USFWS personnel counted nearly 1,600 elk from aircraft in December 1983, but less than 900 the following April. "About 55 percent of elk calves died because of deep, crusted snow," an official told the *Wyoming State Journal.*[9]

By spring 1984, carcasses of mule deer littered Wyoming winter ranges. Across southern Wyoming, pronghorn died in droves, their search for feeding areas hampered by deep, crusted snow. As northern Colorado antelope and mule deer met a similar fate, the Colorado Division of Wildlife initiated an unprecedented emergency program to feed stranded, starving deer.

The most sickening story that I heard came from my hunting pal and conservation colleague, Lloyd Dorsey. He and his wife, Michele, drove to the Denver airport early that spring to escape a winter that wouldn't end. Traveling Wyoming's Interstate 80, they paralleled the Union Pacific Railway where weakened pronghorn had gathered on the railroad grade at winter's apex. The fragile-limbed animals trailed the windblown tracks in a desperate search for food. The news accounts and Lloyd's description of what followed were horrific.

"Bunches and bunches of prongies lay strewn along the tracks. Onrushing trains simply mowed them down," Lloyd related upon his return to Jackson. That corridor of carnage fed scavengers for weeks.

In the end, about 4.7 percent of elk wintering on the NER perished, including fifty-four cows, ninety-six calves, and ninety-two bulls (three-fourths with scabies). The total exceeded losses in recent winters, but by no means was unprecedented. The Jackson herd was not "decimated by starvation," as represented by some. Rather, the episode demonstrated how controversial issues are often the product of complex underlying causes for which scapegoats and symptoms become convenient targets.

There was a belief shared by some folks that the more the refuge fed the elk, the fewer would die. The presumption, of course, was that food was the only limiting factor. That's like suggesting that oxygen-starved trout in tepid water need more mayflies to snap out of their stupor. Dating back to 1968, the year that Buzz Robbins began meticulously searching out and recording winter elk mortalities, I found the opposite effect. The more days that elk were fed, the more elk died. The fewest per-capita deaths were in 1977 and 1981 when no feeding occurred at all.[10] Those were mild winters with below-normal snowfall, a boon to balancing energy intake and expenditure. With little snow, more of the refuge's forage was available. Thus, body fat—a caloric reserve that fuels food-limited animals—lasted longer in winter. Moreover, during mild falls and winters, good grazing extended to areas typically buried by deep snow. Elk remained scattered and migrated to the refuge later, and fewer arrived.

Prevailing conditions, not calendar date, dictated when and if feeding began. Standing forage satisfied about 65 percent of elk diet requirements; pelleted hay provided the other 35 percent. This ratio—and how long we fed elk—varied with annual forage production, elk numbers, and winter snowpack. Finally, a shallow snowpack required less time to melt, hastening soil warming and new vegetation growth in spring. A shallow snowpack effectively truncated winter.

Although the elk losses during winter 1983–84 were distressing, an underlying cause of the public outcry was captured in this April 15, 1984, headline in the *Casper Star Tribune*: "Outfitters say Jackson elk numbers dwindling."

In a letter to the editor of the April 12 edition of the *Jackson Hole Guide*, John Wilbrecht explained: "Ever since the realization that the elk population in the valley has declined this year, it appears some folks are looking for an answer, a 'scapegoat' so to speak."

When John drafted the letter, he conceded that doing so went against Mark Twain's advice: "One should never get into a letter writing contest with a guy who buys his ink by the barrel." But he felt compelled to respond to the previous week's editorial accusing government officials of "Group Think." John's letter went on to rhetorically ask, "Why has the elk herd declined by nearly 3,000 head from the high of several years ago? Simply, the decline is a direct result of planned, well-conceived, intentional hunting regulations and programs successfully implemented with the approval of the public."

This wasn't as much about the refuge providing the wrong kind of feed, in the wrong amount, or the wrong way. It was about how many elk remained in a dwindling herd. Yes, 242 elk had perished over the winter on the refuge, but that wasn't why 5,000 rather than 7,500 elk remained. Filled freezers were to blame.

Like a latent ailment that flares up under stress, elk feeding was an outlet for public frustration. Every refuge manager and biologist before John and me had felt the crush. Elk feeding was necessary to maintain such high numbers, so when the herd declined, the feeding program came under fire.

Among the lessons I learned from winter 1983–84 was to get out in front of an issue, even if it seems unimportant at the time. Because wild animals in the modern world live largely at the behest of our species, effective conservation requires ongoing public discourse. On the one hand, Jackson was an engaged and vocal community when it came to the valley's environment. On the other, the perspectives and interests of even the conservation community (organizations that included the Greater Yellowstone Coalition, Jackson Hole Conservation Alliance, Wyoming Outdoor Council, Jackson Hole Wildlife Foundation, Jackson Hole Outfitters Association, Wyoming Outdoor Council, and Wyoming Wildlife Federation) sometimes conflicted. Enlisting a diverse public's support was often trying, and on no issue was this more evident than the refuge's winter feeding program.

The political response to the winter's controversy was that state legislator H. L. Jensen convened a working group. It included members of CCE, staff from Wyoming Game and Fish Department, John Wilbrecht, and myself. Our charge was to determine changes needed in the refuge feeding program and to provide access for citizens to monitor the operations. For the next two or three years, we chauffeured anyone who wanted a close-up view of elk feeding—something we'd done previously to accommodate educational and civic groups. Requests dwindled quickly as the horrors of calves being excluded from feedlines went unrealized.

Nonetheless, I enjoyed the discussions that developed atop feed trailers, where I could steer people's energies and heartfelt concerns about starving elk toward the management challenges that Wyoming and the NER faced in maintaining so large a herd. For example, soon after the Virginian meeting I requested a donation from the Jackson Hole Outfitters Association, a vocal critic that winter, to help fund a habitat improvement project. Two days after my evening presentation, the refuge received a sizeable check toward the project.

I was no less anxious than the elk for each spring's arrival. As the feedtrucks made their last runs in late March or early April, I breathed a sigh of relief. No major disease outbreak had befallen the elk—an omnipresent cloud of concern that followed refuge managers like a shadow.

As the high arc of the sun passed north of the equator, feedtrucks drew increasingly fewer customers. Elk roamed widely seeking the awakening delicacies sprouting from snow-free knobs and ditch banks. Then almost overnight, a sheen of emerald stirred Poverty Flats' tawny plain to life.

Bluebirds flashed from rock to post; blackbirds and wrens filled Flat Creek's cattail marsh. Great blue herons fished stoically in oxbows. Canada geese tucked the miracle of eggs beneath their breasts. Overhead, the primeval chorus of sandhill cranes announced that spring had come.

Each year one pair of geese laid its eggs among grass and wildflowers on our visitor center's sod roof. One by one, at their parents' urging, the dusky hatchlings leapt into the void and fluttered earthbound like oversize snowflakes. They plopped onto water and were promptly swimming, as though each egg had contained an Olympic training pool.

Visitors asked why this pair chose the rooftop corner of a bustling building, and not an earthbound nest site like more sensible geese. Why a fifteen-foot high dive for their hatchlings' first swim, rather than a waddle to nearby water? The refuge's healthy population of coyotes, skunks, and mink were likely responsible. All were fond of eggs, and a goose's clutch of eight to twelve afforded a fine feast. But skunks and mink were no more plentiful on the NER than most other places. Coyotes, well, that's another story.

Once the elk migrated to summer pastures, that font of carrion protein departed as well. Coyotes were back to full-time mousing, hunting Uinta ground squirrels emerging from winter dens, and eating whatever else these opportunists could find. As it turns out, they were quite good at searching out nests of ground-nesting birds. It seemed that geese were in a perpetual war of wits with terrestrial predators, and every island in refuge ponds and Flat Creek was a coveted nesting site. But encircling moats proved no match for at least one wily coyote.

The NER's public-use specialist, Jim Griffin, was a keen observer of refuge residents. As Jim drove to the refuge maintenance shop one April morning, he spied a robbery in progress. Through binoculars he watched the crime unfold. On the tip of an oblong island a pair of geese had successfully nested for several years. A lone coyote paced the pond's shoreline. Could this be the day the pair's luck ran out? The coyote peered longingly at the hunkered nesting goose, fidgeted, and tested the water with a paw. Suddenly he plunged in and paddled to the island. Despite the defensive goose's battering wings, he mouthed an egg, swam back to the mainland, laid down the egg, dug a shallow hole, and placed the egg inside. One by one Jim watched the coyote make ten such trips. Then he covered the eggs and left without pausing to sample his plunder—a hollow victory for two distraught empty-nesters.

Jim's story only fueled my concern about the low hatching success of refuge geese. I proposed a project to the Jackson High School's shop teacher. With a design I provided, his students fashioned eight wire nesting baskets. Atop steel posts anchored in ponds and Flat Creek's marsh, we fastened the baskets and packed hay for nesting.

The next spring, every basket was occupied and each pair hatched a brood of goslings. This continued for several years until a new problem arose: The refuge was producing too many geese. Tourists complained about the slick of goose poop on the nearby town park's grounds—now a grand grazing lawn for geese. Indeed, you could barely step anywhere without landing in goose grease. Sandals and bare feet were out of the question. The geese were now winning the war of wits, and I had another lesson reinforced: Whenever we tweak nature to our preference or pleasure, there follow reactions or consequences we may not anticipate. John Muir may have phrased it best: "When one tugs at a single thing in nature, he finds it attached to the rest of the world."

I called a halt to replenishing nesting hay in the baskets (each winter elk skated across the ponds and emptied each one). The local goose population leveled off. More tourists picnicked in the park. Refuge coyotes appeared especially pleased.

CHAPTER 6

Disease Disputes

Change is not made without inconvenience, even from worse to better.
—SAMUEL JOHNSON, 1755

In a yawning gray-marbled hallway, I sat on a straight-backed oak bench, gazing at a wall of photographs of Cheyenne, Wyoming's historic notables. I could almost see them talking, their drooping handlebar mustaches and thick mutton chops working as they debated the day's legal matters, or waxed eloquently about their most recent closing statements. What monumental court cases had been heard in the chambers across the hallway, I wondered.

Waiting to be called to the witness stand, I silently reviewed the questions I expected to be asked, but couldn't complete an answer to one before my mind flitted to the next. My thoughts kept returning to one tangential question: Could Olaus Murie have even vaguely foreseen how his discovery of brucellosis in elk would hurl these animals into a political maelstrom?

In 1930, when three of the nine blood samples he drew from elk presented high antibody titers to *Brucella abortus*, what had he thought? In *Elk of North America*, Murie relates that he collected the blood samples to investigate what could be causing cow elk to abort their calves on the NER.[1] He called the disease diagnosed from the three positive samples "infectious abortion." Was his discovery clouded by apprehension over its long-term implications? I'd give up chocolate to hear his response.

Several nineteenth-century names, including Mediterranean fever and Malta fever, were supplanted by brucellosis to "honor" David Bruce.

The Australian doctor had discovered the bacterial cause of this debilitating disease in humans, characterized by body aches, weakness, and undulating fever (giving rise to the commonly applied name, undulant fever). In the livestock literature, brucellosis is commonly called Bang's disease after Danish veterinarian Bernhard Bang. In 1897 Bang isolated *Brucella abortus* as the disease agent responsible for infectious abortion in cattle.

Prior to Murie's discovery, blood samples of Yellowstone National Park bison tested positive for antibodies to *B. abortus* in 1917. Modern consensus among epidemiologists is that the disease found its way to North America in British cattle that were infected. It eventually spread to American bison and elk in the late 1800s or early 1900s. Several other species of *Brucella* can infect many species of animals, including swine, caribou, sheep, goats, dogs, and man.

Because the disease agent is identical and pathology is similar in elk and the bovines—cattle and bison—the disease in all three species is named bovine brucellosis. *Brucella abortus* primarily infects the reproductive organs and lymphatic system of the host. The hallmark sign of the disease is spontaneous abortion during the first pregnancy following infection. In cattle herds, brucellosis reduces calf production, contaminates milk with the bacteria, and encumbers commerce of infected herds under USDA regulations. These effects jeopardize a beef or dairy operation's competitiveness and economic viability. Furthermore, when more than one herd becomes infected, a state may lose its "brucellosis-free" status, invoking sanctions on all cattle producers until the disease has been verifiably purged from the state. Beginning in 2010 the USDA has taken a more nuanced approach to the disease. New rules no longer revoke a state's brucellosis-free status if the disease is detected in two or more cattle herds during a two-year period.

Transmission to humans was once a major problem. With reduction of the number of diseased cattle herds, pasteurization of milk, and adoption of safety precautions among abattoir workers and dairymen, only one to two hundred cases of undulant fever occur annually in the United States. Most of those are occupational infections of veterinarians and disease researchers that are remedied with antibiotics.

The primary significance of brucellosis in elk or bison is not its effects on those species. Calf losses are minimal—about 7 percent of potential reproduction, based on our studies of confined elk at the NER.[2] Rather, under specific conditions, the disease is transmissible from elk and bison to livestock—a defining issue in its ecology and the overriding reason that I was now waiting to testify in federal court.

In 1934 federal and state authorities in concert with livestock producers initiated a Cooperative Brucellosis Eradication Program. The program's goal was to eliminate the disease from cattle and swine in the United States, largely through testing and removal of infected animals and vaccination of uninfected herds.[3,4] As the number of infected cattle herds dwindled from over one hundred thousand in the 1950s to seven hundred in 1992 in the seventeen states still not classified brucellosis-free, the USDA targeted 1998 for complete eradication in cattle. Cattle populations in Wyoming and Montana were designated brucellosis-free in 1985 and in Idaho in 1990. During the 1980s the focus of the disease eradication program in the Rocky Mountains narrowed to the wildlife reservoir.[5,6] Its goal? Prevent reinfection of livestock from wildlife. With the exception of bison in Alberta's Wood Buffalo National Park, infected, free-ranging herds of elk and bison were clustered in the Greater Yellowstone Ecosystem, or GYE, of northwest Wyoming and adjacent areas of Idaho and Montana.

Elk and cattle comingling in southern Jackson Hole
(Bruce Smith)

So, why only there? Biologists and epidemiologists agreed that brucellosis was perpetuated by concentrating some twenty-three thousand elk on western Wyoming's winter feedgrounds. Studies of elk populations in surrounding states not associated with Wyoming's feedground areas showed scant evidence of brucellosis.[7, 8]

Extensive research showed that only reproductively mature females are important in the spread of the disease. Reproductive products (including newborns, aborted fetuses, placentas, and birth fluids) and milk from infected females are all contaminated with *Brucella* bacteria. Like infants inquisitively tasting their surroundings, curious elk, bison, and cattle sometimes lick tissues they encounter at birth sites of others. This oral route is modus operandi of *Brucella*'s "horizontal spread" to other elk, bison, and cattle. "Vertical transmission" from nursing mothers to offspring can also occur.[8, 9]

During 1970–1990, when we regularly screened refuge elk, some 39 percent of mature females tested positive for brucellosis. Results were similar at the twenty-two state feedgrounds where elk were tested.[3] However, not all animals that tested positive were infected. Blood tests merely react to antibodies to *B. abortus*. Some elk may have cleared the disease, while others had acquired immunity to *B. abortus*. Determining a herd's infection rate, not just the presence of antibodies, requires culturing tissues where *B. abortus* tends to congregate—a procedure that requires sacrificing animals. Thus, seroprevalence (the percentage of blood samples that test positive) serves as an index of herd infection in cattle and elk. Repeated sampling suggests trends in infection over time.

Bison are closer relatives of cattle, and presumably more natural hosts for *B. abortus* than are elk. Seroprevalence among adult females ranges from 50 percent in Yellowstone—in a population of three thousand bison that are not fed—to over 80 percent in Jackson Hole. The Jackson bison are more concentrated in winter when they participate in the NER's elk feeding program. Feeding runs from January into April, concurrent with most disease-induced abortions. As in elk, close contact of bison on feedgrounds promotes transmission of *B. abortus* and perpetuates the disease.[10]

Waiting to be summoned, I imagined the ongoing testimony and cross-examinations beyond the facing double doors of Judge Clarence Brimmer's court. For two-and-a-half weeks, I had been sequestered from previous witnesses' testimony. The U.S. attorneys' pretrial interviews had established the substantive testimony of my fellow defense witnesses: wildlife and land managers, veterinarians, and epidemiologists. The opposing lawyers now sought to challenge and discredit.

There was an irony here. I'd chosen to work for the USFWS where the focus was on managing wildlife and their habitat, not politically charged competing issues like timber harvest, energy and mineral extraction, or livestock grazing. Now a livestock disease, one that had traversed the Atlantic to infect North American wildlife, dominated my time. A final irony was that the disease was relatively benign in wildlife. Despite brucellosis, reproduction added 15 to 20 percent each year to the Jackson elk and bison herds. Wildlife managers struggled to control this surplus in both species' populations. Although an elk ran a 50 percent chance of aborting her first pregnancy after infection with brucellosis, only that first calf in her reproductive lifetime was at risk. She either cleared the bacterium or passively harbored it during the remainder of her life. Yet she remained a source of infection to others, like a Typhoid Mary, shedding *B. abortus* with future births.[11, 12]

Brucellosis in northwest Wyoming's elk and bison had become a weekly, almost daily news item. It was as if this pestilence had just been discovered in the 1980s—like finding a Sasquatch village, or unearthing a graveyard of therapod fossils that dwarfed *T. rex*. Two issues gained brucellosis widespread media attention. The first was the killing of 569 bison north of Yellowstone National Park during the winter of 1988–89. After migrating from the park, the bison were killed in Montana, ostensibly to avert brucellosis transmission to cattle. The second issue was this legal action. The Parker Land and Cattle Company out of Dubois, Wyoming, had filed suit against several federal agencies, seeking $1.1 million in compensation, alleging that elk or bison had infected its cattle with brucellosis in 1989. After follow-up testing found more diseased cattle, Parker chose to depopulate—slaughtering his entire herd, all 622 head. In western ranching communities, the brucellosis shock waves were palpable. Infected with brucellosis by cattle a century earlier, elk and bison were now returning the favor—a dreaded threat to the livestock industry.

Some of us saw this as a test case. Were state and federal wildlife managers responsible for protecting livestock from disease? If so, then what other liabilities might follow? Would federal land managers (the U.S. Forest Service and Bureau of Land Management were also named as defendants because Parker leased parcels of those lands to graze his livestock in summer) bear other responsibilities for private livestock? What about naturally occurring poisonous plants that cattle, sheep, and horses might innocently graze? Or predation by wild carnivores on dim-witted prey? A state depredation law already compensated Wyoming stockmen for predator losses, and federal policy authorized limited killing of wildlife with a taste for mutton or beef. Might these concessions morph into open warfare on wildlife for a second time this century?

Inside the courtroom, wildlife biologist Steve Cain was testifying. Steve and I had driven the 450 miles from Jackson to Cheyenne two days earlier on January 21, 1992. This was the third time we'd done so this month, spending twelve days either en route or waiting to testify. Each week we shared a motel room where we remained each day, waiting to be summoned to the federal building by the U.S. attorney. We were bumped from taking the stand both previous weeks by others "with tighter schedules" or more important titles. We no longer maintained work schedules, uncertain how long the case might drag on and when we'd be high enough on the food chain to testify.

You can go over your deposition and research notes only so many times before your brain goes numb. Thankful when 5:00 p.m. arrived each day, we hit every decent restaurant in Cheyenne, often spending hours there discussing everything from previous work experiences to preferred rifle calibers to our personal lives. I recall we both felt fortunate that Carol Statkus (the lead attorney) and Matt Mead were the assistant U.S. attorneys assigned to defend the case.

From my first meeting with her, Carol impressed me as highly competent and well versed in the brucellosis issue. Over the course of this trial, I also found her tenacious. She viewed court proceedings and the necessary preparation as challenging, intellectual exercises. She told me that her edge in defending federal interests was that she tried to outwork the opposition counsel. Moreover, she said, "I have always liked representing natural resource agencies because they care so much about the Wyoming lands and wildlife they manage."

Matt was thirtyish, a few years Carol's junior. His ranching family background afforded him a working knowledge of livestock management. He was also the grandson of former Wyoming governor and U.S. senator Clifford Hansen of Jackson (and Matt was elected Wyoming's thirty-second governor in 2010). I suspect such sharp attorneys could make far more money in private practice, so Carol's and Matt's commitment to the cause of federal law was a given.

When the USDA discovered brucellosis in Parker Land and Cattle Company's registered Black Angus in 1989, Steve had just arrived in Jackson Hole. As my new counterpart at Grand Teton National Park, he would join me in spending many hours over the next fifteen years in meetings, helicopters, and discussions of how best to conserve Jackson Hole's wildlife. We worked for sister agencies, and the elk and bison that summered in Grand Teton National Park all wintered on the NER. So when Parker filed suit against the refuge and park, Steve and I knew we'd be subpoenaed to testify.

I tried to visualize Steve's cross-examination by Stan Hathaway, the lead attorney for the plaintiffs—the cat-and-mouse game designed to frazzle the witness or provoke a gaffe. Hathaway was an imposing figure, a former two-term Wyoming governor and U.S. secretary of interior in the Ford administration. During his deposition "the Governor" (as Hathaway was fond of being called) had blown up at Steve, calling him a "recalcitrant witness." Steve simply wasn't providing answers the opposing counsel hoped to hear. In the courtroom of Hathaway's friend, Judge Brimmer, Steve expected even less geniality from the attorney. On the other hand, Steve was no pushover, and unlikely to be intimidated by the dynamic attorney's legendary table-pounding and verbal bombastics. With a voice timbre like rocks rolling in a wooden bucket, a head of wavy, rust-colored hair, and a face-full of whiskers to match, Steve created his own presence.

Steve's testimony lasted until mid-afternoon. When it ended, the court recessed for fifteen minutes. He found me waiting on my bench.

"Are you done?" I asked, noting he'd testified for almost two hours.

"Done."

He looked relieved, but at the same time a curious smile crossed his face. "How'd it go?" I pressed.

"Better than I expected. Brent Kunz, not Hathaway, cross-examined me."

We'd expected the lawyer who deposed each of us would also cross-examine us in court, and Brent Kunz, Hathaway's younger associate, had deposed me months earlier in Jackson. His questions were thorough and incisive, but his manner was not intimidating. Now my mind began to race. *If Kunz, not Hathaway, cross-examined Steve, could it be that Hathaway would cross-examine me?*

As Carol approached us, she said, "I'll be calling you when court resumes, Bruce. Are you ready?"

"I'll be glad to finally get on with it. Just one question," I said.

"What's that?"

"Who is going to cross-examine me?"

She cast a glance at Steve and replied, "I don't know."

Five minutes after the court reconvened, Carol reappeared through the doors and signaled to me. I followed her down a central aisle between five rows of gallery benches where maybe three dozen spectators sat—some of whom were reporters scratching busily on notepads. We passed through the bar and between two large tables occupied by the defense and plaintiff's legal teams. Hathaway, Kunz, and two associates occupied four leather chairs behind the table to my left. On the right sat Matt Mead. I passed the court recorder and the jury box, but this wasn't a jury trial, so the fourteen juror seats were empty. The bailiff motioned me toward the witness box.

This was my first experience as a courtroom witness, and the first time I'd seen Judge Brimmer. While Brimmer was serving as Wyoming's U.S. attorney, President Gerald Ford appointed him a district court judge to sit on the federal bench in Cheyenne in 1975. He was seventy, stern-looking, and oblivious to my arrival at the witness box.

After I was sworn in, Carol began her examination. A series of concise questions established my qualifications and expertise, especially my credentials over the past ten years at the NER. I testified about my knowledge of brucellosis in refuge elk, and my understanding of elk migrations and distributions, based on the telemetry research Buzz Robbins had begun and I had completed seven years before.

Carol's questioning lasted nearly an hour and a half. Then with a crack of his gavel, Judge Brimmer adjourned court for the day. *But wait!* I wanted to say, *I'm ready to keep going.*

After a restless night I was back in the witness box the next morning. I waited as Hathaway and Kunz conferred over a spread of documents.

"Does plaintiff's counsel have questions for this witness?" Brimmer queried from my left.

I'd done a good job, I thought, of laying out the improbability of refuge elk infecting Parker's cattle thirty miles east across the Continental Divide. The logistics were improbable. Refuge elk rarely ventured that far east. The single radioed elk that did was there during months when brucellosis transmission was unlikely, August through October. Abortions occurred from January into May, births in May and June. Outside those months, *Brucella* remained within an elk's tissues and of no risk to other animals.

"Yes, Your Honor," boomed Stan Hathaway in a voice that commanded the courtroom's attention. He fixed his eyes on me, then rose and circled the table. He began by establishing that I was not a brucellosis expert. I agreed, but stated that I understood the disease's epidemiology and pathology in elk. I was careful not to mention bison, and certainly not cattle. Although I understood quite well that the disease operated similarly in all three species, I was here to testify as an elk expert. Of course, I had as much control over the questions as the sky has over lightning.

Hathaway's questions quickly turned to his belief that the refuge was doing little if anything to control brucellosis in elk and bison. He made a brief recitation of the State of Wyoming's vaccination program on state feedgrounds, and then asserted that refuge staff had resisted the program until directed by Washington to assist. I'd been questioned about this during my deposition, confronted about two letters written to his superiors by Jim Herriges, the Wyoming Game and Fish Department employee charged with the field vaccination of feedground elk.

"What is your response to the allegations that you were uncooperative, and as a result, not as many elk calves as possible were vaccinated?" Brent Kunz had asked at the deposition.

I had responded that Jim Herriges had two missions in his job: to promote the vaccination program, and to biobullet as many elk on feedgrounds as possible. Let me explain. Decades earlier Wyoming had taken a stockman's approach to elk management in western Wyoming, where herds of elk and cattle were infected with brucellosis. Most elk were drawn to feedgrounds in winter to keep them separated from cattle. Because this crowding facilitated transmission of brucellosis among elk, in 1985 Wyoming began vaccinating elk calves on feedgrounds with the same vaccine approved by the USDA to vaccinate cattle. It provided 60 to 70 percent protection against abortion in vaccinated cattle herds. The assumption was that an elk's immune system would respond to the vaccine similarly to a cow's. However, in vaccination studies by the State of Wyoming, the standard cattle dose caused 27 percent of vaccinated elk to abort their calves—the opposite effect desired in a disease that is spread via abortions. Reducing the dosage stopped the vaccine-induced abortions but also likely reduced the vaccine's effectiveness against *B. abortus* in the field.[13, 14]

At the instruction of the director of the USFWS, the refuge accommodated state employees from 1989 through 1991. While riding on feedtrucks, they fired methylcellulose biobullets into the hindquarters of cows and calves. Encapsulated in the bullets was live Strain 19 vaccine. To avoid shooting an animal twice and double-dosing it, each elk also had to be splattered with a paint ball shot from a specialized rifle. The elk weren't crazy about the program, and refuge manager Mike Hedrick and I had our own reservations, which I'd related to Brent Kunz.

Among them, our feedtruck drivers were asked to dribble out the daily hay ration so the elk weren't satiated and therefore would tolerate the vaccinators longer each day. Elk at the state's feedgrounds (for which the biobullet technology was developed) were more tolerant of being vaccinated. There, an average of just six hundred elk were restricted by deep snow to about seventy-five acres, and elk were fed baled hay (which took far longer for elk to eat than alfalfa pellets).

I explained to Kunz that since the refuge had converted to mechanized feeding of pelleted hay in 1975, blood tests showed a significant decline in brucellosis, from 45 percent to 35 percent. I attributed this to faster consumption of pellets and subsequent dispersal of elk from feedlines. Crowding the elk longer to accommodate vaccination appeared counterproductive and to increase stress among the elk. As a less disruptive approach to vaccinate the whole herd, the refuge had advocated incorporating an oral vaccine into their feed.

Another concern was that refuge staff, and some brucellosis experts, remained unconvinced that the Strain 19 vaccine was sufficiently effective in preventing brucellosis infections and reducing abortions. I had explained to Kunz that a more efficacious vaccine and an improved delivery system were needed. Finally, I'd advocated that the vaccination program should be accompanied by a program to monitor its effectiveness in reducing the incidence of brucellosis in refuge elk. "No such evaluation is ongoing or is even possible at present, except for periodically sacrificing elk to culture *Brucella* from tissue samples. This is not practical or acceptable to the public [and not something Wyoming had proposed]. Because it cannot be evaluated, the success or failure is left to speculation and opinion," I had told Kunz.

After three winters of failing to vaccinate large numbers of elk, the state vaccinators had asked Mike Hedrick to further accommodate their program by "shorting" elk rations and to drive over-snow vehicles through the herds to vaccinate. Hedrick had refused. He felt those concessions would further compromise the refuge's mission, without documentable benefit to brucellosis reduction.

As a consequence the state had terminated their "experimental" vaccination of refuge elk after 1991. It was hardly experimental, though, given that results consisted only of tallying numbers of elk vaccinated, rather than any evaluation of disease reduction. Furthermore, experiments, by definition, must be measured against some standard—one or more comparable control groups that do not receive the experimental treatment, in this case Strain 19 vaccine. Only then can the effect of the experiment be measured against other factors that may influence results. No experimental control group existed. Therefore, no experiment took place.

After I had testified to these points in Judge Brimmer's courtroom, Stan Hathaway glared at me. "So the State of Wyoming has been vaccinating elk to protect them and cattle from brucellosis. And the refuge has done nothing, except deny the state the ability to vaccinate refuge elk. Isn't that right?"

"No, Mr. Hathaway. We've taken a different approach."

"A different approach, indeed. Letting that cesspool of disease fester!"

By way of explanation, I ticked off our efforts to lessen all diseases within refuge elk. Our research with radio-instrumented elk identified areas of highest risk of brucellosis transmission from elk to cattle in

Jackson Hole (areas where cattle were grazed among calving elk); our habitat management programs sought to reduce the need to supplementally feed the elk; and our conversion to mechanized feeding reduced the time elk spent crowded on small feeding sites. Blood testing showed that brucellosis had declined since this conversion (a decline that has continued to present, with only 7 to 20 percent of females testing positive from 2000 to 2009).

My words seemed to make no impression, like pebbles hurled against a stone wall. After blustering again that the refuge had refused the only real effort being made to control brucellosis—vaccination—Hathaway suggested the result of our obstructionism was that refuge elk had infected Parker's cattle. I responded that there were several independent lines of evidence suggesting the probability of that was remote. Our monitoring of radioed elk from 1978 to 1984 produced over five thousand relocations. Only 12 percent of those elk summered east of the NER toward the Continental Divide. "No relocations occurred on the Parker Ranch or their grazing leases, or for that matter anywhere east of the Continental Divide when transmission of brucellosis could occur. A new telemetry study of 115 elk captured in 1990 and 1991 produced another 5,200 relocations to date. None was east of the Continental Divide."

I noted that ear tag returns from eleven thousand hunter-harvested elk, all captured and marked in the Jackson herd unit, indicated only 4.4 percent interchange with adjacent elk herd units. Based upon that rate of interchange, only some seventy-five seropositive elk wintering on the NER might leave the herd unit in any one year. Those elk had gone in all directions, north, south, west, and east, so only a very small number may have ever crossed the Divide onto lands used by Parker cattle.

I paused briefly, too briefly for Hathaway to interject another question, and summarized, "These data show that the risk of brucellosis transmission from elk wintering on the NER to cattle is largely confined to Teton County. But there have been no cases of transmission occurring as far back as the records go. Some 2,500 elk wintering on or adjacent to the three State of Wyoming–operated feedgrounds in the Gros Ventre drainage summer much closer to the Parker grazing allotments and in much larger numbers than NER elk."

At that point I turned to Judge Brimmer. "Your Honor, may I go to the map to point this out?"

A U.S. Forest Service map covering the Jackson elk herd's distribution and adjacent lands east of the Divide had been mounted on foam board and propped on an easel to the right of the witness box. Parker's home ranch and federal grazing allotments were outlined in felt-tipped marker.

"You may," the judge somberly nodded.

Standing beside the map, I pointed to the three state-operated Gros Ventre feedgrounds and to the Continental Divide, and then traced the known summer distribution of Gros Ventre feedground elk. "Those animals are far closer to Mr. Parker's allotments, more likely to have crossed the Divide to calve, and more likely to have mingled with his cattle—that is, if any Jackson elk did so."

I saw the expression on the Governor's face harden as he stalked back to the witness box. "Mr. Smith, you really don't know where those elk with radios go, do you? You told this court yourself in yesterday's testimony that to locate them, you have to triangulate them from known ground locations. So if they go into the wilderness, or over the Continental Divide, you wouldn't know that, would you?"

He finished his mini-tirade with his chin jutting nearly into the witness box.

"Yes, I would know where they go, Mr. Hathaway," I responded deliberately, anticipating his next question.

"How could you?" he boomed, as a mist of saliva sprayed my chin and jacket. "You can't follow them everywhere!"

"We track elk that travel long distances by airplane, Governor."

He cocked his head and looked curiously at me for a moment. I wasn't sure if it was in response to my use of his favored appellation, or that he was caught off guard that I used aircraft to locate wide-ranging elk in rugged, roadless areas. *How could that be?* He had a copy of my manuscript. I could see it there on the table in front of Brent Kunz. The Methods section clearly described our telemetry protocols.

"From airplanes? How could you do that?! You said yourself that you had to get the radio signals from fixed locations. You'd have to stop the airplane to do that!" he exclaimed, looking like a cat about to pounce on a mouse.

"Mr. Hathaway, I would never want the airplane to stop when it's in the air," I answered, doing my best to restrain the smile I felt crease my face.

The courtroom erupted in rolling laughter. I glanced to see the judge, too, was enjoying a chuckle at his longtime friend's expense.

Hathaway whirled around, his arms tether-balling from his sides, and then came back at me. "Then you can't find the elk from the air!" he recovered with an air of triumph.

"Actually, we can," I countered and briefly described the procedure for finding a telemetry signal's location by centering it in the aircraft's ever-tightening circles.

"We map the radio's position. Eighty percent of the time, we observe the radioed elk, or the group that it's in," I concluded.

With that, the Governor stormed back to the plaintiff's table, hesitated, and barked, "I have no more questions for this witness."

With a furtive smile betraying her amusement, Carol offered no redirect. Judge Brimmer dismissed me.

Stan Hathaway died October 5, 2005, at age eighty-one. A four-story building in downtown Cheyenne, housing state judicial, health, and family services offices, was named in his honor. Following his brief stint as secretary of the interior in 1975, he won praise as a stalwart, sincere, and honest litigator during his three decades of law partnership with Brent Kunz. However, *Parker Land and Cattle Company vs. the United States* was not among his legal victories.

After five months Judge Clarence Brimmer ruled, finding for the federal government and exempting all agencies from any liability. A collective sigh of relief rushed from private and government wildlife interests. With no apparent cattle source for Parker's brucellosis—based on testimony from his ranch manager and USDA veterinarians—the gun targeted elk and bison. Consequently, Steve Cain's testimony about the improbability of Jackson Hole bison infecting Parker's cattle, and my testimony about NER elk were pivotal in the court's decision. At least, I like to think so.

In the end the preponderance of evidence did not implicate Jackson wildlife. There was no direct evidence of how Parker's cattle became infected, whether from cattle, or bison, or elk, much less which specific animals. As plaintiff, Parker's burden of proof was substantial. However, in his findings and conclusions, Judge Brimmer repeatedly referred to the federal agencies as "negligent" for failing to control brucellosis. He stopped short of calling the NER a cesspool of disease, the phrase Stan Hathaway coined during the trial and every newspaper parroted. But according to Brimmer, the State of Wyoming wore the white hat. Only they were vaccinating elk. The implication was clear: The feds were intractable hoof-draggers when it came to brucellosis.

Here is the stark reality. The standard protocol for purging brucellosis from a cattle herd is to repeatedly test and remove infected animals—a prolonged process, to be sure. Instead, producers often choose the same course as Parker—depopulate and start over to get back in business. Likewise, the only certain means of eradicating brucellosis from western Wyoming and Yellowstone Park would be to kill all elk and bison comprising the disease reservoir. Logistically possible? Probably. Just call in the military for some "shock and awe."

But given the economic, social, ecological, and symbolic importance of these populations—some 120,000 elk and 4,000 bison at that time—the predictable public outrage would be politically intolerable. These charismatic bison and elk draw tourists and hunters from all over the world and stoke local economies. In fact, neither federal nor state law mandates eradication of brucellosis in wildlife. Although Judge Brimmer's opinion in the *Parker* case urged more intensive federal management efforts against the disease, it did not suggest that wildlife brucellosis must be—or even could be—eradicated. In a *Land and Water Law Review* article on the case, Robert Keiter and Peter Froelicher observed:

> . . . the decision does not indicate that federal officials are legally obligated to take any particular management actions. In fact, the absence of any congressional policy on wildlife brucellosis suggests that federal officials are under no legal obligation to protect domestic livestock from infected wildlife. Under federal law, therefore, wildlife and cattle should be able to coexist on the public domain, notwithstanding the brucellosis risk.[15]

There was considerable fallout from the *Parker* decision. Livestock producers redoubled their efforts to vaccinate cattle. To limit burgeoning elk numbers, Wyoming and federal wildlife managers offered hunters the option of buying a second license to harvest two elk in certain hunting areas of Jackson Hole. Wyoming and the NER also initiated a bison hunt on the refuge. Wyoming accelerated its elk vaccination program—both in the field and in the public relations arena. And in 1994 the Greater Yellowstone Interagency Brucellosis Committee (GYIBC) was formed to coordinate state-federal actions.

"When in doubt, appoint a committee" is a common government response to problems. That tactic temporarily gets decision-makers off the hook from those calling for real action. Accordingly, formation of the GYIBC was a show of unity for eleven federal and state agencies in the GYE (U.S. Forest Service, Park Service, Fish and Wildlife Service, Bureau of Land Management, and Animal and Plant Health Inspection Service, and each state's wildlife and agriculture departments from Idaho, Montana, and Wyoming). They were doing something to address the problem. They must be; they convened a symposium in 1994 and well-publicized meetings three times a year.

To be fair, the GYIBC tempered the level of discourse and brought focus to the issue of brucellosis (and money for everything from press releases to research). It even produced as its first position statement a document on winter feeding. The opening sentences read, "The evidence is overwhelming that winter feeding of elk has proven to perpetuate and enhance the spread of diseases, especially brucellosis. Once certain contagious diseases become endemic within a population of elk, bison, or other wildlife, they become very difficult, if not impossible, to eradicate. Consequently, promotion or initiation of new wildlife feeding grounds in the states of Montana, Idaho, and Wyoming would be contrary to the mission statement and goals of the GYIBC."[16]

Idaho took this issue quite seriously after brucellosis was detected in two elk herds in southeastern Idaho in 1998. With the state having just regained its cattle brucellosis-free status in 1990, Governor Phil Batt established a Wildlife Brucellosis Task Force. This agency-citizen advisory committee recommended actions to eliminate or minimize the number of elk being artificially concentrated around annual winter feedgrounds in four eastern Idaho elk herds. Although elk feeding in

Idaho was junior league in comparison to Wyoming, many of these elk interchanged with western Wyoming's brucellosis-infected feedground elk—the likely source of the Idaho disease. Along with hunting, Idaho's trapping and testing of elk—destroying brucellosis-seropositive animals and translocating seronegative animals to suitable habitat elsewhere—served to reduce elk numbers and the impetus for feeding. Elk feeding in eastern Idaho remains on schedule for complete elimination of this nexus of brucellosis in wildlife.[17]

On the other hand, the GYIBC's position on feedgrounds had little effect on Wyoming. To the present, not one feedground has been eliminated in Wyoming, and the number of elk that the Wyoming Game and Fish Commission authorizes to be fed remains unchanged. Similarly, no changes in feeding occurred at the NER through 2006, though not for lack of desire. In 1995 refuge manager Mike Hedrick requested that Wyoming Game and Fish Department consider reducing elk numbers to a maximum of 5,500 on the NER. In a half-page response, director John Talbot cordially declined.

To some degree this disparity between Idaho and Wyoming indicates how entrenched the feedground mentality was in Wyoming and what a political hot potato feedgrounds and diseased elk had become. Turf wars and political expediency trumped what was good for the elk. Maybe the most symbolic indication of the difficulty, or intractability, of agencies with differing missions and political constituencies agreeing was the months-long dispute over the logo for the GYIBC's letterhead. Imprinted beside the words "Greater Yellowstone Interagency Brucellosis Committee" were a bison and an elk. Several of us from member wildlife management agencies questioned why an Angus or Hereford shouldn't appear as the third leg of the stool. After all, were it not for cows, the disease wouldn't cross agency radar screens, and the GYIBC would not exist. But other members argued, "No need to point the finger at the livestock industry. They have a program to manage the disease, and a commitment to eliminate brucellosis in cattle by 1998."

"Yes," I replied. "But cattle are the reason we are focused on this disease. Whether transmitted from bison and elk or from other cattle, I think they remain part of the problem."

The GYIBC letterhead remains cattle-free still today.

After most of the United States was classified brucellosis-free, several states threatened sanctions against importation of Wyoming beef, concerned about wildlife transmitting the disease to cattle in the northwestern part of the state. Wyoming responded in 1997 by requesting that the USDA review the state's cattle brucellosis program. The review prescribed extensive testing and complete calfhood vaccination of cattle in western Wyoming—an inconvenience and expense largely borne by livestock producers.

Pressure mounted from Wyoming to resume vaccination of elk at the NER. The new refuge manager, Barry Reiswig, resisted, noting the disruption of the NER's feeding program during the 1989–1991 vaccination venture, and the questionable efficacy of Strain 19 in elk. Under increasing pressure from Wyoming governor Jim Geringer, the USFWS's Washington office directed the NER in 1997 to review the effectiveness of Strain 19 in controlling brucellosis. Dr. Tom Roffe, the NER's veterinary contact at the National Wildlife Health Center in Wisconsin, and I were charged with conducting the review. We evaluated the Wyoming Game and Fish Department's clinical vaccine research and their ballistic vaccination program at state-operated feedgrounds from 1985 to 1997.

Tom and I pored over the design and results of their vaccine trials and trends in blood tests of feedground elk. Our August 1997 report to the USFWS's regional director in Denver was unflattering. Because of flawed experimental designs and interpretation of results in all clinical trials, we concluded that the efficacy of Strain 19 could not be judged. Furthermore, the state failed to experimentally demonstrate vaccine benefits on brucellosis among feedground elk.

A decline in brucellosis at the Greys River feedground—where elk had been vaccinated and blood-tested longest—was mirrored by a decline at the NER, subsequent to the refuge's conversion to mechanized feeding of pelleted hay. Was either, or both, the cause of brucellosis declines? (After 2000, brucellosis seroprevalence at Greys River inexplicably spiked to pre-vaccination levels despite continued vaccination each year, while seroprevalence has continued to decline at the NER.) Tom and I concluded:

Efforts to reduce dependency of elk on supplemental feed, by increasing the productivity of winter ranges and reducing elk populations to numbers nearer the carrying capacities of available habitat, should be pursued to reduce brucellosis infection and protect elk against infection with other exotic diseases. Vaccination may best augment the brucellosis reduction effort when a vaccine that is demonstrated to be efficacious can be widely administered to the elk herds without enhancing the crowding of animals.[13]

This infuriated state officials, who publicly decried our review as biased. So manager Reiswig sent the "Smith and Roffe report" and all the state's data to biostatisticians and epidemiologists at three universities for independent reviews. Their interpretations were the same. In his report, Dr. Edward O. Garton, University of Idaho, bluntly summed up Wyoming's vaccination program:

It appears to me that the vaccination program of elk in Wyoming has been carried out on the basis primarily of hope and faith that it will lead to increased calf survival rather than on the basis of solid evidence that such vaccination will reduce fetal losses among Wyoming elk populations. Alternately, such a program has been instituted for political reasons due to the need for Wyoming Game and Fish Department to demonstrate to the ranching community and their legislators that the Department is doing what they can to protect Wyoming's brucellosis-free status.[18]

After receiving these experts' reports in early 1998, Reiswig sent copies to state officials and made them available to the public. Immediately, the State of Wyoming sued the federal government to assert authority over wildlife on the NER and to force vaccination of elk. The 1999 ruling on that case, again from Judge Brimmer, found for the federal government, reasserting the statutory authority of the secretary of the interior over wildlife on national wildlife refuge lands. This was a significant reaffirmation of long-standing law.[19]

Simultaneously, the USFWS funded a four-year vaccination study by Roffe and his colleagues. The USFWS felt this research was warranted so that all parties could discuss the efficacy of Strain 19 based on rigorously conducted, peer-reviewed, published research. Those clinical trials showed that Strain 19 provided protection against abortion in only 25 percent of elk, at best, and no detectable protection against becoming infected. The research concluded, "Based on these data, single calfhood vaccination with S19 has low efficacy, will likely have only little to moderate effect on *Brucella* prevalence in elk, and is unlikely to eradicate the disease in wildlife in the GYE."[14]

In their 1993 legal analysis, Keiter and Froelicher stated, "But as unpopular as an elk feedground closure program may be with both ranching and wildlife interests, it is nonetheless an essential component of any comprehensive brucellosis policy. Otherwise, the disease will persist and continue to spread in wildlife populations, and perhaps necessitate even more drastic measures in the future."[15]

Despite Judge Brimmer's ruling, the political winds blew stiffly against us after 2000. Wyoming appealed and the Tenth Circuit Court of Appeals remanded the case back to Judge Brimmer for reconsideration of one of the three counts he'd dismissed: whether the U.S. government had complied with a provision in the National Wildlife Refuge System Improvement Act requiring the federal government to "... ensure effective coordination, interaction, and cooperation with owners of land adjoining refuges and the fish and wildlife agenc[ies] of the States...."[20] Rather than contest more legal action by Wyoming, the USFWS chose to settle out of court in June 2002. Wyoming got what it wanted. The NER prepared an environmental assessment for a reinstated vaccination program—a perfunctory exercise. Wyoming began pelting elk with biobullets again in early 2003, a folly that continues as I write in 2010.

Despite years of contrary evidence, state wildlife officials tacitly tout Strain 19's efficacy in elk and promote vaccination as a fundamental solution to the elk brucellosis problem. But realistically, to expect a vaccine developed for a bovid to similarly fire up the immune system of a cervid is no different than commanding an elk to "moo" and repeating the exercise in hopes that it will.

If this sounds harshly critical of Wyoming officials, it's because I could see a train wreck coming. Over the years, I'd grown fond of the

Jackson elk, dedicated to their health and place in the GYE's tapestry of life, and stubborn enough not to "go along to get along." Wyoming had painted itself into a corner, entrenched in an agri-industry approach to elk management of feeding and vaccinating.

Then in 2006 the state went a page further in the animal husbandry-man's handbook. Wyoming Game and Fish Department began a five-year test-and-slaughter program at the Muddy Creek feedground near Pinedale. While this was called a "pilot project," many Jackson Hole observers worried it was destined for expansion elsewhere. Elk testing positive for brucellosis were trucked to an Idaho packing plant. Over the first four years, biologists captured 1,845 elk and slaughtered 162, only half of which actually were infected with brucellosis based on subsequent tissue culture.

Department veterinarian Terry Kreeger told a state legislative committee in May 2009 that the program was proving expensive. He reported that $1 million had been spent so far, translating to about $13,000 to kill each infected elk. He added that the slaughtered elk were processed and given to the public for consumption.

In response, state representative Matt Teeters observed, "It would be cheaper to buy them lobster."[21]

But where elk management is concerned, Wyoming is bipolar. East of the Continental Divide, elk are not fed in winter. Instead they're managed like most North American elk, by working with private landowners and federal land managers to conserve and improve habitats, and by keeping elk numbers in balance with available range. Where the continent's waters part, so does Wyoming's philosophy about managing elk.

In the years since I left Jackson Hole, not much has changed. Cattle herds of Idaho, Montana, and Wyoming ranging across the GYE again contracted brucellosis (Wyoming in 2004, Idaho in 2005, and Montana in 2008). Infected herds were quarantined, tested, and depopulated to clean up each outbreak. In the process, each state lost its brucellosis-free status for a year or more until each state complied with USDA disease abatement requirements. The Idaho and Wyoming outbreaks occurred adjacent to elk feedgrounds. By default, those elk were considered the source of cattle infection. The source of the disease in the Montana cattle herd was not reported. Another Wyoming cattle herd within the state's elk feedground complex broke with brucellosis in 2007. Wyoming retained its class-free disease status following rapid depopulation of that herd. And in late 2010 three more Wyoming cattle herds in the GYE became infected with brucellosis.

This scenario is sure to repeat itself. Western Wyoming's feedgrounds remain recycling centers for *Brucella* in elk and bison and an unremitting source of cattle infection. Diseased elk that spill into adjacent Idaho perpetuate the disease there. Montana has seen an uptick in brucellosis of its unfed elk herds adjacent to Yellowstone Park. Commingling with the park's chronically infected bison—and western Wyoming's feedground elk—serves as a source of brucellosis transmission. Since 2000, Yellowstone bison have been trapped and over three thousand testing positive for brucellosis have been slaughtered. Elk that are restricted to park winter ranges by boundary hunts and others that gather on private ranchland-refuges to avoid hunters perpetuate a level of infection that maintains brucellosis. If we are going to beat brucellosis in wildlife, all three states and federal land managers must remedy these unresolved issues.

CHAPTER 7

Train Wreck

There's a real need for scientists to get (their results) out of the lab, so that the public can understand that things are never black-and-white.
—DR. ELIZABETH WILLIAMS, FEBRUARY 2004 INTERVIEW ABOUT CHRONIC WASTING DISEASE IN *HIGH COUNTRY NEWS*

After retiring from federal service, I left Jackson, but the Jackson elk herd and its challenges did not leave me. On no issue was this truer than chronic wasting disease, or CWD. This was the train wreck I saw brewing, with western Wyoming's elk feedgrounds fertile ground for a perfect storm.

Among a group of degenerative brain diseases that affect species as diverse as cattle, cats, mink, and man, CWD uniquely affects North American deer species. As I noted in Chapter 1, CWD was not known in the elk and deer of Jackson Hole, or elsewhere in western Wyoming during my twenty-two years at the NER. As I write now in 2010, it still isn't—or more accurately, it's not yet been detected.

In 2005 I received a call from Lloyd Dorsey. Lloyd was then the Jackson field representative for the Greater Yellowstone Coalition, a nonprofit organization dedicated to protecting the land, water, and wildlife of the eighteen-million-acre GYE. He asked if I would consider writing an analysis of the connection between western Wyoming's feedgrounds and diseases in elk and bison. Dr. Markus Peterson, veterinarian and professor in the Department of Wildlife and Fishery Sciences at Texas A&M University, was contracted to write on the same topic. These independently prepared papers became supporting documentation for a 2008 lawsuit by the Greater Yellowstone Coalition and four other conservation organizations contesting the Department of Interior's recently released Draft Bison and Elk Management Plan and Environmental Impact Statement (EIS) for the Jackson bison and elk herds.[1,2,3]

Brucellosis, CWD, and other diseases exacerbated by the crowding of animals were at the heart of the litigants' case. The court ruling in 2010 found for the defendant. That decision is under appeal as I write.

This isn't the only recent lawsuit filed over feeding of wildlife. After the first CWD-infected white-tailed deer was discovered in Michigan in August 2008, the state's Department of Natural Resources imposed a ban on baiting and feeding of deer and elk throughout the Lower Peninsula. Citizens practiced these activities to attract deer during hunting season and to enhance recreational viewing of animals in winter. The ban was litigated but upheld in court. The judge ruled that the department had the statutory authority, based its decision on scientific principles, and had included the proposed elimination of baiting and feeding in its CWD management plan developed in 2002 after the disease was discovered nearby in Wisconsin.[4]

Besides the 2004 and 2007 outbreaks of brucellosis in cattle near Wyoming's feedgrounds, three additional events in 2008 generated a flurry of news reports and intensified criticism of wildlife management agencies. First, Bridger-Teton National Forest issued twenty-year permits reauthorizing several elk feedgrounds operated by Wyoming on forest lands. (A consortium of environmental organizations unsuccessfully appealed the decision on grounds that the NEPA process paid only cursory attention to disease impacts.) Then in mid-October 2008 the Wyoming Game and Fish Department announced that a moose had tested positive for CWD near Bedford, Wyoming. The moose had been euthanized for disease-testing in February that year, but seven months passed before this first case of CWD in western Wyoming was diagnosed from tissue samples.

That same week, another press release reported results of a CWD study involving forty female elk, captured as healthy calves on the NER in 2002 and trucked to Wyoming Game and Fish Department's Sybille research center (where CWD had previously killed research animals). The news release indicated that thirty-one of the forty elk had died of CWD. Because most of the elk had reached reproductive age before dying, a department spokesman concluded, "in the presence of CWD it appears the elk in this study would maintain a stable or increasing population."

Other scientists and I thought this an astonishing statement. These research animals died while protected from other diseases, predation, accidents, and hunting, all of which limits increases in free-ranging elk. Yet three-quarters died while still young adults.

Throughout October, newspaper headlines about these events flowed like champagne in a World Series champion's locker room. "Wasting disease found in Bedford," "How did moose get CWD?", "Elk study reignites controversy," "Groups call for disease action," "Wildlife disease debate heats up." My guest editorial, "State agencies ignore danger of CWD," appeared in the *Jackson Hole News and Guide* on November 5, 2008. No longer in Uncle Sam's employ, I offered my candid perspective on the lack of proactive management.

> *It seems Wyoming continues to publicly assert that without having seen dozens or hundreds of elk suffering a CWD epizootic on feedgrounds, citizens should not worry that could happen. That's like saying that because we have not seen our power plants, ports, and transportation hubs attacked by terrorists, providing those targets security is unwarranted.*
>
> *Until Wyoming addresses the root cause of disease issues in western Wyoming's elk (and bison) . . . elk will remain vulnerable to infection and die-offs from emerging diseases.*

So how did things get to this point? CWD was originally observed in confined deer in Colorado's wildlife research pens near Fort Collins in the 1960s. Wildlife biology professor Dr. Bill Alldredge, who worked as a technician at the facility at the time, referred to it as "the mysterious deer dying disease."

CWD cropped up at about the same time in animals confined in Wyoming's wildlife research pens in Sybille Canyon. The concurrent eruption of the disease was probably more than coincidence. Animals had been exchanged between those facilities. Still, the disease's initial source remained a mystery.

During the 1980s wildlife disease expert Dr. Elizabeth Williams and her colleagues established that the disease had infected wild mule deer and elk adjacent to both research facilities, as well as elk in Rocky Mountain

National Park. Initially, the distribution of this perplexing disease—known nowhere else in wild cervids—remained localized, either because too few individuals served as infective vectors or because testing of wild herds was lacking or too limited elsewhere. But during the 1990s CWD was discovered more widely both in captive, farmed herds and in free-ranging populations. By 2005 deer (mule and white-tailed) and/or elk in fourteen states and two Canadian provinces were infected (in six additional states, wild or captive deer have since been detected with CWD). That year in Colorado, the first wild moose joined the list of stricken species. Caribou remained the only endemic North American cervid free of the disease.

Asked in 2002 how CWD was spreading, Dr. Bruce Chesebro, a leading researcher at the National Institutes of Health's Rocky Mountain Laboratories, answered, "By truck. It is being moved around in these game farms, and it is leaking out in the wildlife. Until you close down the game farms, you can kill all the wildlife you want, and you will not halt the spread of the disease." Indeed, trace-backs often led to infected game farms from which animals were shipped to new outbreak sites.[5]

Reported prevalence rates among captive elk have ranged as high as 59 percent in a South Dakota elk farm that tested positive for CWD.[6, 7] Cervids in infected game farms were depopulated—destroyed by U.S. Department of Agriculture and state officials to eliminate the disease's source—rendering uncertain what eventual prevalences might be realized in protracted epidemics. During the first five months of 2002, Colorado alone killed and burned 1,449 elk from game farms according to Lynn Creekmore of the USDA. That same year, the Canadian Wildlife Federation implored the Canadian Minister of Agriculture to institute a ban and decommission all cervid game farms in Canada. The federation noted that as of July 2002 thousands of captive deer and elk had been slaughtered in Alberta and Saskatchewan at a cost to the government of over one hundred million dollars in Saskatchewan alone.[8, 9]

Researchers tried to eradicate the disease in the Fort Collins, Colorado, research facilities. They killed and removed the surviving deer and elk, turned the top foot of soil in pastures, and sprayed the entire area with a powerful chlorine disinfectant. A year later twelve wild elk were brought to the facilities, and within three years the elk began dying of CWD. Similar cleanup of Wyoming's Sybille elk pens also failed. Recent experiments have shown how prions accumulate in soils where they resist environmental and chemical degradation. In the California lab of Dr. Stanley Prusiner, who won the Nobel Prize in medicine for discovering prions in 1997, scientists demonstrated the shedding of infective doses of prions in feces of deer.[10] Prions may also be shed, transmitted, and contaminate the environment via animal fluids and other tissues, prompting authorities to believe that recurrent die-offs will follow return of cervids to CWD-infected sites.[11, 12, 13, 14, 15, 16]

Much of what we need to know about limiting the impact of emerging diseases we learned during the nineteenth century. In our own species, tainted drinking water and crowded, unsanitary living conditions breed pathogens and disease transmission, and weaken human immunocompetence.[17] The same is true for our animal food production systems. High densities and unsanitary conditions provide magnificent laboratories for pathogens to infect abundant hosts and develop more successful forms. As William McNeill, the University of Chicago historian of disease ecology, wrote about the AIDS pandemic:

> *It is obvious that as virus host populations (or potential host populations) increase, there is concomitant increase in the probability of major evolutionary changes in virus populations due to increased opportunities for replication, mutation, recombination, and selection. As the world population of humans (and of their livestock animals and plants) increase, the probability for new viral disease outbreaks must inevitably increase as well. AIDS is not the first "new" virus disease of humans, and it will not be the last.*[18]

Whether it be humans living in squalor, chickens warehoused fifty thousand per level in two-story poultry factories, or overstocked wildlife, disease exacerbation is a common thread. Game farms in the United States and Canada have suffered recurrent outbreaks of bovine tuberculosis (another deadly disease affecting many mammal species) over the past twenty years. Among the reservations that scientists and conservationists have voiced about game farms is the potential for disease eruptions and subsequent transmission to wild herds.[19, 20] In 2006, for example, 160 elk escaped from an Idaho game farm just west of Grand Teton and Yellowstone National Parks. The owner had refused disease-testing of his herd by state officials, heightening concerns that the escaped animals represented a potential threat to wild elk.

CWD in wild cervids is relentlessly increasing—its geographic distribution expanding and its prevalence trending up. In Wyoming the number of deer-hunting units with CWD infection increased by two to seven units annually from 2003 to 2010. In 2005 infected deer were found west of Thermopolis, Wyoming, just eighty miles east of the Continental Divide and the Jackson elk herd. At the same time, several of the twenty-five elk I'd captured and radio-collared on the Gros Ventre feedgrounds migrated east of the Continental Divide and spent summer within sixty miles of infected deer. Ironically, the probable path that CWD might take to western Wyoming's feedgrounds was across the Wind River Indian Reservation—where herds of deer and elk I'd helped restore provided an east–west migratory conduit for CWD.

Although prevalence of CWD in the nearest infected deer herds was very low—about 3 percent—this was the disease's blueprint. Along its front, one or two deer or elk would initially test positive among hundreds examined. Then as more animals were exposed, infection rate increased. Prevalence exceeds 25 percent in areas of Colorado and Wyoming where it has been longest established (and measured 48 percent in 2010 in Converse County, Wyoming, in a mule deer herd that had declined by half during the previous decade). Testing of elk in Colorado's Rocky Mountain National Park in 2008 showed CWD prevalence had reached 11 percent.[21] Culling began in 2009 to reduce overabundant elk numbers, thereby limiting vegetation damage and hopefully curbing CWD in the park. But Rocky Mountain Park's elk are not fed in winter, nor are deer and elk east of the Continental Divide in Wyoming. In western Wyoming, from Jackson Hole to the Green River basin, it's a different story altogether.

I'm reminded of a statement by Dr. Edwin Kilbourne about the prudence of disease preparedness. Kilbourne, who became known as the "emperor" of human influenza, had argued as a young researcher in 1976 that the U.S. government prepare for mass vaccination of the public in anticipation of a pandemic. What alarmed him more than the regularity of decade-ending flu epidemics since the 1940s was a startling discovery in 1976: A Fort Dix army recruit had died of an influenza virus closely related to the H1N1 virus responsible for forty to one hundred million human deaths during the 1918 pandemic. Amid division in the scientific community about the likelihood of a pandemic, the pharmaceutical industry was reluctant to produce millions of vaccine doses without federal indemnification, and the Ford administration was gun-shy of stoking election-year alarm. As it turned out, the 1976 pandemic was a nonevent. Yet the healthcare community's eyes were opened to its limitations to effectively rally to a threat. Dr. Kilbourne defended his advocacy of a massive vaccination effort by saying, "Better a vaccine without an epidemic, than an epidemic without a vaccine."[17]

For CWD, no effective vaccine exists. There are no therapeutic treatments, only preventive measures—the point that Dr. Tom Roffe, the U.S. Fish and Wildlife Service wildlife veterinarian who spoke before me, advised at a CWD forum in Jackson Hole in February 2004. As the last of four speakers, my remarks reinforced that message:

When I began talking about the threat of CWD arriving at the National Elk Refuge and adjacent Wyoming elk feedgrounds, my concern was generally met with three reactions: apathy, denial that such a thing would ever happen, or anger that I dared suggest such a far-fetched notion. That was two years ago. With what we know now about CWD, its potential to move across the landscape, and its potential to reach high prevalence when animals are confined or fed, it's time to move past denial and anger. Given the unique and insidious nature of this disease agent, it will be impossible to roll back the clock once CWD is in our midst.

The northwestward advance of CWD has generated conflict in Wyoming's environmental/sportsman community. Many conservationists are impatient with wildlife agencies' resistance to reassessing the wisdom of feeding thousands of elk. Outfitting and organized hunting groups protest that dismantling of elk feedgrounds isn't in the animals' (or their) best interests. "There's no proof," some have insisted, that CWD would create more than a mild decline in feedground elk numbers, while others claim that CWD is already there with no ill effects. And besides, forcing the elk to subsist on their own would wreak starvation and death on far more elk than would CWD. Feedgrounds are fixtures in Wyoming, like its bucking bronco license plate, Devil's Tower, and horizontal snowstorms in December.

The "mild decline" contention assumes that the rate of infection on feedgrounds will mimic the 1 to 10 percent typical of free-ranging elk in southeastern Wyoming. Indeed, such a low prevalence has had negligible effects on populations of elk in Wyoming and Colorado. Citing such evidence, officials in state government have been among the most ardent defenders of feedgrounds (at least publicly). But the Wyoming Game and Fish Department employs some excellent professionals who support the party line with reluctance.

In 2005 Wyoming produced a CWD management plan. Like an earlier plan in 2002, the retooled version failed to proactively tackle state and federal elk feedgrounds. The main thrust was surveillance—testing harvested animals and sick animals suspected of being diseased. This collection of heads (from which the necessary tissues are taken) began in GTNP and the NER in 1996 to check for CWD and bovine tuberculosis. Tuberculosis continues to crop up in cattle in several states and provinces, free-ranging deer in Minnesota and Michigan, plus elk and bison in certain Canadian parks. The disease's transmissibility among livestock and wildlife—and potentially to humans—is also a risk to the well-being of feedground elk and bison.[19]

Wyoming's draft 2005 CWD plan, floated for public comment, stated, "Although prevalence of CWD in free-ranging elk is only 2 to 3 percent [approximately an order of magnitude less than that found in deer], scientific research has indicated that the prevalence of CWD in captive elk can exceed 50 percent. This level of prevalence in captive elk, combined with the density of thousands of elk inhabiting feedgrounds for several months, suggests the possibility of much higher prevalence rates in feedground elk, possibly resulting in a concomitant reduction in elk numbers." In the final plan, this wording was changed to "prevalence of CWD in captive elk has been higher [than 2 to 3 percent]. Elk densities on feedgrounds may result in prevalence levels found in captive elk. It is unknown at this time what impact prevalences exceeding 2 to 3 percent will have on free-ranging populations."[22]

The plan goes on to discourage private feeding of deer and elk because "CWD is more efficiently transmitted when these animals are concentrated. Private feeding may lead to localized concentrations of environmental contamination with the CWD agent." Alternatives to public feeding of thousands of elk—thousands more than citizens feed—were not evaluated in the plan.

Don't get me wrong. I strongly support conducting surveillance to ascertain the distribution and prevalence of CWD. But going no further is like checking the air pressure in your car's tires, and then pulling into traffic after finding one flat. Just once I wanted to hear a state biologist or manager declare in public our mutual concern that feeding was a time bomb waiting to happen.

Actually, this did happen once—loudly and clearly—in the Wyoming Game and Fish Department's own newspaper, *Wyoming Wildlife News*. In a lengthy 2000 article, three state employees—the brucellosis biologist and two veterinarians—laid out the issues in "Feeding wildlife: a recipe for disaster." In a summary paragraph, the authors stated, "The evidence is undeniable. Wildlife are adapted to survive winter without supplemental feeding. Feeding causes many more problems to wildlife than it solves. Additionally, it can be harmful to humans and domestic animals."[23]

The federal government too, particularly the USFWS, was not lily white. When opportunity arose to advocate policy changes, the NER's superiors in Denver and Washington deferred to state prerogatives. So when refuge manager Barry Reiswig was pressed by his supervisor in Denver, "What are your contingency plans should CWD develop in refuge elk?"

Barry's comments were characteristically to the point: "(1) Dig a big hole with a dozer or obtain an incinerator. (2) You round up and shoot all suspect [diseased] animals. (3) You cover the hole with dirt or incinerate all killed animals."

He added, "Once CWD reaches the refuge, the time for contingencies is long past."

In the Jackson Hole region there were many willing to speak truth to power on CWD and feedgrounds. Among the most persistent were conservation leaders Franz Camenzind of the Jackson Hole Conservation

Alliance, Lloyd Dorsey of the Greater Yellowstone Coalition, Meredith Taylor of the Wyoming Outdoor Council, and Shane Moore.

Shane was a self-employed Jackson resident educated as a wildlife biologist. We'd talk conservation and our shared love of wildlife and wildlands from time to time. Generally this was at the local athletic club where I'd see Shane when his wildlife filmmaking career didn't take him to Alaska, Patagonia, or the Kalahari. His commitment to Jackson Hole's wildlife was exemplified when he conceived and organized the CWD workshop of February 2004 at Snow King Resort.

Shane and the others I mentioned were conservationists in the great sense of the word—in the Teddy Roosevelt tradition. Like so many conservationists with no ax to grind and nothing to gain personally, he simply wanted his children to enjoy the wealth of healthy wildlife that he felt privileged to observe and hunt from boyhood to adult in Jackson Hole. What greater gift than to pass on to future generations this great legacy of wildlife and wildlands we've inherited.

During the past decade many state, federal, and provincial officials have worked to limit the spread of CWD, including restricting transport of animals from infected areas and depopulating infected herds in game farms. Colorado tried to reduce CWD in wild mule deer through experimental herd reductions. Wisconsin went a step further after finding CWD in deer in 2002. That state's Department of Natural Resources sought complete eradication by killing thousands of white-tailed deer with special hunts and culling programs to reduce deer densities. Deer were collected and stored in refrigerated tractor-trailers until their brains and lymph nodes could be removed for diagnostic testing. Because it remains uncertain if CWD can be transmitted to humans (the World Health Organization, Centers for Disease Control, and several states, including the Wyoming Department of Health, recommend against human consumption of diseased deer), Wisconsin's Department of Natural Resources faced the daunting task of disposing of the carcasses. Truckloads of dead deer were initially hauled to landfills, but concern arose that prions might leach into groundwater. So giant incinerators became fiery graveyards for diseased deer, roasting their remains to ashes. Wisconsin spent twenty-seven million dollars through 2006 (much of this in federal earmarks) to control CWD—a cost that impacted other department programs. Budget cuts reduced funding for CWD control in subsequent years.

These efforts to stem the geographic spread of CWD and quash the disease have met with limited success. The distribution of CWD in Colorado continues to expand. In 2009, Wisconsin officials estimated from infection rates in sampled deer that CWD prevalence continues to increase 4 percent annually.

Leading CWD scientists Drs. Elizabeth Williams and Mike Miller wrote in 2002 that high animal densities and feeding programs significantly elevate the risk of disease amplification (increasing the number of infected animals) in deer and elk by increasing direct and indirect (through environmental contamination) routes of transmission.[24] In a subsequent paper, Miller and colleagues modeled the spread of CWD in infected deer herds. They found that where environmental contamination is significant, that route of transmission was nearly four times more likely to explain the observed spread of disease than transmission by direct contact between infected and susceptible deer.[25] Dr. Erdem Tamguney, professor of neurodegenerative diseases, was more direct. "If you think of areas where these animals congest, you would find higher concentrations of feces in those areas. Feedgrounds would be a very good way of spreading this disease. Sick and healthy animals come together."[26]

As the nearest surrogates for Wyoming's feedgrounds, the record of game farms and research pens is instructive. Without a test to detect the presence of prions in the environment, judging the accumulation of the disease agent on feedgrounds is relegated to the health of the elk themselves—their own canary in the coal mine. It may be true that little can be done to slow the spread of CWD in the wild. But the risk of its amplification can be lessened by reducing animal densities. And merely modifying feeding protocols does not mitigate the enhanced disease transmission of CWD compared to halting the attraction of animals to feedsites, as demonstrated in Wisconsin white-tailed deer.[27] Rather than reacting after CWD arrives, responsible officials would be wise to proactively mitigate the disease's effects, should it be introduced.

Whatever survival benefits a highly resilient animal like elk may accrue from hay handouts will be offset by the consequences of CWD and other infectious diseases. In feedground conditions other elk diseases become chronic, among them brucellosis, scabies, foot rot, and hemorrhagic septicemia (the latter two are bacterial diseases that periodically kill elk on the NER).

What's more, a recent study comparing physiology of elk on nineteen Wyoming feedgrounds to eleven unfed, free-ranging populations found that increased density may provoke a stress response. Glucocorticoid concentrations (inflammation and stress can escalate production of these steroidal hormones) excreted in feces of feedground elk were 31 percent higher than among elk that were not fed. Likewise, rates of aggression increased significantly when elk were fed.[28] Given the harmful effects that chronically elevated glucocorticoids have on immune function of mammals,[29] could elevated stress and compromised immune efficiency be contributing to disease prevalence on elk feedgrounds? For emerging diseases like CWD and others beyond the horizon, investing in habitat rather than hay may forestall the worst ecological outcomes.

The report from a CWD workshop in Madison, Wisconsin, identified one additional element that could limit amplification of CWD: predators. It stated, "The absence of predators may allow sick animals a longer period in which to spread CWD."[30] Like weak calves, limpers, and toothless wonders, animals debilitated by CWD would quickly be culled by large carnivores—an elegant natural check on the spread of disease. Near Boulder, Colorado, mountain lions and the CWD-infected mule deer population they preyed on were studied. Although healthy deer lived nearly four years longer than CWD-infected deer (CWD-affected deer were preferentially preyed on by lions), the spread of CWD continued, as did the twenty-year population decline of deer.[31]

However, mountain lions are solitary ambush predators; packs of gray wolves chase and single out disadvantaged prey, what David Mech and other wolf biologists have called the "sanitation effect" of predation. Recent modeling suggests wolf predation may suppress CWD emergence or prevalence in deer.[32] For the overstuffed numbers of elk on feedgrounds, however, there may be too few wolves to keep pace with disease epizootics.

As analogues to predators, scavengers remove carrion from the environment and the disease agents they harbor, such as *Brucella abortus*. Ravens, eagles, and particularly coyotes patrol the NER like prison guards. Aborted fetuses on the NER last an average of twenty-seven hours, whereas on Wyoming's elk feedgrounds (where coyotes aren't protected) fetuses remain for forty-one hours and the number of elk contacting them is significantly higher.[33]

As I write, western Wyoming sits on pins and needles, waiting for this ecological drama to play out. Its westward march across Wyoming has brought CWD perilously close to world-class elk and mule deer populations numbering over two hundred thousand in the Greater Yellowstone Ecosystem.

Should CWD infect herds of elk drawn to postage-stamp feedsites, a foreseeable cascade of consequences will unfold over years, and maybe decades. Feedgrounds will become de facto biological "Superfund" sites contaminated with infectious prions proven highly resistant to environmental and chemical degradation. Adjacent to a town of nine thousand residents, and supporting part of Jackson's domestic water supply, the NER will face a daunting and sensitive challenge to dispose of diseased elk. Instead of partially fencing elk *in* the NER as now, managers may be compelled to fence them *out*. As elk herds decline, predators and scavengers will have to adjust. Black bears, coyotes, mountain lions, bald eagles, grizzly bears, and gray wolves will need to find alternate food sources or slip in abundance. Under increasing predatory pressure, other prey species also susceptible to CWD—mule deer, whitetails, and moose—will suffer a double blow. Hunting quotas will unavoidably shrink, diminishing hunter recreation and their spending at area businesses.

In a worst-case scenario, Wyoming will receive a national black eye—one surpassing its repute for contributing to maintenance of brucellosis in elk. Elk in eastern Idaho that interchange with elk on Wyoming's feedgrounds will be at risk. Elk that roam Yellowstone Park could be next, since they share summer ranges with Jackson elk. The region's economic engine, the tourism industry, may suffer (even if CWD is not found to be transmissible to humans), and public demand may force Wyoming and the federal government to belatedly do what should have been done before. "Phase out feedgrounds" will emerge a battle cry. In the aftermath, brucellosis may become no more than a footnote in the annals of western Wyoming's elk management failure.

Cynics call such projections overreaction, and sometimes worse. But to suggest that CWD may never reach Wyoming's feedgrounds—and that therefore its worst effects are unnecessary to thwart—reminds me of denials of the growing global climate crisis. In *The End of Nature*, Bill McKibben dismissed such obduracy this way: "To declare, as some editorialists have done, that the warming has not yet appeared and therefore the theory is wrong is like arguing that a woman hasn't yet given birth and therefore isn't pregnant."[34]

As with climate change, why wait? Responsibly curbing the risk of epidemic infection before CWD arrives will spawn secondary benefits. Brucellosis will fade over time from western Wyoming's elk herds, and other density-dependent disease threats also will wane.

Reducing elk herds to sustainable numbers will not prevent CWD from killing elk, but it's an alternative supported by professional wisdom. In a 2005 *Casper Star Tribune* article ("How big is the threat?"), Colorado's Dr. Mike Miller observed, "From what we've seen to date, there are few diseases that can completely wipe out a wildlife population. However, if CWD were to become sufficiently prevalent [in the GYE], it could conceivably lower elk abundance and lead to other effects on that system."[35]

In the rosiest scenarios, CWD may fortuitously fail to infect feedground elk. Or maybe a "cure" for CWD lies within reasonable reach of medical technology. Maybe the costs of developing therapeutic tools will rise above other pressing national needs. But if not, then the wildlife of western Wyoming and its residents will pay a high price in coming years. Just as climate scientists agree there is a fast-approaching tipping point to stem accumulation of greenhouse gases, the march of CWD toward thousands of feedground elk is undeniable. Prompt action by responsible federal and state officials may yet avert a disease disaster.

CHAPTER 8

The Right Questions

Because the struggle for life is incessant, this unceasing process promotes endless slow changes in bodily form as living creatures are subjected to different natural environments, different enemies, and all the vicissitudes against which life has struggled down the ages.
—LOREN EISELEY, 1959, *THE IMMENSE JOURNEY*

I am a fly fisherman, but I grew up using a cane pole with chalk line and hook tied onto the end—no reel to confuse the process of lobbing worms onto water. By age nine or ten, I and most neighborhood kids owned one of those fancy spinning outfits with a Johnson or Shakespeare reel. Then at ten or eleven, my great-uncle Len gave me his split cane fly rod. He once used that pretty four-piece bamboo to entice brook trout and bass to strike fur and feather concoctions on western Michigan's lakes and streams. From bluegills and bass on poppers, I soon graduated to lashing the local trout waters with mayfly and caddis patterns.

In truth, fly-fishing contributed to my decision to finish my college degree somewhere in the West. To a working-class kid in the 1950s and '60s, the West was still frontier—a great open space of cowboys and cattle and wild animals, a realm only recently invaded by *Sports Afield* photographers. Their glossy images of glistening trout plucked from cascading streams amid snowcapped peaks set my mind swirling. Without either of us knowing its significance a half century ago, Uncle Len's gift would channel a young naturalist west.

But the connection between fishing and a science career runs deeper. For me the pursuit of scientific investigation is akin to exploring a newly found trout stream. Each turn reveals a novel and often unexpected set of circumstances. If designed and carried out properly, the outcome of biological study is never certain. Each step of data collection and analysis may land an unexpected catch. Like multiple casts delivered to a riffle, alternative hypotheses are conceived and tested—striving to raise a fish from the depths and knowledge from nature's mysterious sea.

My early concerns that my Jackson Hole experience would prove unrewarding faded as my research endeavors expanded, triggered in large part by my return to college in 1988. Among the ongoing challenges dogging Jackson's state and federal wildlife officials was how to identify and measure factors that limited the elk herd. To wisely prescribe hunting seasons, managers needed to understand how natural processes affected the herd's rate of increase and the surplus of elk available to hunters. The Jackson Hole Cooperative Elk Studies Group conceived a study of these matters, but the work was beyond the scope of the state and federal agencies' personnel. Money, or rather lack thereof, impeded contracting the work. So when I decided to tackle it myself, I knew that grant acquisition would be easier if I ran this multiyear project through a university. To conduct the research, I would need the State of Wyoming's approval to capture and radio-tag dozens of newborn elk. The University of Wyoming was the logical choice of schools. Following a boatload of coursework during the 1988–89 academic year, I began my dissertation research in spring 1990. While continuing my refuge responsibilities, I effectively juggled two jobs for the next four years.

Compelling the study were two previous investigations. A 1989 book on the management of the Jackson elk herd by Dr. Mark Boyce—who would serve on my graduate committee—concluded that the primary limiting factors of the herd were hunter harvest and survival of calves. Boyce also identified a shift in the herd's summer distribution from two decades before. He attributed this change to greater vulnerability and hunter harvest of elk on national forest lands than of elk that spent summer in Grand Teton National Park (GTNP).[1] In our study of radio-collared elk, Buzz Robbins and I confirmed Boyce's conclusions that elk harvests had altered elk distributions (see Chapter 3).[2]

With this disparity in harvests now well understood, both studies identified two outstanding research needs. Could Grand Teton's elk numbers be limited by low calf survival? And could numbers also be limited by dispersal of juvenile elk to less densely occupied national forest lands? The underlying premise of both questions was this: Crowding or food competition among animals in GTNP may foster outward dispersal or reduced survival of calves. These questions were more than academic because GTNP hosted the only big-game hunt in a national park in the lower forty-eight states—a distinction not unnoticed by anti-hunting groups who sought to end the practice.

Both matters—measuring calf survival and dispersal—would require marking two samples of newborn calves, one born inside and another born outside GTNP. As such, this was a comparative study, with the Jackson elk herd partitioned into adjacent study areas. To measure annual effects of weather and other uncontrollable phenomena on both dispersal and survival, I planned to capture calves for three consecutive years, 1990, 1991, and 1992.

The overriding concern of elk managers was that the Jackson elk herd was some four thousand animals over the management target of eleven thousand elk in 1989. Significantly, GTNP elk were the most difficult to harvest, and some managers believed numbers in GTNP had increased disproportionately. Most lands in the park were closed to hunting and almost all those elk migrated directly to the NER where they were fed in winter. With limited hunting opportunity and low winter mortality, controlling their numbers was problematic. Without significant natural control—predation, other calf mortality, or juvenile dispersal out of GTNP—the Jackson herd would remain overpopulated, requiring more winter feeding and consequent crowding and disease.

The ironic and inescapable reality was that human interference was wholly at fault. Lost migrations to historic winter ranges, exacerbated by winter feeding and artificially imposed security zones for elk, concocted a cascading witch's brew of unintended consequences. Before any additional intervention took place, I sought to better understand how the system was responding. Over the course of the next three years, the 145 elk calves I captured and radio-monitored would offer some answers.

From the airport near Jackson we followed the Snake River north, then Jerry Ewen banked the Hiller UH-12E helicopter west along Cotton-wood Creek. Flanking Jerry on the cramped bench seat, Billy Helprin and I peered through the acrylic bubble with high anticipation. Billy was one of my two seasonal assistants. I'd met him at the Teton Science School, north of Jackson, where he had worked as an environmental educator. Now we sought to educate ourselves in the art of capturing newborn elk.

The year before, I had learned the basics. A colleague of mine, Francis Singer, had invited me to Yellowstone Park to help with his own study of elk calf survival. On a glorious morning we choppered across Gardners Hole and the Lamar Valley, catching eight baby elk and fitting each with an expandable radio collar. Now it was May 25, 1990, and over the next three weeks—when 80 percent of the year's calves would arrive—I needed to capture and mark fifty or more newborns in Jackson Hole.

Alan Strassler, the author, and Billy Helprin with the Hiller helicopter
(Jerry Ewen)

Like Billy and me, Jerry was new to this. Elk capture from helicopter was not on his long résumé of piloting skills. We would all learn the fine points of this work together, given that capturing elk calves was a consummate team effort. Flying along Cottonwood Creek, we spotted a group of females ducking through a canopy of freshly erupted leaves. After a couple of circles we spotted a calf.

"There," exclaimed Billy. "Just now crossing the creek."

I remember the excitement of anticipating this day and rehearsing the handling procedures in my mind. Now, just ten minutes in the air, I had my initial opportunity. We landed on a terrace twice the height of the cottonwoods in the stream corridor below. Billy and I unplugged the avionics cords from our helmets, piled out, and headed for the calf's last known location.

In reality our first attempted calf capture was like a Laurel and Hardy episode. I was skeptical when the calf crossed Cottonwood Creek, swollen with snowmelt. After chasing the calf across the creek and then back again, I found this was no neonate, but a rambunctious tyke a week or so old. Drenched to the crotch and laughing at ourselves, Billy and I retreated up the terrace bank to the helicopter.

Airborne again, we approached a forested terrace west of the Snake River. On a slope that plunged from the tangle of lodgepole pine, a lone cow elk stared back at us. From the edge of an ivory-trunked aspen grove, she stood stock still near a thicket of snowberry and sagebrush, two hundred feet above a sage-studded plain below. Should she have a calf, we'd need to land on that lower terrace and hike up to her.

Elk seek solitude when they are ready to deliver, an anti-predator strategy to avoid attracting unwanted attention. Lone females, I would come to learn, are often harbingers of a newborn nearby. On our second circle, I spotted a flash that was more rust-colored than the cow's shedding coat. Tucked thirty yards away in a thicket, I saw the calf more completely on our next pass overhead. The calf's mother had unwittingly helped me when twice she'd curled that graceful neck in her offspring's direction. That sentinel instinct was a behavioral cue I'd obligingly exploit again and again with other dutiful mothers.

Billy and I made mental notes of the calf's hideaway before Jerry set the Hiller down far beneath the elk. Grabbing the pack with its assortment of capture equipment, Billy followed as I wove my way through clutching sagebrush up the slope. When we reached the edge of the thicket, Billy circled to where the calf had been facing. As he became the calf's point of focus, I stole to the opposite side and stalked closer. I was but ten feet away when I finally glimpsed a shred of rust-brown through the brush. After several quick steps I lunged and pinned the calf beneath my chest, bracing my fall with my hands.

It gave a piercing squeal out of fright, not from any harm done it. I slipped one elastic band of the neoprene blindfold under the chin and one behind the calf's ears, then hog-tied both hind legs and one front, rodeo-style, in a wrap of velcro strap.

From the edge of the forest above us where she had nervously retreated, the mother responded with a sharp alarm bark, and then another. In the days ahead, we often saw small calves instinctively drop into hiding at the alarm bark of their mothers. This behavior serves them well for the first week or so of life until calves have grown big and robust enough to join the safety of herd life. While new calves hide as if frozen, no more than an ear twitch and pulsing black nostrils to give them away, their mothers may graze and rest at a considerable distance. I recall one calf I caught that appeared to be abandoned, until I watched its mother return to it from one-third mile away.

A mother returns and suckles her calf six to ten times daily. During this "hider stage" when they expend little energy, I found that female calves gained nearly three pounds and males three-and-a-half pounds per day. As an additional precaution during these nursing bouts, the cow elk consumes the calf's urine and feces, and licks the calf extensively to diminish giveaway scent. Similar protective avoidance has proven successful maternal behavior for other species as well, including deer and moose.

Now Billy and I went deliberately through the protocol we'd rehearsed in dry runs. With calipers I measured the eruption of the middle pair of incisors (5.2 millimeters), the upper canines (barely through the gum), new hoof growth (9.2 millimeters), and the diameter and condition of the umbilicus (11.5 millimeters with a dry scab). From these measurements and the hard nature of the hooves and dewclaws, I would later determine that this male calf was four days old. A fifty-two-pound calf such as this was remarkably strong. The hobble—a necessary precaution should he try to escape—protected him and us. Yet enveloped in the blindfold's darkness, the calf was surprisingly relaxed until I hooked a spring scale through the hobble and suspended him upside down. Then he let us know he didn't appreciate being treated like a sack of potatoes. After several kicks of protest the scale's indicator settled, and I lowered our study's first member back to the ground.

After the final step of fitting the radio collar around the calf's neck, we removed the hobble and blindfold and slipped away. Beneath the towering Tetons cloaked in winter's wardrobe with spring still buried below, we grinned and inhaled the scene. Our joy was distinct to this kind of work, privileged to learn the ways of this new addition to the Jackson elk herd—that is, if he escaped the perils awaiting every newborn elk.

This was the first of twenty-nine elk I would capture west of the Snake River in GTNP during 1990. I radio-collared another twenty-four east of the Snake, not quite the fifty-fifty split I had planned. But considering that far fewer elk calved in the east where thicker vegetation also made spotting calves harder, it was a pretty fair first year.

Author with three-day-old elk calf that was radio-collared
(Don Katnik, US Fish and Wildlife Service)

Biologist Doug Brimeyer and pilot Bob Hawkins with captured elk calf
(Bruce Smith)

Biologist Steve Cain with captured elk calf

(Bruce Smith)

I captured calves on foot and horseback, but by far the lion's share were caught using the Hiller helicopter. Although the cow-calf bond is tenacious and mothers sometimes watched us from close range, I worried that our work might trigger some mothers to desert calves we captured. Indeed, some marking studies of newborns of North American ungulates reported rates of abandonment measuring 1 to 28 percent—a troubling circumstance that confounds research results and dismays biologists whose lifework is dedicated to these animals.[3] So beyond precautionary handling protocols, I located their radios from fixed-wing aircraft three times a week, and was heartened to find that none of our marked calves was abandoned.

To more regularly check their status and follow their movements, my technicians and I monitored the radio signals of each elk—once after daybreak and again ten to twelve hours later, seven days a week through July. We'd built four fixed radio-tracking stations surrounding the areas where most calves were captured (the southern half of GTNP and adjacent Bridger-Teton National Forest). Each station was a six-foot-square, fiberglass-roofed, plywood shack with an eighteen-foot steel mast topped with a pair of huge twelve-element antennas that boasted a potential receiving range of twenty miles.

Inside the shack, one of us rotated the mast while listening through headphones for the signal of each calf. Where the signal was loudest, a pointer indicated its direction on a compass rosette. Simultaneously, my coworkers recorded signal azimuths at the other tracking stations. Each morning the one who packed his or her laptop computer called the others for their compass bearings every half hour. As the bearings were entered, the location where each calf's azimuths intersected appeared like magic on a blue LCD map.

Listening for most of two hours to electronic beeping was a tiring routine, particularly when signals were faint, faded in and out, or were masked by citizen-band conversations, including the local pizza delivery guy. Although we were eager to learn the whereabouts of each elk, our communications about number so-and-so held no special meaning. We

Alan Strassler and the author repairing a radio telemetry tower
(Billy Helprin, US Fish and Wildlife Service)

needed something more tangible than chronological ID numbers. So in 1991 we began naming each calf we captured.

Some names came quite readily from a geographic landmark: Davis we captured on Davis Hill, Rosie atop Rosie's Ridge; Mystic we found in the heart of the 1981 Mystic Isle burn; and Mardy we seized within view of Mardy Murie's house. Unique capture circumstances spawned names for others. Tubbs was particularly hefty for a two-day-old. Tag-along followed us partway back to the helicopter. Big Mama was the calf whose outsize mother threatened to stomp us. And when we snatched Swan, two trumpeter swans honked overhead.

For a time we even named calves after ourselves or other people. But that soon ended. When we learned of her namesake's death, for example, someone had to break the news to Kathy. We also learned never to bestow a charmed name. As fate would have it, Lucky was eaten a week later by a bear.

Some calves left a special impression. These are the stories of three.

Whenever I rode horseback during calving season, I shouldered a day pack stuffed with radio collars and capture equipment. Whether I was off to investigate an elk whose radio collar beeped double-fast (indicating its owner may be dead), or I was bound for some other task, I just might chance upon a newborn elk.

One day toward the end of the 1992 calving season (and with my flight budget depleted and the helicopter returned to its stable in Greybull, Wyoming), I hoped to add another calf or two to our present sample of forty-eight. Besides, my favorite refuge horse looked like he could use some work.

Bud (short for Budweiser) was a tall, bay gelding with a feathery blaze and four white socks. I liked his temperament when hazing elk on the refuge, and his eagerness to set a fast pace. We made a good working team. If coworkers joined me, they'd ride Mich (short for Michelob) or Red (short for Red).

Across an undulating tract of monotypic sagebrush, Bud and I headed toward a solitary blemish of pines. As we approached, a lone cow elk bolted out. I'd searched for calves with Bud before and I sensed he took it as great sport. So with a minimum of reining or footwork, he quickly started circling the two-acre patch of lodgepole pines. From beneath a clump of perimeter sagebrush, a calf dodged into the trees. For several minutes thereafter we played a game of hide-and-seek. After finding its hiding place, I dismounted, dropped the reins, and pulled off a successful stalk. While I worked the calf and filled out the paperwork, Bud grazed toward where I kneeled and nudged my shoulder. As my other hand stroked the calf, I rubbed its namesake's muzzle. *Yes, old horse, this "Bud's" for you.*

Kathy McFarland was a soft-spoken biologist fresh out of college when I hired her in 1991 to fill Billy Helprin's position. She was a dedicated field technician who loved the outdoors and the thrill of catching and handling elk calves as much as Billy or I did.

On a crisp June morning cruising over a sea of sagebrush, we spotted a calf in a nondescript hiding place. When we landed and seized the three-day-old as easily as a rag doll, no special name came to mind. After weighing and radio-collaring him, I laid this thirty-nine-pound male (a touch small for his age) beneath a thickly crowned bush where we had found him hiding. Freed from their blindfold and hobbles, younger calves often remained bedded while older ones were more likely to bound away. However, this was no ordinary elk; he promptly bounced to his feet, backed stiffly away, then lowered his head and charged. By now I had caught 102 calves and had never witnessed this behavior. I was sitting on the ground gathering calipers and other equipment when his head smacked into my shoulder.

I was both stunned and amused at the little guy's bravado, but once was not enough. Twice more he backed deliberately away and followed with a resolute head butt. When I pushed him back, he bucked, then boxed his front hooves at me. After that final assault, I'd had enough. I leapt to my feet and shooed him away. In disbelief Kathy and I gawked at each other and then she said, "Bucky. His name should be Bucky."

Because my project was on a tight budget, efficiency was a constant concern. I recruited and trained volunteers to help with fieldwork, and scrounged used equipment whenever I could. Helicopter charters constituted a major but necessary expense that could be reduced only by improving our capture rate. So I continually challenged myself and my flying companions to more adeptly ferret out calves.

Because older calves already had survived those vulnerable, early first days, I wanted to catch the youngest calves—those more likely to be bedded and concealed from predators. "Older calves make biased samples," I told my assistants.

After a super-size mug of coffee, better sunglasses topped my list of accessories that might provide an edge. I bought a pair of aviator Ray Bans with fancy photochromatic amber lenses that seemed just the ticket to penetrate early-morning glare and still highlight the flash of a calf's ginger coat.

The morning after my purchase, we cruised over a mosaic of overgrown sagebrush and aspen-splotched landscape that concealed calves the way cloudy water hides fish from osprey. Flying with me that day

Kathy McFarland on horseback approaching an elk calf lying near its afterbirth
(Bruce Smith)

in 1991 was Alan Strassler, an affable Massachusetts transplant who'd worked extensively with elk and other wildlife across the West. I liked Al's good humor—including his impersonations that ranged from Bill Murray in *Caddyshack* to the *Saturday Night Live* character Mr. Bill—but I especially valued the way he questioned different aspects of our work. That made me consider how I might do things better.

This was Al's second year working for me, and spotting calves had become competition. By 10:00 a.m. we'd collared five, each of them spotted by me. Yes! The Ray Bans were working. Then we flew nearly forty minutes more, before Al spotted number six. As I crept behind him through waist-high sagebrush to make my final lunge, the calf bolted from his bed. After ungracefully wrestling him to the ground and slipping the blindfold over his eyes, I heard Al laughing. Besides a nasty scratch across my forehead, I had the twisted frames of my new Ray Bans dangling from one ear. The calf's conquest that day made his christening a no-brainer. At five days old, "Ray Bans" had made his mark.

The explosive power of species to produce surplus offspring is a fundamental tenet of evolution. Considering the thousands of seeds a plant may produce, the hundreds of eggs an insect may lay, the dozens of offspring a mouse may bear, or even the potential of an elk herd to double every four or five years, the Earth would soon be overpopulated with these and other species. Humans too, as pointed out in Thomas Malthus's 1798 treatise, *An Essay on the Principle of Population*, have the potential to double their numbers every twenty-five years, unless checked by environmental constraints.[4] But nature possesses a vigilant system of checks and balances that curbs unrestrained growth by ensuring that large numbers of offspring do not survive to adulthood and reproduce. Like the beaks of Darwin's Galápagos finches, his breeding experiments with orchids and pigeons informed him that no two individuals were alike. Without variation, there would be no chance to weed out the less fit and advance more desirable traits. It was nature's filter, not the breeder, Darwin surmised, that did the selecting in the wild. Implying correctly that chance variation played a significant role in natural selection, Darwin wrote, "What a trifling difference must often decide which shall survive and which perish."[5]

Who survives and who dies are of equal importance to a population or species' persistence. For elk and most other species, those first two tenuous months of life are the time of greatest vulnerability, when limited size and energy reserves, inexperience, and environmental constraints conspire to cull the less fit. Accordingly, I'd try to correlate their survival with those traits of newborn elk subject to nature's filter.

Based on these concepts, Darwin formulated the theory of "descent with modification," not to be termed evolution until the publication of *The Descent of Man and Selection in Relation to Sex* in 1871, twelve years after *The Origin of Species* shook the world.[5, 6] Although he was confident that this process of weeding the less fit from a population was at work, the mechanism of *how* individual traits were passed on from one generation to the next escaped him.

In one of science's great leaps forward, the Modern Synthesis of the mid-twentieth century integrated evolution and population biology with genetics and molecular biology. The Modern Synthesis advanced theory about *how* evolution works at the level of genes, individuals, and populations by proposing an observable, measurable mechanism for natural selection. The landmark discovery of DNA by Watson and Crick, development of electron microscopy, DNA fingerprinting, and molecular biology's ever-emerging technology provided scientists the tools to elucidate how genetic inheritance, mutation, and gene flow advanced individual traits, and therefore individual survival and reproduction. Because lineages that survive create more offspring in each generation, their hereditary material comes to predominate in a population over many generations.

Natural selection helps explain not only how populations are shaped by their environment, but how population density—through resource limitation and behavioral competition—can limit and hone populations as well. As competition among individuals in a population increases, malnutrition, disease transmission, and other factors intensify selection. This, too, I would need to consider in my doctoral research.

Previously focused on a hands-on career as a management biologist, I'd never had occasion to examine theoretical aspects of my field. It wasn't required and I wasn't all that interested. But this was different! Aside from the practical reasons to study calf survival—what limited the surplus of elk to be taken by hunters—observing how disease, predation, weather, and other forces of nature (potentially exacerbated by elk density) influenced individual elk survival might provide a sliver of new evidence to this science of evolutionary biology. Jackson Hole would prove a suitable and exciting outdoor laboratory for investigating a small slice of this grand scheme.

At its best, research—like shrewd management—yields the most useful products when the right questions are asked. To conduct consequential research—studies that may yield more than transient results—a field scientist must start by doing two things: scrutinize existing research pertinent to the problem he will study, and understand the ecological system in which he will be working. These prerequisites sharpen one's thinking about what questions need asking. Like peeling layers from an onion, the surface questions often mask those that are most important.

I crafted my dissertation's blueprint and field methods carefully. As much as why elk calves died, I wanted to know why some were predisposed to an early demise. What underlying conditions—the ultimately fatal factors—led to each calf's proximate cause of death, that final coup de grace such as predation or disease?

This was challenging work in a wildland laboratory. Each dead calf presented a figurative crime scene where forensic evidence rapidly faded. Carcasses were scavenged and scattered; opportunistic bacteria masked primary disease agents; and whole animals could vanish, as when swallowed by a river at flood stage. To help combat odds stacked against us, we monitored our calves twice daily to improve our chances of finding carcasses when fresh. I was on call twenty-four hours a day to respond when any of my crew detected a mortality signal. To do the job right, I enlisted the help of a top wildlife pathologist, Dr. Beth Williams, from the Wyoming State Veterinary Lab in Laramie. She performed exhaustive diagnostic tests on tissues or whole animals I recovered and shipped to her.

With the help of many others, I would learn the details of who survived and who did not. Individual calf characteristics, annual weather, disease, and predator conditions were all data of interest. In the process of gathering the evidence, I would gain an even deeper affection for the elk of Jackson Hole.

CHAPTER 9

Who Lives, Who Dies

It is almost a law of science, the more indirect the evidence, the more polarized the debate. The more direct the evidence, the less the answers look either–or.

—JONATHAN WEINER, 1995, *THE BEAK OF THE FINCH*

I sought to understand what limited survival of newborn elk. Numbers of calves per one hundred cows recorded from refuge feedtrucks were lower than on some State of Wyoming feedgrounds and in many unfed elk populations, and yet the Jackson elk population was stable. Critics who favored bountiful elk blamed Jackson's low calf-to-cow ratios on one of two causes: inadequate winter feeding or excessive predation. As mountain lion numbers increased, grizzlies ranged south of Yellowstone National Park, and reintroduction of gray wolves to Yellowstone was proposed, the inevitable and alarming conclusion to some Wyoming observers was clear: The Jackson elk population would plummet, leaving fewer for hunters and tourists.

I suspected the equation was not quite this simple, and the upshot not so dire. Elk numbers had fluctuated during the refuge's seventy-five-year history (see Appendix A), and winter counts had actually trended upward since the early 1980s. Calf ratios were low, yes, averaging twenty-nine calves per hundred cows in recent years. Yet when Buzz Robbins had measured pregnancy rates of refuge elk during 1976–1982, 87 percent of adults (two years old or more) and 17 percent of yearlings were pregnant—quite typical of other elk herds. After accounting for brucellosis losses, Buzz and I calculated that sixty-three of every hundred cows (yearling and older) potentially produced calves.[1] So why had the expected

The annual winter elk classification count from refuge feedtrucks
(Angus Thuermer, *Jackson Hole News and Guide*)

number of calves born (sixty-three calves per hundred cows) declined to twenty-nine per one hundred observed six months later on the refuge?

With the elk herd hovering around fifteen thousand in the winter of 1988–89—four thousand above Wyoming's desired population size—many federal and state wildlife managers had the opposite concern: How to design hunting seasons to reduce the herd? In western Wyoming this was serious business. Like politics, the celebrity invasion, and tourist dollar trends, the status of the elk permeated Jackson's café and saloon conversations. Strong opinions grew stronger when shared and repeated.

The practical purposes of my research—those objectives attracting financial support of agencies and nonprofit organizations—were to learn what percent of calves survived, and for those that did not, why they died. Was it as simple as more predators, more predation? Was winter feeding somehow responsible? Were more obscure or complex processes at play? And what were the prescient implications for elk conservation and management?

Over three calving seasons, twenty-two calves (15 percent of the 145 I had radio-collared) died during their first month of life—the neonatal period. Predators killed fifteen (black bears eleven and coyotes four), while the remaining seven succumbed to disease, malnutrition, or accidents.[2] Two previous studies of elk calf survival—one in central Idaho in the 1970s and one in Yellowstone National Park in the late 1980s—both found higher rates of mortality, primarily from predation. In Idaho, black bears and lions killed thirty of fifty-four young elk. In Yellowstone, grizzly bears and coyotes accounted for most of the 31 percent of newborn calves that died. Both studies found calf survival improved immensely beyond one month of age.[3,4] Following this initial period of vulnerability, surviving calves in my study were likewise all but bombproof until the fall hunting season began.

Investigating animals killed by large meat-eaters is always exciting. While I was seeking newborn elk to collar, carnivores hunted them for meals. From partially eaten calves I displaced black bears, including a female and her three rambunctious cubs. Bone fragments, the head, and partial hide of another calf were scattered some distance from the source of the radio collar's beeping signal. My colleagues and I searched intensively but could not find the six-inch-diameter vinyl collar. Finally, on hands and knees, with the volume of the receiver minimized, I figured it out. The collar was underground, beneath a log; a coyote had buried the collar and covered the hideaway with forest litter.

An equally intriguing case occurred in the backcountry of GTNP. From the telemetry receiver in his Maule aircraft, pilot Fred Reed and I determined that a calf had died near the shore of Jackson Lake. After boating across the lake to Moran Bay and searching the shoreline, Kathy McFarland and I realized the radio signal wasn't on land. Plying the bay, we found the calf floating offshore. Skin contusions and battered bones showed that the calf had been whisked downstream by the nearby creek that entered the bay. A narrows some two hundred yards upstream required a spooky leap of several feet to cross thundering Moran Creek—something negotiated by hundreds of elk, but a feat only an unhinged human would have tried. Unlike their strong-swimming cousin the moose—which I observed paddling with newborns across Jackson Lake's bays—elk migrated around, preferring thick vegetation, rocky terrain, and snowmelt-swollen torrents instead.

Kathy McFarland locating drowned elk calf (seen floating at the end of the antenna)
(Bruce Smith)

Older elk were swallowed by icy currents as well. A calf I radioed in 1992 drowned several years later in that same creek. Pummeled and swept by the spring flood, I found her wedged in a logjam at the creek's outlet to the bay. These were not isolated events. In June 1997 we boated to Moran Bay once more. Pilot Gary Lust had located the mortality signal of another calf's radio. As Kathy, Susan Patla, and I searched the bay's margin from a Boston Whaler, we were stunned to discover the partially eaten and rotting carcasses of six elk littering the shore. After routing a reluctant black bear from one calf's remains, we found contusions on the torso and head that attested it too had taken a wild ride down Moran Creek. Another showed similar battering, but the other calves and adults were too scavenged or decomposed to tell us their story.

We grid-searched the bay, seeking the radioed calf Gary had heard. The transmitter faithfully called from its watery grave. How many more elk lay undiscovered on the bottom was anyone's guess, but Moran wasn't the only place where swift currents challenged Jackson elk. Young calves also drowned—though none of my radioed sample—crossing the Buffalo Fork and Snake Rivers. The northward migration to summer range fatefully coincided with the annual flood of high water.

Such travails are not unique to elk. While fishing an Idaho creek early one July, I found a mule deer lodged in a tangle of overhanging brush. The fawn had apparently been swept away when the stream raged with runoff two or three weeks earlier. I've also found porcupines, skunks, and Hereford calves drowned in streams. Whether it's the victims' inferior size, strength, and instincts at fault, or poor maternal judgment, a few are selected against while the majority survive.

The rate of loss of our radioed calves was unexpectedly low—given that half as many calves showed up on the refuge in winter as pregnancy rates indicated were born. Much of the difference I resolved. Each August Steve Cain and I counted and classified elk from helicopter throughout the central valley of GTNP. The calf-to-cow ratios we recorded in GTNP were 28 percent less than the ratios expected from pregnancy rates. Besides the 15 percent mortality of my radioed elk calves, an additional 13 percent of calves must have died. How could this be? Based on research by others of deer and caribou, I knew that estimates of neonatal mortality from captured and radioed animals are always downward-biased. That is, like my measurement of 15 percent mortality, other investigators have also concluded they measured only part—about half in one case—of the true rate of mortality in the population at large. The undetected losses include stillbirths, calves rejected and abandoned by their mothers, nonviable births, and predation immediately after birth. These perinatal losses occur from within minutes to a day or two after birth. From studies of red deer and caribou, we know that more than half of mortality occurs within forty-eight hours of birth. The calves I captured ranged from a few hours to seven days old, averaging 3.3 days. I had no chance of capturing any of the younger calves that had already died. Thus, among every one hundred calves born, twenty-eight did not survive a month—fifteen of which I was able to document by radiotelemetry and an estimated thirteen more I could not.[2]

Although 28 percent neonatal mortality did not completely explain why winter calf-to-cow ratios were lower than expected on the refuge, other findings allayed some citizens' fears. Calf birth weights were similar to those reported elsewhere. We discovered no calamitous diseases among newborns (although two viral forms of enterocolitis, an intestinal inflammation we found, had not been reported in free-ranging elk calves). Calves were not dying left and right. Predators were not pushing the population toward the brink. However, most research and all public attitudes share a decidedly short shelf life.

In Idaho, Yellowstone Park, and Jackson Hole, predators—primarily bears—killed most of the calves that died. Black bears were common in Jackson Hole. They killed elk neonates I captured both east and west of the Snake River, and in similar proportions. But with black bears a component of the valley's fauna for thousands of years, and hunted spring and fall as a trophy game species in Wyoming (including over bait), nothing indicated that they threatened the persistence of elk. Not that anyone suggested that. Indeed, most people didn't realize that lunching black bears were the leading cause of calf mortality. It was something rarely witnessed in the wild. With coyotes the only other predator of neonates I

The cased hide of an elk calf killed and eaten by a black bear
(Bruce Smith)

recorded, the Jackson herd seemed destined to produce an annual surplus of three thousand elk for hunters ad infinitum (see Appendix A).

But conditions are seldom static in nature, and Jackson Hole would prove no exception. The black bear's big cousin, the grizzly, was rebounding from historically low numbers. A century of persecution had contracted the range of this emblem of wildness by 95 percent. A reversal of fate was made possible by the plummeting population's listing as a federally threatened species in 1973. The remaining 150 to 200 individuals survived largely inside Yellowstone Park. Ever so slowly, efforts to protect both bears and people—by bear-proofing everything from garbage cans to cabins and closing open pit dumps—rescued Yellowstone's grizzlies from their slide toward extinction. Increased numbers fostered pioneering of vacant ranges well beyond Yellowstone's boundaries—invisible property lines of little ecological import to grizzly bears and other wide-ranging wildlife.[5]

Recovery of Yellowstone's bears—like Old Faithful geyser, long a symbol of the world's first national park—was lauded as a success story by some. Others were less sure. Bears increasingly clashed with human interests beyond the park, and a particular hot spot lay east of Moran, Wyoming. Trouble was brewing there.

Yellowstone's grizzly bears are among the most predatory in the world. As some ventured into new ranges, they not only found the GYE's bounty of wild ungulates to their liking, but they also encountered tens of thousands of domestic sheep and cattle. Livestock graze U.S. Forest Service and Bureau of Land Management lands in summer and fall—a century-old practice consistent with those agencies' multiple-use policies. In addition to hosting a commercial airport and conducting an elk reduction program, GTNP is also unique among U.S. national parks in permitting cattle grazing on lands east of the Snake River. One of these allotments, Elk Ranch East, bordered Bridger-Teton National Forest lands where cattle grazed the Blackrock–Spread Creek allotment. In total these 175 square miles were grazed in summer by more than two thousand cattle during the 1990s. And once again, it was grizzly range.[6]

In 1993, the year after my doctoral study ended, a spike in deaths of Hereford calves grazing the Blackrock–Spread Creek allotment alarmed the livestock's owner. Investigation by Wyoming and federal officials confirmed that many of the dead cattle, thirty-one calves, were killed by grizzly bears. The telltale way in which bears deliver the coup de grace was unmistakable, biting the head and neck then deftly peeling back the hide to feed. Wyoming Game and Fish Department biologists Dave Moody and Chuck Anderson initiated a three-year study in 1994 to determine the number of bears in the area and how many were preying on cattle. Offending bears would be removed to ease the conflict.

Wyoming may have the most liberal compensation law for wildlife damage in the nation. The state not only compensates landowners for crop damage, it pays ranchers the fair market value of livestock lost to predators, including cattle and sheep killed on public lands. Through 1998, 108 cattle were seriously injured or killed in grizzly bear attacks on Blackrock–Spread Creek. Wyoming compensated the rancher $158,000 and spent another $300,000 trying to manage the conflict. Bears killed another thirty-five cattle nearby in GTNP. Thus, Wyoming had two reasons to halt the depredations: to limit payments for lost livestock, and to quell the outrage of the Wyoming Farm Bureau and stockmen's associations.[7, 8]

During the summers from 1994 to 1996, Moody and Anderson captured twenty-four black bears and eighteen grizzlies in snares and culvert traps on the affected grazing allotments.[6] The number of grizzlies surprised most everyone. Seventeen bears of each species were fitted with radio transmitters. Although several grizzlies were removed—transported to cattle-free wilderness—cattle losses continued as the situation became politically charged. All the way to Washington, D.C., it drew attention, and not the good kind. When state officials captured and euthanized a six-hundred-pound male who was a repeat offender, wildlife interests took particular note. Wildlife was protected in GTNP, and 86 percent of the Blackrock–Spread Creek allotment was designated critical habitat for bears under the Interagency Grizzly Bear Management Guidelines. These were public lands, and the grizzly bear was a threatened species. Cows were not.

Like many Jackson Hole residents, I sympathized with the rancher, but agonized that the threatened bears were under the gun. Having captured elk calves where this clash now brewed, I knew the allotments' luxuriant tapestry of Douglas-fir forest, aspen groves, and meadows well. Hundreds of elk congregated on those Forest Service and Park Service lands each May, giving birth and raising their young. Some remained all summer, although the majority migrated north to the Teton Wilderness Area or Yellowstone Park after calving.

At the 1996 annual meeting of the Jackson Hole Cooperative Elk Studies Group, I offered a hypothesis to state and federal biologists and managers. Pioneering grizzly bears had discovered a bounty of newborn elk calves and decided this was a dining experience not to be missed. As calves grew bigger and stronger, most readily fled from bears or migrated with their mothers elsewhere. Quite timely for the bears, cowboys trailed the cattle to the Blackrock–Spread Creek and adjacent GTNP lands just as chasing calves no longer rewarded bears with elk protein. The carnivorous habits of some bears turned to bovine calves.

Although the theory was plausible, there was no evidence to support it. During 1990–92 the grizzlies killed none of the 145 calves I radioed. However, the cattle losses didn't spike until the following year. The idea of repeating my earlier investigation to test this hypothesis gained momentum, fueled by a changing large-carnivore landscape. Mountain lion numbers were also increasing—a trend reported throughout much of the West. From 1972 to 1992, Jackson area hunters had harvested only three lions, compared to twenty-six during 1994–99, and four more were killed in motor vehicle collisions. Finally, the reintroduction of wolves into Yellowstone Park in 1995 and 1996 only escalated the controversy. Funding commitments from federal and state agencies and private donors soon followed amid the polarized debate over cattle predation by grizzlies, a heated anti-predator political climate, and a burgeoning Jackson elk herd that exceeded the state's population objective of eleven thousand by seven thousand animals in late 1996.

Grand Teton National Park offered to pay one-third of my salary over the next five years to pursue the research and other studies of elk in the park—an incentive that compelled the USFWS to commit my time. With first year's funding obligated by the end of 1996, I again enlisted the assistance of Dr. Beth Williams to analyze the remains of calves, and state forensic expert, Tom Moore, to identify predator hair samples collected from mortality sites. As before, I circulated the research proposal to state and federal agency personnel for peer review to ensure its scientific rigor and consideration of everyone's interests.

At daybreak on May 28, 1997, my first helicopter flight left the Jackson Hole airport to capture elk. This study, like the one completed five years earlier, would span three years and, in all but two respects, replicate the methods and experimental design of the previous study. First, to assess physiological status and disease exposure, I collected ten milliliters of blood from captured calves. Secondly, instead of expandable radio collars, I attached radio ear tags to calves. The transmitters were ironically left over from another mortality study in which Moody and Anderson had investigated grizzly predation on cattle in the Blackrock–Spread Creek allotment. The transmitters that had previously been worn by bovine calves would now be attached to the ears of 153 elk calves during 1997–99.

My objectives were to evaluate:

1. Whether increased predator populations were increasing elk calf mortality.

2. Whether mortality by new predators (grizzlies, lions, and wolves) was compensatory—that is, did it reduce mortality by black bears, coyotes, or other causes, or was it additive to causes of neonatal mortality I recorded during the early 1990s?

3. And, maybe of greatest interest to resource managers, were grizzly bears preying on elk calves where bear depredations on cattle were occurring?

These three years of study offered an additional opportunity. Would the variation in winter feeding, elk population size, or other environmental factors over a six-year span of time alter what I'd learned five years earlier about what influenced elk calf survival?

As in my earlier study, calves died from predation, disease, and accidents. Average birth weights were similar throughout the six years and uncorrelated with the ration or duration of elk winter feeding. Other results were strikingly different as neonatal mortality nearly doubled from 15 percent to 28 percent. Corrected for undocumented perinatal losses, mortality was 45 percent compared to 28 percent in the earlier study.[9]

Grizzly bear pursuing an elk calf as its mother looks on
(Diana Stratton)

Grizzly bear closing in on an elk calf
(Diana Stratton)

In addition to black bear and coyote predation, six calves were killed by grizzly bears and two by mountain lions in the late 1990s. Wolves, on the other hand, had no measurable effect. One pack established a territory and produced six pups in my east study area, but this didn't happen until 1999. The chances of even one of the fifty-seven calves captured and radioed that year being killed by so few wolves were statistically slim.

Yellowstone's Interagency Grizzly Bear Study Team estimated that bear numbers doubled during the 1990s across an expanding domain that included lands east of the Snake River. However, lands where I captured calves to the west were all but grizzly-free, and that geographic dichotomy mirrored the locations where grizzlies killed elk calves.[5, 9]

As in the early 1990s, the mortality rate east and west of the Snake River was similar; however, the proportion of calves killed by bears during 1997–99 more than doubled to the east while remaining similar west of the river. In the latter study, both bear species killed calves east of the river, while diseases and accidents were four times less prevalent there than to the west. This appeared to be a case of compensation, where predation partially replaced other causes of mortality (disease and accidents, which also had accounted for a greater proportion of calf losses in the early 1990s). Two calves killed by bears suffered preexisting bacterial infections. A third calf killed by a grizzly and another killed by a coyote had experienced difficult births (we had captured both at chaotic birth sites where brush lay broken and ground plowed by hooves). Both calves had been weak, and scrapes and contusions marred their heads and shoulders. All four of these elk may have died from their predisposing conditions had predators not found them.[9]

These instances of predisposing ailments along with the variety of nonpredatory causes of death (seventeen of the total sixty-four mortalities died of accidents or disease) were among the two studies' most unexpected results. We recovered and examined the complete carcasses of calves that drowned and others with viral enteritis, bacterial pneumonia, brucellosis, encephalitis, meningitis, malnutrition, and congenital abnormalities that included a ruptured umbilical cord, dystocia (difficult birth), and the bizarre anomaly of a calf born without a right ventricle in its heart. As a group they were younger when captured than all the other calves, suggesting that newborns with such rarely reported conditions don't survive long.

As I considered why calf mortality had increased, I suspected bears preying more aggressively on elk calves might be a symptom of some underlying cause. Other evidence supported this conclusion.

Blood chemistries of the calves that survived the neonatal period suggested they were in better health or received more milk than those calves that died. Accordingly, those that died may have been less thrifty or grown more slowly, predisposing them to predation. I hadn't collected blood from calves during the early 1990s—a missed opportunity I regret—so I couldn't relate increased mortality during the late 1990s to declining animal condition over time. Or could I? Other circumstances of the fates of these young elk filled in pieces of the puzzle.

I discovered that the calves I captured from 1997 to 1999 grew more slowly than those captured during the early 1990s. Calves that were one day old or less (considered birth weights) were similar in weight, but by the time they reached two to seven days old, they weighed 16 percent less than in the early 1990s. Why, I wondered, did calves grow more slowly during the late 1990s?

The elk population was some three thousand animals larger, and that could potentially increase competition for food among mothers. In studies of several species of deer and domestic animals, suboptimal foraging conditions adversely affected milk production of dams, and subsequently the growth rate and survival of offspring. Growth occurs fastest in the first few weeks of an elk's life when energetic demands on mothers for milk are greatest. Did a growing elk herd translate to poorer calf survival? A subsequent analysis by Dr. Bruce Lubow and myself cast doubt on this possibility. Twenty years of elk population data suggested that any such density-dependent mechanism was likely swamped by winter feeding.[10] That left me to consider other environmental factors, causes independent of herd size.

Among the forces driving natural selection, vagaries of weather often reign supreme. Quite simply, April temperatures in Jackson Hole set in motion a series of cascading events.

April is the month in northwest Wyoming that forage "green-up" typically begins. This new vegetative growth is far more nutritious than cured forage, more nourishing even than the rations of alfalfa fed to refuge elk. Indeed, termination of each winter's feed season is dependent on spring greening, which varies from year to year.[11] In Yellowstone Park, for example, the onset of green-up varied by as much as a month.[12] Likewise, the end date of feeding during my twenty-two years at the refuge ranged from March 20 to April 22. During the last three years of my research, April temperatures were below normal, whereas they were average to above normal from 1990 to 1992. Beyond this simple index of temperature statistics, I confirmed reduced green biomass across elk calving areas from 1997 to 1999 from satellite-derived images.[9]

In years of unseasonably cool April temperatures and delayed spring green-up, both recovery of body condition lost in winter and milk production of gravid females may suffer. Reduced milk yields, in turn, diminish growth rates of new calves. Undernourished, slower-growing calves experience higher mortality and for a longer period of time postpartum. In my earlier study, all calves reaching one month of age survived. But half a decade later, they died as much as fifty-six days after birth, including five predations by black and grizzly bears of calves forty-two or more days old. Throughout all six years of study, mortality was concentrated on individuals with low birth weights. It followed that those who grow more slowly may also be more vulnerable, as in the late 1990s.

In my research this nutritionally mediated variation in annual calf survival was expressed as changes in bear predation. But the dynamic was driven by more than calf vulnerability. Bears, like humans, are omnivorous. They consume grass and nuts, bulbs and berries, insects and larvae, fish and mammals, and they eat carrion as an opportunistic protein source. Bears' twenty-four/seven food mart is a mix of what's in season and can be grazed or caught. In the Greater Yellowstone Ecosystem, grizzly bears consume more protein from large mammals than populations elsewhere on the continent.[13] In part this is due to the tremendous concentration of ungulates in the GYE, including eight wild species totaling 164,000 animals, plus 230,000 cattle and 60,000 domestic sheep.[14] Although successful attacks on full-grown deer, elk, and moose do occasionally occur—primarily winter-weakened animals and other compromised unfortunates—far more neonates fall to bears than older individuals. The black bear is likewise a skilled predator of newborn deer, moose, and elk.[15, 16]

Bears hunt more by scent than sight. Because elk calves are "hiders" for the first week or so after birth, they are less vulnerable to sight hunters like cats. Thus, bears' highly evolved olfactory lobes serve them well during the period when calves remain concealed.

Female grizzly and yearling offspring eating an elk calf
(Diana Stratton)

Beyond being born of adequate weight and in a year when milk yields were high, luck certainly favored some calves and frowned on others. In a landscape filled with large carnivores, a mother's experience and nurturing care may mean the difference between tasting your next meal and becoming someone else's. During our capture flights, I watched elk mothers rush in to protect calves against would-be attackers. One harassed a black bear; others chased coyotes, sandhill cranes, and even grouse away from their secreted young. One mercilessly hounded a porcupine—a connoisseur of tree bark—until I feared it would be stomped, with both mama elk and porky regretting the encounter. On two occasions protective elk charged within striking range as I handled their babies. I've also observed elk mothers in Yellowstone chase grizzly bears intent on their calves. Devoted mothers though they are, warding off determined bears is often a lost cause for even the most dogged elk.

In late May and June, both black and grizzly bears converge on meadows, sagelands, and aspen groves shared with elk. These are biologically special areas where female elk gather each year to deliver the next generation. Grizzly bear expert John Craighead felt grizzlies may travel to elk calving areas specifically to prey on calves.[17] Certainly the same logic may apply to the equally proficient black bear. Alternatively, these lush plant communities may attract both elk and bears simply by virtue of their luxuriant grazing. But when spring winds blow cold and forage is spare, adaptable bears may turn to alternate food sources. On the heels of a long winter's fast, the nutritional payoff of prowling the undergrowth for thirty-five-pound protein packages could become habit forming.

If bears can learn to hunt young elk, should we not expect them to do the same with what are drolly called "slow elk"? The less aggressive black bear appears disinclined to do so, though they readily scavenge cattle carcasses. But some grizzly bears are another story, as in the Blackrock–Spread Creek and adjacent GTNP cattle grazing allotments. Grizzlies began killing cattle in late June and July, but they killed five of six radioed elk calves before June 19, before cattle were permitted to graze those lands each year. This supported my hypothesis that predatory bears traveled to the grazing allotments before cattle were turned out, ostensibly in search of elk calves. Rather than continuing the same practice and expecting different results, I and others suggested that ranchers be offered incentives to graze their stock on alternate summer pastures. If the GYE's grizzly bears are to persist, secure habitats where they can hunt elk calves, pine nuts, and bistort roots are essential.

With restored gray wolves now denning and hunting on the Blackrock–Spread Creek and GTNP allotments, managing those federal lands for wildlife would seem to better serve the public interest. Indeed, reason prevailed in 2003 when the Walton family voluntarily ceded their permit to graze cattle on the Blackrock–Spread Creek allotment. From a coalition of conservation and hunting groups the family accepted a $250,000 incentive to graze their cows on private land. The longtime grazing permits on the adjacent GTNP lands remain; however, the ranchers have voluntarily not turned cattle onto the allotments in recent years. Grizzlies, wolves, and elk still share the area, while conflicts with cattle have faded.

One of the great evolutionists, David Lack of England, once responded to a question about the great tits of Oxford, the bird species he studied exhaustively. "Well, I can't answer that question," Lack replied, "because

I only have seventeen years of data." Similarly, if I had only studied calf survival from 1990 to 1992, my inferences about mortality and its causes would have reflected a relatively favorable set of environmental conditions for elk.

Numerous long-term studies have shown the environmental sensitivity of populations. Peter and Rosemary Grant studied evolution among thirteen species of finches on the Galápagos Islands, the same finches that kindled Darwin's early thinking about variation and natural selection. Over twenty years of observation, the Grants recorded how the effects of a drought and two El Niños accelerated success or failure of reproduction and survival of each species, and consequently selection for individual traits.[18] On time scales as short as ten years, biologist Dolph Schluter and colleagues have measured evolutionary changes in species of stickleback fish when introduced into new environments or when competition from other species was relaxed.[19] Long-term studies of red deer in Scotland, grizzly bears in Yellowstone, and gray wolves on Isle Royale have illuminated how animals cope with environmental variation, and how any one snapshot of a system we observe can be misleading.

As scientists gather more data, their insights into dynamic processes sharpen. In math and the physical sciences, answers are concrete, unfettered by meiosis and chromosomes. In the natural sciences, each problem doesn't have a correct answer or solution, but rather a variety of answers approaching truth to varying degrees. It is pattern that scientists seek, understanding there will be wobbles in trend lines, outliers, and anomalies. That is why we use inferential statistics to state results as probabilities. For example, with 95 percent confidence I concluded that daily weight gains of calves were lower during 1997–99 than in 1990–92.

The influence of April's growing conditions on the annual survival rate of elk was a parsimonious discovery. An ocean away, British and Scottish scientists likewise found that differences in spring temperatures correlated with annual survival of red deer calves.[20] In science the true test for credibility is replication. When results from experiments replicated across space or repeated in time concur, they strengthen conclusions that take on generality. Hypotheses unsupported by repeated testing are rejected like contestants eliminated from a spelling bee.

Since my dissertation research, another nine studies of elk calf survival have been completed in Oregon, Washington, Idaho, Montana, and

Wyoming. A recent synthesis of all those studies found the following patterns.

Among the twelve elk populations studied in the Northwest (each supporting three to five species of large carnivores), survival during the first three months of life ranged from 31 to 84 percent. Neonatal survival greater than 40 percent was capable of increasing elk populations. Predation was the leading cause of mortality. In study areas with four and five large predator species, competition among predators diminished the proportion of calves killed by lions, coyotes, and wolves, but not bears. That is, as the most successful predators on elk neonates, only bears additively decreased survival of calves regardless of the competition. Where wolves were restored, they were the least significant predator on newborn elk. The synthesis also found that climatic conditions interacted with competition among species of predators to limit the impact of predation on neonatal mortality. As I found in Jackson elk, when spring weather was unfavorable, predators killed some calves that likely would have died of other causes. Lastly, the synthesis concluded that efforts to increase elk populations through predator control may prove futile. The effects of weather and competition between predators may thwart any benefits of this management approach.[21]

Beyond assessing survival of neonates, radiotelemetry provided two other opportunities: the means to test my hypothesis that dispersal of elk may limit herd growth, and the prospect of measuring the ultimate fate of each elk, whether neonate or older. Some unnerving moments awaited as I tracked down mortality signals during fall, winter, and spring.

The afternoon of October 30, 1990, Billy Helprin called and informed me that a transmitter was beating double time in eastern GTNP. "Do you want any help tracking it down?" he asked.

Sometimes others joined me to investigate an elk's undoing. Beyond the welcome help, companionship was a safety precaution. But in 1990 grizzlies were not part of the predator/scavenger community I expected to encounter in GTNP. I replied, "No. It was probably shot by a hunter. I'll just head there tomorrow. Shouldn't take too long."

The elk hunting season in GTNP had opened ten days earlier. I suspected a hunter had discarded elk #52's collar where she'd met her end. Based on the position Billy and Al triangulated from the telemetry towers, this would only be a two-mile hike.

In a steady snow I set out the following afternoon. Expecting to find only the elk's collar and entrails, instead I found the radio collar encircling the neck of what remained of a 250-pound elk. From it two packed trails led to bed sites beneath thickly crowned fir trees. Both trails clearly registered four-inch-diameter paw prints of a mountain lion—likely a big male. Other tracks showed that the cat had just bounded away.

An elk kill may feed a lion three days or more—less if usurped by a grizzly or pack of wolves. Thus, solitary hunters like most cats and bears are hard-wired to conceal a partly consumed carcass. In this case the cat had crowned the elk's remains beneath debris ranging from pine needles to five-inch-diameter logs. Social carnivores like the canids or African lions need not bother with such precautions. To them a kill is no more than a one-course meal, and gamely defended by the group as a whole.

Without further thought I uncovered and examined the carcass over the next half hour. When I finished, just enough daylight remained for the hike back to the truck. With nothing pressing in Jackson, I decided instead to track the lion for a while through the ten inches of fresh powder. This wouldn't be the first time my backcountry fieldwork had ended with a hike by flashlight.

After he'd bolted from the kill site at my approach, the lion crossed a small stream, then angled upslope. Following his bounding tracks another seventy-five yards, I was stunned to find that the big cat paused directly upslope of the carcass. The snow impression told all. He'd sat facing downslope where I worked.

A chill shook my body. I *too* was potential prey. What had he contemplated about this weak human who'd displaced him from *his* kill? Was he simply amused? I suspect not. Hunting prey for a living is serious work. A kill usurped by another meant hunger, and a poorly executed attempt on quarry the size of an elk could cause grave injury, even death. An old lion that curled up and died next to a refuge feed shed one winter had two broken canines—sufficient cause to explain his wasted body.

How long he watched from his vantage point I couldn't tell. But a dozen bounds could well have ended his vigil, and my research. Instead, he'd padded upslope through a deepening forest where I pursued with fascination, and a watchful eye ahead. At times he'd duck beneath low-spreading branches. Once he burrowed through a tangle of underbrush and limbs from two fallen giants, rather than detour around. Farther on he leaped five feet onto the trunk of another downed fir, though he could have crept beneath. Such is the life of the hunter turned hunted: slinking through cover to remain concealed, yet risking a vantage point to appraise the pursuer. Each move, each decision, is the finely tuned handiwork of a hunter living among other deadly hunters. As light slipped from the forest, my nerves turned my steps toward the truck.

In September 1998 Gary Lust circled his Maule over the north slope of the Teton Range's 12,605-foot Mount Moran, zeroing in on the source of a mortality signal, two thousand feet above Jackson Lake. I'd not been on Moran since a friend and I had summited the peak in July 1993, a week after a two-foot snowfall buried our camp at ten thousand feet on our first attempt. Two days after circling the mortality signal, I crossed Jackson Lake in a Boston Whaler.

After nearly two hours of brush-busting up Moran's northeastern slope, I found the ear-tag transmitter still attached to the devoured calf's left ear. The pile of brush and duff adjacent the carcass, the intact empty hide, the fifty-foot drag trail, the signs of struggle and death at the kill site, and finally the paired punctures in the rear of the cranium all told the story: another lion kill.

This was just one among 125 elk (42 percent of those 298 I had radioed) that didn't live until its first birthday. Of 234 that survived the first two months of life, hunters killed twenty-seven during fall and another thirty died over winter, December through April. Lions killed a number of those, four confirmed and others I suspected but too little remained to tell "who dunnit." After wolves arrived at the refuge in 1999, they killed a radioed calf in February—the only radioed elk I knew to be killed by wolves through April 2004 when I left Jackson Hole. For others that died in winter and spring, extensive scavenging masked cause of death. Some fell to disease, including periodic outbreaks of septicemic pasteurellosis

Mount Moran in August with elk in foreground
(Bruce Smith)

on the NER, a deadly bacterial infection responsible for at least three deaths of radioed calves. Others may have been the undiscovered victims of hunters' bullets. Over the years I found that for every five elk harvested, another unretrieved animal died of gunshot wounds. As their wounds compromised their mobility or became infected, predators finished some while others slowly slipped away.

Of course, keeping tabs on each captured animal was limited by the battery life of its radio transmitter. So I went elk hunting during feeding seasons from atop the refuge feed trailers. Armed with a fifty-caliber rifle and aluminum darts filled with a narcotic immobilizing drug, I replaced the tattered collars and colored ear-tag transmitters of calves with more durable collars sporting six years of battery power. Over fourteen years of these catch-and-release hunting outings, some old-timers wore three or four different collars, changing looks with the times. Eric Cole, the current refuge biologist, still tuned in the signals of the six that remained in 2011.

In fall 2008, #7—a sturdy female—was the lone survivor from the original fifty-three captured in 1990. It now seems a shame I gave her no name on that dew-drenched morning when I stroked her russet coat. When I

The author darting elk on the National Elk Refuge
(Kathy McFarland, US Fish and Wildlife Service)

replaced her calf collar in March 1992, I pressed my face against her barreled ribcage, felt the rise and fall of her lungs, and heard the life-giving rhythm of a heart weighing several times my own. The pungent aroma of fermented cellulose hung on her breath. She embodied all the wonder of a species so well adapted to environmental conditions from desert to boreal forest, coastal redwoods to alpine meadows, wilderness to the edge of exurban sprawl. I felt privileged to touch this life as only my profession permitted. Still she remained nameless, one among thousands of elk.

Over eighteen years this grand dam endured the rigors of winter's minus-thirty-degree temperatures, crusted spring snows, summer droughts, and migrations to and from her summer home in GTNP. She outwitted orange-clad hunters and enriched the Jackson herd with maybe a dozen offspring—regal males who've filled autumnal evenings with resonant bugling, and females who've now produced many calves of their own. Each bolstered this most wondrous of elk herds, grazed verdant meadows, and in turn fed a menagerie of predators, scavengers, and decomposers. Bones and antlers enrich hungry soils that in turn nourish wheatgrass and groundsel, feeding this ancient cycle.

The original sample of 298 calves, plus another 51 yearling females I darted and radio-collared on the refuge, served as markers of the herd's seasonal distribution and the timing and progress of each fall's migration. They were also the basis for evaluating my second hypothesis of how the elk herd might be limited. I postulated that if elk density in GTNP caused excessive competition for food resources, some elk may disperse to adjacent summer ranges, for example, the Teton Wilderness Area. Indeed, some calves that summered in GTNP did disperse in subsequent years, but this outflow was offset by others that moved into the park.[22] Taking this a step further, if significant numbers of elk left the Jackson herd, this could limit population growth. This also proved not the case. Although five radioed elk spent a winter or summer outside the boundaries of the Jackson elk herd unit, all but one (harvested just west of Jackson) returned to the herd later. The Yellowstone River drainage in southeastern Yellowstone Park was primarily where these elk strayed and mingled with elk from two other herds that winter east of the Continental Divide. But this was only part of the story.

In this book's first chapter, I told of radio-collaring twenty-five elk on winter feedgrounds in the Gros Ventre drainage. Following their

Author, Fernando Escobedo, and Kathy McFarland radio-collaring an immobilized adult female elk
(US Fish and Wildlife Service)

radio transmitters over the next two years showed that they had much lower fidelity to the Jackson elk herd than the 474 elk radioed since 1978 in western parts of the herd unit. Fully one-third of those twenty-five elk summered elsewhere—in the Green River drainage to the south, or east of the Continental Divide in the Wind River country. Two of those animals did not return, while two others were harvested in their newly adopted homes. A fifth elk vanished from the airways, likely hauled away in a pickup after someone's successful hunting outing, or having dispersed beyond our aerial telemetry range.

Before monitoring this sample of Gros Ventre elk, the Jackson herd was considered "non-leaky," that is, less than 10 percent left its human-drawn boundaries for greener pastures elsewhere. Assuming this sample of radioed animals is representative of the three thousand elk that occupy the Gros Ventre drainage, some one thousand head may mingle with other herds to the east and south. Most leave only seasonally—and therefore aren't lost to the Jackson herd—but on their return may bring with them new pathogens they have acquired. Uncertain is the degree of influx of elk and deer from adjacent ranges. However, radioed mule deer from as far south as Pinedale migrate each summer to Jackson Hole.[23] And one fall

Releasing a newly radio-collared yearling elk on the National Elk Refuge
(US Fish and Wildlife Service)

two elk radio-collared 160 miles distant in southwest Montana showed up at the refuge for alfalfa à la carte. Within the encircling stronghold of towering mountains, the Jackson elk seemed secure from outside threats. Now we know better. And this is a chilling prospect as CWD creeps nearer.

Some of my research findings ran counter to popular opinion, and none more than the relationship of winter mortality to winter feeding—perhaps because it was counterintuitive or proponents of feeding wanted their beliefs justified. Regardless, years of recordkeeping showed that more elk died in winters of more feeding at the NER. Feeding wasn't causative of mortality, just a response by managers to tough times and no panacea for long winters' energetic drain on elk.

Why also didn't winter feeding produce bigger calves than in unfed elk herds? Why were these calves a typical thirty-five pounds if larger calves survive better? Calf birth weights reflect genetic potential and prenatal investment by mothers. Prenatal investment is expensive, and a large female in excellent condition is more likely to bear an optimum size calf than one that is not. Delimited by the maximum size that the birth canal can accommodate and some minimum size that promotes a calf's viability, optimum size lies somewhere in between. Thus, average calf birth weights were similar during all six years of my studies as well as during the 1978–82 refuge feeding trials, as well as similar to birth weights in other herds.

On the subject of elk calf survival, it would be easy, even understandable in the absence of data, to believe that more calves died simply because there were more predators. Indeed, predation was higher in the late 1990s, but the proportion of all losses attributable to predators (76 percent) did not differ significantly from the earlier study (68 percent). On the other hand, the proportion of disease-related deaths declined and necropsies showed that predators, especially bears, killed compromised animals. Compared to the early 1990s, all evidence suggested that the 1997–99 cohorts were more vulnerable to predators because of lower rates of growth, and remained vulnerable for twice as long.

Finally, even though adult survival invariably exceeds survival of juveniles, population trends are far more sensitive to changes in survival of adult female elk than survival of calves.[10, 24] The primary reasons are that half of all calves are males and calves have much higher winter mortality (and therefore, like all males, some females may never bear young). Given that 90 percent of adult mortality of Jackson elk resulted from hunting (compared to 39 percent for calves), human hunters have a greater effect on elk numbers than predators or other natural mortality. The decline in neonatal survival during the 1990s reduced the harvestable surplus of elk in fall by an estimated 13 percent, and suppressed the annual finite rate of increase (the yearly growth rate) of the Jackson herd only slightly, from an estimated 1.26 to 1.23.[9, 25]

Many of the traits we admire most in elk—their strength and speed, doting maternal care, well-heeled social order, and above all their resilience—are products of adaptation to extremes of weather, and their coevolution with grazing competitors and especially large carnivores. Still, the small victory of resolving bear predation of cattle on the Blackrock–Spread Creek allotment to the benefit of grizzlies did not carry over to a resounding public acceptance of more large carnivores sharing the elk's domain.

My research findings that bears, lions, and coyotes only modestly low-ered the Jackson herd's annual surplus allayed some fears, even as a new unease was mounting. Again it centered on a large carnivore. Wolves had come to Jackson Hole. Because wolves kill elk and other large mammals twelve months a year (compared to bears and coyotes, which take them opportunistically during calving season), are notoriously fecund, and hunt in packs (unlike mountain lions), wolves represented a greater threat to depressing the elk herd's growth.

My curiosity as a scientist led me to hatch a new proposal to learn how this fifth large carnivore might affect the Jackson elk. For the public and policy-makers, I wanted to provide reliable data that might mediate both the awe and loathing accompanying wolves' colonization of west-ern Wyoming. However, Grand Teton National Park's contribution to my salary had ended, and on the heels of my previous two studies I found resource agencies had little interest in supporting more research on elk survival. I too would be a spectator witnessing the restoration of this top-rung carnivore unfold.

CHAPTER 10

When Wolves Call

I've always said that the best wolf habitat resides in the human heart.
You have to leave a little space for them to live.
—ED BANGS, USFWS WOLF RECOVERY COORDINATOR

I twirled the three-element antenna in a narrowing arc to where the *ping-ping-ping* rose loudest above the receiver's static hiss. Lloyd and I trained our binoculars where the antenna pointed. The radio signal's unvarying, twice-per-second cadence announced, "Dead elk here." Across the sweeping valley cloaked in pines and fir, the odds weren't good we'd spot the elk, or the scavengers on her remains.

Unlike humans, elk and most other wildlife do not sleep for seven to eight hours straight. Forever vigilant to potential danger, interludes of unconsciousness are limited to cat-napping. Even the longest of resting bouts are interrupted by enough movement to ensure that the drop of mercury in a transmitter's mortality switch will contact the electrodes at either end of the glass tube, thus completing the electrical circuit within four hours. The transmitter continues announcing "This elk is alive." But more information is available. The more a signal modulates in amplitude, the more active the elk—actively feeding or running.

All this I found quite fascinating early in my career while surreptitiously eavesdropping on radioed mountain goats in western Montana (my master's degree research) or deer and pronghorn in north-central Wyoming (duties of my first wildlife job). Now I was more interested in the fate of elk #240. Was she really dead? Did the collar now lie beside her remains, the product of a lion attack or a hunter's bullet? Or had the collar deteriorated and fallen from her neck, and #240 now roamed miles from here? If she was still alive, the mortality switch had malfunctioned—something I'd experienced just twice before. Do this kind of work long enough and those bugaboos arise.

Then Lloyd announced, "I see a cow elk."

Bedded and mostly concealed by trees, the bronzed body materialized in my raised binoculars. Encircling her chocolate mane was the dirty gray band of a radio collar.

On Saturday I'd asked Lloyd Dorsey to join me in recovering elk #240's collar. On a flight to locate radioed elk wintering beyond the refuge, I had found her mortality signal where she had apparently died in the Gros Ventre Wilderness. Knowing this was one of Lloyd's favorite places in the world, I was sure I'd have a companion on a snowshoe trek. I was right.

I had met Lloyd fifteen years or so earlier. We hiked, hunted, fished, and discussed resource management and politics—the latter usually over beers and in an effort to save the world from its most pressing problems. I enjoyed his sense of humor and the intensity with which he threw himself into the citizen conservation arena, first with the Wyoming Wildlife Federation and then as the western Wyoming representative for the Greater Yellowstone Coalition.

It was mid-December 2001, the time of year when cross-country skis or snowshoes provide the best transportation in areas closed to over-snow vehicles. But snow at the Grizzly Lake trailhead was shallow for that time of year, so we zipped gaiters over our pac boots and headed out on foot. After an hour of hiking, I spotted something in the snow ahead.

Among the pleasures of field research are the unexpected discoveries along the way while pursuing your planned work. This was one of those occasions when following my curiosity or instincts was rewarded with the chance to unravel a mystery.

Beneath the spreading overhead branches of several Douglas-fir trees, we spotted the remains of a mule deer. The head, spine, shoulder blades, pelvis, and leg bones of a four-by-four-point buck lay still articulated and attached by the hide on a packed area of snow. Blood spotted the snow and smeared the remaining flesh, and several tears incised the hide. Coyote tracks were immediately evident—two-and-one-half-inch-long impressions—but other canid tracks measuring four by four inches dwarfed the coyotes'. Wolves had been here too.

Coyotes are among the messiest of killers. Ripping and tearing at prey the size of this formerly 175-pound deer, they would slash and harry to bring it down. If several had overwhelmed it, the feasting would be chaotic and the carcass likely scattered. However, the firm white tallow encased by the femur indicated this was a healthy deer, and it was unlikely that even several coyotes had killed it. Assessing which predator was responsible, I knew that wolves wouldn't surrender a kill to coyotes unless they were finished eating and had moved on. Obscuring some coyote tracks were those of wolves; they had been here last.

While Lloyd examined the teeth to estimate the buck's age, I searched upslope and found more tracks. At more than three inches long and wide, they were more rounded than canid tracks and no telltale claw marks showed. Cats retract their claws during travel to keep them sharp, but extend them when tree climbing, fighting, killing, and occasionally when ascending steep slopes. Mingled with the large tracks of an adult cat were many more just half that size. I presumed that a female with one and probably more cubs had also feasted on the deer. Why else was she here? The cat tracks milled in the deadfall, then headed as a group upslope. *Probably two kittens,* I surmised where the tracks parted briefly. I called Lloyd to have a look, then we returned with this knowledge to the carcass.

Skinning back the hide from the upper neck muscles, I found hemorrhaging around the trachea. Lions kill their prey efficiently, either by suffocating bites to the throat or by crushing the cervical vertebrae or skull. The attack is over in minutes, unless the cat is inexperienced or miscalculates.

I had investigated a dead radio-collared calf in March 1992 that apparently died of a thwarted lion attack. My field necropsy revealed a badly infected bite wound to the side of the neck that did not damage any vitals. The spacing of the canine punctures suggested a lion. Concealed in a thicket of young firs, the calf had died in a bedded position (likely of septicemia) and had gone undetected by scavengers.

Our deer was basically intact, minus its organs and most of the flesh. The killer had opened the carcass quite neatly—ventrally, based on where the skin was severed—then fed on the exposed edibles. And finally, and maybe most tellingly, the stomach lay several yards away. Lions disdain digestive tracts and their contents. At other lion kills I found the stomach and most of the intestines deposited several yards from the carcass, and often covered by debris. Lions are meat eaters; they don't eat stinking stomachs!

With enthusiastic gestures I re-created the scene for Lloyd as I imagined it took place: The female lion hid her cubs in the underbrush to hunt the mulie buck. Either she detected and stalked the deer, or it happened to pass where she crouched in ambush. She attacked with lighting speed, latching onto his throat with powerful jaws as her claws secured a hold on his shoulders and neck, dragging him down to the ground. She released her stranglehold after his thrashing had ended, then dragged the body in her jaws to a more concealed place I had found several yards away. There she split open the hide and peritoneal muscles along the belly. Before she began lapping blood from the body cavity, she called to her kittens to join her at the feast. Finishing the free blood, she severed and removed the internal organs, spilling them onto the adjacent snow, and separated the digestive tract from the remaining offal and dragged it some distance away. She and her cubs ate the lungs, heart, liver, and kidneys first. They rested nearby until their hunger returned later that day, or the next, and continued feeding on the buck's flesh.

At some point, probably the day after the kill, one or more coyotes happened along. Perhaps they harried the cats. More concerned with her cubs' safety than defending her kill, the lion retreated. The coyotes tore hungrily at the carcass, dragging it to the flat location where we found it. The scattered remnants of ribs were probably their doing. Judging by the freshness of their tracks, they had been here within the last day, but so had the wolves that displaced them. As with the coyotes, I could not determine from the jumble of tracks how many wolves had dined. Regardless, the mulie was a meal served to three species.

Satisfied with my detective work, I watched Lloyd nod his head, then snap some pictures of the scene. They might show up in some future slide presentation he would give about predator-prey relationships. Predators, especially those of game animals, were a constant source of curiosity and controversy that were part and parcel of his conservation work. And wolves just seemed to evoke more passion among folks than other predators.

With some final comments about our good fortune in stumbling onto this drama, we hoisted our packs and continued on. Tracks of a lone coyote headed roughly in the direction of #240's radio collar. I decided to follow. Despite how common coyotes were on the refuge, I always enjoyed seeing them. Beyond the next ridge, maybe we could catch him pouncing on a subnivean mouse, or in zigzag pursuit of a snowshoe hare, or perched on an outcrop preparing a "yip-yip-howl" to a potential mate.

Ten minutes of hiking and we stopped at a disturbance in the snow, tinged with fresh blood. Wolf tracks had intercepted the coyote's, a scuffle had apparently ensued, and then both sets of tracks bounded south through the foot of snow.

An adult wolf outweighs a thirty-pound coyote by three or four times. This coyote was lucky to escape with his life. As we keenly followed the unfolding theater in the snow, twice more the wolf overtook and rolled the coyote. More blood. I began to feel sorry for the underdog as I often do at lopsided sporting events. Where wolves and coyotes are sympatric, coyotes become more furtive, necessarily timid. If not, they become dead. As closely related canine predators, wolves simply seek to reduce the competition. On the other hand, the red fox, which typically feeds on small mammals and birds, often prospers in the presence of wolves. Wolves attack coyotes, but pay little attention to foxes, which in turn coyotes view as unwelcome competitors with overlapping food habits. As coyote numbers decline and survivors grow wary, foxes do well. This chain of events occurred in Yellowstone National Park when gray wolves were reintroduced in 1995 and 1996 after a sixty-year absence. Bob Crabtree and colleagues, who have studied Yellowstone's coyotes for twenty years, found the song dog's numbers declined by half following wolf restoration.[1] From a pre-wolf rate of 90 percent, annual survival of the park's coyotes dropped to just two out of three. Then an adjustment took place. Since 2001, coyotes have rebounded somewhat, due to lessons learned about wolves and an uptick in rodent numbers (the coyote's main food source). However, in contrast to their freewheeling ways and large packs before wolves, they now live in smaller groups with smaller territories or as vagabond "floaters."[2]

While scientists like Crabtree and Yellowstone's wolf project coordinator, Douglas Smith, record a host of ecological changes across the park's restored wolf landscape, vocal public factions have taken sides in a heated debate. Are wolves good or bad for Yellowstone, its elk and coyotes, and other wildlife? Inevitably such judgments are the dominion of human values, extraneous in the shifting ancient struggle of survival in the natural world.

When it comes to wolves, the history is almost as complicated as the present. For two centuries, as immigrants pioneered western North America, they sought to rid the landscape of possible threats to themselves, their crops, and their livestock. Most came from areas of the eastern United States or parts of Europe where wolves were vilified and intensely persecuted. These attitudes and solutions were likewise visited on Western predators.

Attitudes toward wildlife changed during the early 1900s as immigration patterns shifted and rural dwellers increasingly flocked to cities. Freed from a largely utilitarian connection to nature, more and more citizens came to appreciate wild animals and wild places from a more benevolent perspective. But as Harvard professor Steven Kellert observed, "This 'kinder and gentler' attitude hardly prevailed toward large carnivores."[3] Open warfare, with full government support, was waged on anything with big canine teeth—bears, bobcats, cougars, coyotes, wolves, and wolverines. Grizzly bears were purged from most of the American West by 1922. California's estimated ten thousand bears were gone by 1925. However, no predator was more detested than the gray wolf. Between 1887 and 1907, more than twenty thousand were killed in Wyoming alone. Stockmen's associations, such as the Fish Creek Wolf Association in Jackson Hole, focused like a laser on exterminating wolves.[4] Facing extreme human prejudice and persecution, wolves found no future in the American West, including Jackson Hole.

In a 1907 U.S. Forest Service "cookbook" on killing wolves, Vernon Bailey wrote:

> *The chief objective of the report is to put in the hands of every hunter, trapper, forest ranger, and ranchman directions for trapping, poisoning, and hunting wolves and finding the dens of young. If these directions are followed it is believed that the wolves can be so reduced in number that their depredations will cease to be a serious menace to stock raising.*

*Their complete extermination on the western range is not, how-
ever, to be expected in the near future, and it is only by constant and
concerted effort that their numbers can be kept down sufficiently to
prevent serious depredations.*[5]

Mr. Bailey underestimated the tenacity of Westerners. In the Yellowstone region and elsewhere in the lower forty-eight states, wolves
were wiped out by 1930. It's true that a century ago many stock growers
lost significant numbers of animals to predators. What's often lost in this
war on predators is that unregulated hunting had caused the decimation
of their wild prey. Out of necessity wolves, mountain lions, and others
turned ever more to livestock as a source of food.

When wolves were listed as a threatened species in 1974, the only
New World wolves left outside Alaska and Canada inhabited northern
Minnesota and Lake Superior's Isle Royale (arriving there in the 1940s).
Years later wolves pioneered into Wisconsin and Michigan's Upper Pen-
insula, eventually establishing new populations. Finally, small numbers
of wolves that dispersed south from Canada recolonized the Glacier
National Park area of Montana during the 1980s.

After years of planning, preparation, public hearings, and research
contracts to estimate wolf impacts on the region's ungulates and the
human socioeconomy, it happened. The record of decision on the Yellowstone Wolf Environmental Impact Statement was signed in 1994. After
130 public meetings and 180,000 written comments on the draft EIS, the
policy debate concluded. Thirty-one wolves were translocated from Canada to Yellowstone in 1995 and 1996. After acclimation in large holding
pens, all were released and restored to the park's native fauna within a year.
All the Holocene large carnivores roamed the core of the GYE once again.

Yet one thing was clear: The closer people lived to the park, the more
unfavorable were their opinions on wolf restoration. Stockmen and big-
game outfitters were predictably least enthralled by the prospect. After
all, wolves are designed to kill large, four-legged mammals, which historically fueled government-supported efforts to shoot, trap, and poison, and
ultimately purge tens of thousands of wolves from the lower forty-eight
states. But a fundamental issue was not livestock or wildlife predation, or
even the possibility of attacks on people. As Joel Berger explained in *The*

Better to Eat You With, "It was about property rights and state independence, not that of a greater good or a benevolent goal. It was about local interests versus the will of America's resounding endorsement for restoration and conservation."[6]

As a biologist I saw the debate often reduced to a dichotomy of the moral imperative or the folly of restoring wolves. Hailed as both ecological keystone and murderous scourge, the wolf generated hysteria like no other species. I recall a comment someone made on a field trip I led onto the refuge after wolves had arrived in Jackson Hole. Following several disparaging remarks about those "bloodthirsty murderers," he concluded, "I wouldn't mind wolves so much if they just wouldn't kill our deer and elk."

I had to respond. "Wolves wouldn't have large slashing and tearing teeth if they were intended to eat cabbage."

Wolves are predestined to a life of hunting, as surely as dung beetles must gobble manure. As obligate carnivores, they have specialized in killing large mammals over the ages. Although my remark probably didn't endear me to the gentleman, it distilled the truth of the matter.

On January 6, 1999, the first gray wolves in seventy years set foot on the NER. The previous fall, Yellowstone's six-member Soda Butte Pack had made forays into the Buffalo Fork valley, fifteen miles north of the refuge. This was not a welcomed occasion by many in Wyoming. Fathers and grandfathers of some had helped rid the range of this bane. Among their detractors, some hunters saw wolves as the death knell of western Wyoming's bounteous elk, moose, and deer herds. These worries were grounded in the reality that predator-free populations typically have lower rates of mortality than those with large carnivores, and lower mortality often translates to higher densities of ungulates on the range. However, Wyoming's ungulates lived among bears, lions, and coyotes, and had coevolved with wolves over thousands of years. Were wolves so totally destructive, their prey would not have persisted. A fundamental question regarding the GYE's big game was this: Would their primordial fear of wolves return quickly or belatedly after the jolt of a predation blitzkrieg?

My first glimpse of wild wolves was in Yellowstone's Soda Butte valley. On a crisp June morning, a friend and I were treated to a choir of soaring howls. As first light awakened a dew-covered meadow nestled amid old-growth spruce, three large canids—one silver and two black—lifted their heads in ancestral lament. I was close enough to see vapor surging from their muzzles, and the experience remains etched in my mind's eye. On a December 1998 telemetry flight eighteen months later, these same wolves and their offspring were the first I saw in Jackson Hole. As our Maule aircraft circled overhead, pilot Gary Lust and I watched five apparitions—some silvery gray, the others coal black—negotiate more than two feet of snow like Hermann Meier manhandling a Super G course. The fall elk migration through the Teton Wilderness was nearly ended. We saw no elk nearby, just these graceful creatures cavorting among sullen pines as sunlight sparkled and danced through their snowspray.

In dawn's light three weeks later, I drove onto the refuge to survey range conditions. We had not yet begun winter feeding, so the elk were

Gray wolf
(Yellowstone National Park)

widely scattered. At the north end of Miller Butte—a solitary limestone ridge that rises 500 feet above the surrounding grasslands and marshes—several ravens flushed from a depression, a telltale sign of some unfortunate's demise. I stopped to have a look. Below the bank lay a freshly dead and partially eaten cow elk. More than half of the gaunt animal's flesh remained. A coyote skulked a hundred yards distant. I removed the tools of the trade from my truck—meat saw, ax, and pack containing a skinning knife, whirl-pac and ziplock plastic bags, and a clipboard full of prenumbered forms for recording mortalities. As I approached the steaming carcass, I saw their tracks in the snow. *Wolves!*

I had expected wolves to show up at the refuge. Why not? As my fellow combat Marines and I would say, this was a target-rich environment, and the wide-ranging nature of wolves was sure to eventually lead them here. Now the hair bristled on my neck as I witnessed their return after a decades-long absence. Refuge staff periodically received reports of wolves from hunters and from passersby traveling the highway adjacent the NER's west boundary. But in those early years of the Yellowstone wolf project, at least one wolf in every pack was radio-collared to monitor pack movements. Wolf project biologists Ed Bangs and Mike Jimenez would have notified the refuge that wolves were headed our way.

Granted, the NER hosts some very large coyotes. With lots of carrion to eat and full protection from exploitation—like all other refuge wildlife, except the elk that were hunted each fall—refuge coyotes grew older, bolder, and sometimes larger than elsewhere. They also hunted in packs on occasion, behavior most laymen associate with wolves. Confusion of husky coyotes with Yellowstone's reintroduced wolves was not unexpected. I had checked out a number of such reports, only to find coyotes each time. But surrounding this carcass were the four-inch tracks of wolves.

Besides the massive amount of spilled blood, I noticed that the flesh had been peeled from the dead elk's nose. Coyotes certainly do this, but usually not until most of the entrails and muscles are devoured. Skinning back the hide revealed that tooth punctures had pierced the shoulder and neck. I cracked open a femur and found the contents red and gelatinous, wholly depleted of fat. Upon opening her mouth I was startled to see that the eight incisiform teeth were worn to the gum. *This old girl's days were numbered.* I worked my knife alongside the middle pair of incisors and dislodged the roots from the jaw. These would be sent to the wildlife lab in Laramie, along with those of all other elk mortalities this winter. By July I'd know just how old she was. In the meantime, having seen teeth of hundreds of dead elk whose ages were deciphered, I knew that she was ancient, at least twenty.

When Tom Moore's report arrived five months later, I immediately leafed to the spreadsheet's entry for the January 6 mortality. In the "Age" column appeared the number 29. In the seventeen years since our staff and I began collecting teeth, this was the oldest elk recorded at the refuge. I let the reality sink in. *Twenty-nine. The first wolves to hunt the refuge in seventy years had killed the oldest of 2,215 elk that had died since my arrival!* Something probably unworthy of Guinness's book, but a coincidence I regarded as astonishing.

In Yellowstone Park, biologist Doug Smith was finding that elk comprised nearly 95 percent of the wolves' diets. Wolf biologists anticipated the same among Jackson Hole's buffet of elk. During the winter of 1998–99, 119 elk died on the refuge. This represented 1.6 percent of the 7,300 wintering elk. During the previous twenty-five pre-wolf winters, an average 1.4 percent of the herd perished each winter. Most were the weak, old, crippled, diseased, and otherwise least fit that had reached their end during western Wyoming's sometimes grueling, always testing winters. As I overheard one salty resident of the valley assert, "Jackson Hole has ten months of winter and two months of tough sledding!"

When high-pressure systems blanket "The Hole," steep temperature inversions trap the coldest air against the valley floor, sometimes for days on end. You learn to check the wood supply before one of those arrives. Outdoor enthusiasts can drive up Teton Pass to find the temperature thirty degrees warmer than in town. Elk cannot. Locked in subzero morning fog, frost veneers the hardiest animals. Those lacking insulating body fat lose precious heat. Some mornings as my feedtruck approached, the escaping vapor from their breath and bodies formed a hovering cloud above two thousand animals. *Cervus strato-nimbus.*

A newly formed pack of three wolves, the Gros Ventre pack, had joined the Soda Butte wolves later in January at the mother of all smorgasbords. They partitioned refuge prey, with Soda Butte patrolling north and the Gros Ventre pack encamped to the south. Of the 119 elk mortalities that the refuge staff found that winter, I assigned a probable cause of death to sixty. Half were killed by wolves. By extrapolation, wolves may have killed about sixty elk during winter 1998–99 on the NER.

Among the thirty known wolf kills, two-thirds were calves from seven to ten months old. Nine of the remaining ten were cows that averaged an amazing nineteen years old. The wolves concentrated on the very young and the very aged. In Yellowstone Park too, calves and aged cows—averaging fourteen years of age—were disproportionately selected by wolves.[7] One year's data does not a pattern make, however. So in a presentation to the North American Interagency Wolf Conference in 2001, I presented data from the previous three winters of wolf presence on the refuge. During the winter of 1999–2000, wolves killed only twelve of forty-nine elk that died, one bull, six calves, and five cows averaging sixteen years old. The following year, wolves rarely were observed on the refuge and were not known to kill any elk. Wolves increasingly roamed the Gros Ventre and Buffalo Fork valleys farther north. They hunted elk at the State of Wyoming's three feedgrounds in the Gros Ventre drainage and elk scattered across winter ranges where they were not fed. An average of just twenty-three elk per winter, just 0.3 percent of the refuge herd, were killed from 2001 to 2008 by a growing population of wolves in Jackson Hole—fewer than the fifty-one elk killed per year on Jackson Hole highways from 2002 to 2010. During 2009 and 2010, wolf use of the refuge was still more limited and accounted for just thirteen known elk kills, according to refuge biologist Eric Cole. Who would have guessed? They seemed to turn up their noses at the refuge's awesome prey base. Or did they?

During that first winter that wolves were on the refuge, the elk were truly naïve. I recall watching the Gros Ventre pack, its sibling black females and 130-pound silver-gray male, easily approach and sort a victim from a bewildered band of elk. Those elk acted as though they had nothing to fear—just three big coyotes casually checking to see if anyone was at death's doorstep before stalking more mice. I was gripped by anticipation as the elk nonchalantly fed. The wolves padded forward single file, made a half circle around the dispassionate animals, and charged their ranks. Chaos and a brief, lethal chase ensued.

Some observers were lucky enough (or completely aghast) to see the big dogs take down an elk within easy viewing of the horse-drawn sleigh they rode. For years this contractor had provided a world-class wildlife experience to thirty thousand riders annually; each winter the elk and coyotes had been the highlights of the outing. Now they were upstaged by wolves. In a sleigh's close quarters the sight of a wolf made for some animated conversations. An occasional exchange erupted between pro- and anti-wolf factions, including debate about this population being exempt from human exploitation, except in cases of livestock depredation. The refuge's policy was complete protection of wolves, as required under the federal Endangered Species Act.

As the refuge biologist, I tried to remain neutral on wolf restoration. The refuge's legal mandates and published results of the predator's relationship to prey populations guided my thinking. This objective viewpoint was tested one frosty morning in 1999, however, when I was introduced to the concept of "surplus killing." Passing through a locked gate north of Miller Butte, a line of six calves lay steaming in the snow. As I walked from one to the next, the telltale killing pattern was apparent. Ripped legs and necks and the swath of elk hoofprints accompanied by the bounding tracks of wolves completed the story. Only the last calf killed had been fed on that morning. I found the scene gut-wrenching.

Although Game and Fish Department biologist Doug Brimeyer and I investigated one other such case—four calves killed by the same pack a month later—these two cases proved to be exceptions to the wolves' hunting tactics. I didn't observe additional episodes or hear reports from others over the next five years. In other places too, wolves, coyotes, hyenas, and other predators have been recorded killing surplus prey they did not eat (although predators may return to feed on carcasses later). Although these are rare cases, they clearly reinforce in a visceral way the hostility many people feel toward wolves.

A more contentious issue involves wolf predation on livestock, and also the killing of dogs. Far removed from their ancestral roots of wild bovids and ovids, the rancher's stock lack the instincts and athleticism to ward off attacks. Despite programs by Defenders of Wildlife and state agencies to compensate ranchers for bona fide predator losses, fear and loathing of wolves still run deep in most Western communities. Sportsmen and outfitters tend to view them as unwanted competitors, whereas wolf advocates point to their keystone role in balancing ungulate numbers and protecting habitats from overgrazing. Others admire wolves' fascinating social and play behavior, so reminiscent of man's best friend. I know people from each of these camps. I also know that accommodating wolves and those who love and hate them is no easy task for state and federal resource managers. The middle ground is often elusive.

Unlike solitary hunters, such as mountain lions and bears, wolves hunt cooperatively. Chasing, scattering, and sorting out vulnerable targets, their killing often takes place in plain view. But like the unheard tree that falls like thunder in the forest, an elk ambushed from an unseen cliff is equally prey of the cat. The wolf's work may be untidy as well as conspicuous, but the result makes no difference to the elk.

Wolves' lot in life is to slay the biggest of animals. That on occasion they do so in excess, for reasons we may or may not understand, makes them no different than another top-rung carnivore—us. Our own excesses and the damage we inflict on our environment—so poignantly detailed in writings such as *Bloodties* by Ted Kerasote—dwarf occasional feeding frenzies by wolves, hyenas, or bears. The uneaten wolf kill goes "unwasted," devoured by others. By nature's impartial calling, wolves endure by eating species its foremost competitor holds dear. The core question is this: Should we be nature's arbiter, to pick and choose which species go and which stay? Have we a God-given license or prerogative earned by a big brain? Are we no less compelled to steward and care for other creatures than for our common man? Can we find a way to share?

It is not my intent to diminish the ranchers' predicament in wolf country. The unnerving financial impacts of livestock losses deserve redress. Within the framework of laws that protect private property, we are compelled to compensate this loss of commodity and forestall future losses as federal and state agencies have been doing. But wildlife are communal property. Like herbivores, wolves and other predators are ecological agents, and in a montage of biodiversity all have their roles.

By the wolves' second winter, refuge elk had been to school. When wolves approached, instead of waiting to be bitten or scattering with abandon, elk stood their ground and closed ranks into a tight, defensive knot. Some of the largest cows would face the wolves, daring them to advance. On occasion I watched these matriarchs give chase, running wolves a short distance, before returning to the safety of their cohorts. Such standoffs seemed to leave the wolves perplexed, even frustrated, and more pointedly hungry. I watched wolves change their tactics, increasingly seeking out individuals that were easier marks. Single elk (signifying to me, and certainly to wolves, a compromised animal) or small groups composed largely of calves became preferred targets. Across the refuge's open grasslands, lessons were being learned by all. Just as elk soon differentiated between coyotes and their burly cousins, ravens shadowed hunting wolves, envisaged purveyors of future venison.

Coyotes too, were also on a steep learning curve. Although they benefited by scavenging deserted wolf kills, they paid a price. I recall one such day in February 1999. The fiancée of my friend John Kremer, the resident Natural Resources Conservation Service conservationist, tagged along with me during a morning in the field. Tracy was visiting from Florida, and John asked if I would show her some wolves. "Sure," I said. "Tell her to dress warm." Recalling the morning's weather report calling for a high of ten degrees, I added, "Tell her to wear *everything* she brought from Jacksonville."

We drove north of Jackson on the highway skirting the refuge's western boundary. Abruptly, I pulled to the roadside. Something had caught my eye. Dashing across Miller Butte was a coyote, and in loping pursuit came the Gros Ventre pack, the black females in the lead with the brawny male trailing lower on the Butte. The coyote sent up a snowy vapor trail as it frantically glanced back at the pursuers. The wolves were closing in, even though their gait appeared relaxed. Their long legs propelled them in great bounding strides, compared to the staccato scamper of the coyote. In a bid for sanctuary, the coyote veered downslope and without hesitation leaped into Winegar Springs, a shallow, spring-fed pond some thirty yards wide. As he splashed and paddled outward, the male wolf headed straight for him while the females stopped to watch the show. Near the middle of the pond, the coyote found a spot where he could touch bottom and turned to await his fate. The silver wolf reached the coyote's entry point, sniffed a bit, then studied the coyote.

With the two related canines filling the field of view of a sixty-power spotting scope, I anticipated the inevitable. "Do you want to take a closer look?" I asked Tracy, who was taking it in through binoculars while I set up the scope.

"You bet," she said, as the big wolf—nicknamed "Houdini" by the Yellowstone wolf project staff—coolly sat down on the shore.

Houdini, officially designated wolf #29, was one of the thirty-one wolves reintroduced to Yellowstone from Canada. He was a pup at the time but quickly developed a reputation for his rapid growth and uncanny ability to find ways out of his holding pen. As Doug Smith told me, he was the only wolf that figured out how to get out of a pen. And he did it twice. After the second time, the wolf project team chose to let him roam rather than recapture and return him to his penmates.

One day after #29's second escape, Doug was walking the perimeter of the holding pen and noticed a clump of wolf hair dangling from the overhanging panel of the pen's chain-link fencing. Houdini had apparently jumped to the wire panel and snatched it in his teeth. Supported by his teeth alone, he somehow gained footing on the panel and worked his way over the top. His heroics took a toll, however. When Doug next captured and examined him, several teeth were broken and seemingly unusable. Still, he continued to successfully kill elk and survived for several years after his arrival in Jackson Hole. The episode prompted Doug to conclude that a wolf's success in hunting is as much about jaw strength—a crushing power of 1,200 pounds per square inch—as it is about sharp teeth.

From my vantage point, Houdini's eyes seemed to bore into the coyote, but he made no move to assault him. After ten to fifteen minutes, he apparently lost interest and wandered off. Only once did he glance back at the pathetic animal shuddering shoulder-deep in the pond.

I drove to the opposite side of Miller Butte to show Tracy the four mountain lions that had taken up residence in the cliffs. For forty-four days the female and her three kittens put on quite a show as wildlife enthusiasts and photographers gathered roadside from sunrise until dusk. They weren't stirring today, but fifty hopeful onlookers, some tending cameras with lenses the size of bazookas, confirmed they were within the yawning blackness of two limestone caves above. Not far above the caves, a dozen bighorn sheep wove single file across the talus and outcrops, but no curious felines materialized. Judging that the cats could linger indoors until evening, I drove back to the highway.

Between the highway and Miller Butte, tawny swaths of cattails interrupted the otherwise white landscape. Through a rift in the cattails we saw the wolves, and something else. Like charcoal briquettes on white linen, the two female wolves lay on the snow, facing each other. Between them, a coyote cowered just paces from each. Through the spotting scope, it appeared to be the same beleaguered animal from the pond, his coat slicked flat against his back. The wolves lay fully stretched, sometimes resting chin on paws, appraising just when to end his misery. Intermittently one would raise its head, as I anticipated the final act. The coyote hunkered dully, like the condemned awaiting his fate.

Clearly outmatched, chilled from his watery escapade, and now surrounded, he seemed resigned. *Just get it over with!* Two magpies perched atop the cattails and a raven hopped expectantly nearby. But to my surprise the wolves soon stood and stretched, and nonchalantly wandered off. Maybe we had missed the attack. Or maybe this was all a game. If so, I remarked to Tracy, how easily it could end whenever the wolves wanted. For now, play was suspended due to lack of interest.

Across Montana, Wyoming, and Idaho (wolves were also reintroduced to central Idaho in 1995), the drama of wolves' return has unfolded over the past decade and a half. While many thrill to the sights and sounds of this top-rung carnivore's homecoming, those in the anti-wolf camp grow increasingly angry and distressed. As wolves multiply beyond scientists' modeled predictions, tempers flare and lawsuits are filed. Yet projections of the livestock industry's demise and collapse of big-game populations and vanished hunting opportunities have proven at least premature. While it's true that wolf depredations on domestic sheep and cattle have grown with wolf populations, wildlife numbers have held steady overall. Fifteen years following wolf reintroduction, Idaho and Wyoming populations of elk—wolves' preferred prey—were 97 percent of 1994 levels (totaling well over 200,000). During that time, wolf numbers have increased from zero to 1,150 in those two states. In Montana, where a 1994 population of forty-eight wolves has swelled to 500, elk numbers have actually increased by 50 percent—94,000 to 150,000.[8] However, wolf predation is not distributed equally. Yellowstone's northern range elk have markedly declined, for example, at least in part due to wolves. While some tout restoration of the gray wolf to the Northern Rockies' wilds as a major conservation success, others adamantly label it a federal boondoggle. Yet one thing is clear, the GYE is now a more diverse and beguiling place—more complete, in ecological parlance.

In May 2009 the Department of Interior removed wolf populations in Idaho and Montana (and also wolves that had dispersed and colonized parts of Washington, Oregon, and Utah, and along with Wyoming were considered part of the Northern Rockies wolf population) from protections afforded by the Endangered Species Act. Management of wolves, like other resident wildlife, reverted to those respective state wildlife management agencies. Only in Wyoming, where state elected officials seem bent on reducing wolves to a number near zero, did Endangered Species Act protections remain in place. In 2009, for the first time in the contiguous United States, fair-chase hunts were held in Montana and Idaho. Notwithstanding a harvest of 260 wolves, the Northern Rocky Mountains population increased by 4 percent. Then in August 2010 a federal court returned protection under the Endangered Species Act to wolves in all six states. Public outcry, litigation, federal rulemaking, and even federal legislation called to reverse that latest court decision. Finally, in March 2011 the federal government struck a deal with wildlife advocates to remove some 1,200 wolves in Idaho and Montana from the endangered species list. Before a federal judge's concurrence might finalize the agreement, a startling development circumvented the court and the Endangered Species Act. A rider on the 2011 budget reconciliation bill removed wolves from federal protection in Idaho and Montana and in parts of Oregon, Utah, and Washington (but not in Wyoming, which has yet to produce an approved wolf conservation plan). By the time this book is in print, however, more twists in the road to wolf restoration and management will surely transpire.

As U.S. Fish and Wildlife Service wolf recovery coordinator Ed Bangs observed, "People often give wolves supernatural powers for good or evil." Although cloaked in folklore and fairytale mystique, wolves are just another animal trying to earn a living with the instincts and adaptations natural selection has honed. But in a modern world so dominated by human hegemony, wolves will require science-based management to limit conflicts with our socioeconomic interests. To temper the effect of wolf predation on livestock—exceeding 250 cattle and sheep confirmed killed annually in recent years—federal authorities have aggressively removed depredating wolves. In fact, this lethal management (about 10 percent of the population annually) has been a leading cause of wolf mortality during wolf restoration. Despite losses of 26 percent of the wolf population due to all causes annually, wolf numbers continue to expand, as do conflicts with livestock.[7, 8] Wolves need not be seen as incompatible with humans, and transferring their conservation and management to the states will advance that commission. Professionally managed as a valued member of our wildlife heritage, wolves will continue to delight wildlife enthusiasts and serve an important ecological role into the future.

Back in the Gros Ventre Wilderness, Lloyd and I assured each other again that the elk we were watching a half mile distant was collared—and quite alive. Lowering his binoculars, Lloyd grinned through a graying beard frosted white around his mouth. "Thought she was dead?" he grinned.

"Guess she got better," I answered.

Later that winter, riding atop a horse-drawn sled heaped with hay bales, I spotted elk #240 among several hundred others on the state's Alkali feedground twelve miles east of the NER. Five years after I first captured her in 1997 as a yearling on the refuge, I darted her and replaced her malfunctioning radio collar. Another fourteen years later in 2011, she still wanders the Gros Ventre, raising her calves among lions, coyotes, bears, and the howl of wolves.

Like fences, freeways, firearms, and feedtrucks, wolves became a part of the lives of refuge elk. Since 2004, wolves have frequented the refuge to varying but generally increasing degrees. In 2005, the year after my departure, the first wolves in at least seventy-five years denned on the NER. They bore a new generation of wolves on the refuge, as did other packs in four of the ensuing five years.

Unlike fences, freeways, or firearms, it's wolves that sort out the less-fit members of a herd. And it's wolves and other keen predators that cultivate their instincts, that in turn help perpetuate elk in the face of adversity. Wolves had returned to Jackson Hole. Despite the doomsayers' fears, the Jackson herd remained 10 to 20 percent above the state's population objective of eleven thousand elk. The age-old arms race between predator and prey remains a stalemate. The NER remains a haven for too many elk.

CHAPTER 11

Nitrogen

The success of the movement to preserve the elk has been measured and evaluated in terms of elk numbers, not in land use values.
—JOHN CRAIGHEAD, 1952, "A BIOLOGICAL AND ECONOMIC APPRAISAL OF THE JACKSON HOLE ELK HERD"

The Jackson herd is among the largest in North America, rivaling the White River herd of Colorado and the elk that grace Yellowstone Park's northern range. Roaming two of the premier U.S. national parks and the only national wildlife refuge set aside for elk, the Jackson herd is justifiably our national elk herd. But perhaps most remarkable are the annual migrations the elk undertake. My field assistant Marjean Heisler was right. When I arrived at the NER in 1982, she told me that the grandeur of the elk could not fully be appreciated without traveling the span of their migration processions. The longest originate beyond the Buffalo Fork valley—the northern extreme of Jackson Hole—in a jumble of high ridges and soaring plateaus of the Teton Wilderness Area and Yellowstone National Park.

That first summer, Marjean and I crested Two Ocean Plateau on horseback. Sixty miles north of the refuge, and twenty miles from the nearest road, we were as far from civilization as one can get in the lower forty-eight states. Before us unrolled a sea of lavender lupine drenched in alpenglow. Beyond shimmered the azure waters of Yellowstone Lake, the largest freshwater body above seven thousand feet in North America. There pelicans nest, schools of native cutthroat trout swim, and river otters, bald eagles, ospreys, and grizzly bears hunt these fish in the shallows and in spawning streams. From the wash of lupine, heads of bedded elk poked like periscopes, ogling us yet unafraid of our presence. We turned our horses Bud and Red south to Two Ocean Pass where Atlantic and Pacific Creeks arise from a single rivulet, then spill down opposite sides of the continent's spine. These are the lofty headwaters of the Mississippi and Columbia Rivers. Here Jackson elk intermingle with three other great elk herds, each of which migrates to its own distant winter range when snow buries the high country beneath a crystalline hush. Following Pacific Creek, we passed Enos Lake where trumpeter swans—the continent's largest waterfowl—challenge the elements. The lake's short ice-free season barely allows a single resolute pair to nurture their two or three nestlings to flight stage before the waters freeze solid again.

Pacific Creek emerges from the Teton Wilderness and joins the Snake River in GTNP, thirty airline miles from Two Ocean Plateau. From there the elk's journey is only half complete. Yet what makes the migration even more astounding is that we had just ridden but one of many convergent pathways from the high country. Beneath the towering Teton peaks, across the terraces of the Snake River plain, throngs of elk weave southward, merging in a mesmerizing display each fall. In the New World only Alaska's migratory herds of caribou exceed the splendor of this mammalian march.

Like fluid passing through a grand topographic funnel from nearly two thousand square miles of summer range, this fall flight for food ends at the NER, separated from Jackson's art galleries and fine restaurants only by eight feet of woven-wire fence. Along the way, some elk find adequate winter habitat in the Spread Creek, Buffalo Fork, and Gros Ventre River valleys. Migrations for 60 to 70 percent, however, end at the NER and a sliver of national forest lands along its eastern boundary.

The spring migration is a more leisurely affair. Like the end of refuge feeding, the northward exodus depends upon snowmelt, the warming of soil temperatures, and appearance of new vegetative growth. Once green-up measuring an inch in height covers the southern half of the refuge, the thousands of elk no longer can outstrip the profusion of sprouting grasses and forbs. The migration begins about three weeks after winter feeding concludes and progresses in pulses. As snow recedes from the Gros Ventre Hills, animals probe the Gros Ventre floodplain, eventually flooding across the Kelly Hayfields in dozens and hundreds. Kelly residents are

Spring migration from the National Elk Refuge
(Bruce Smith)

treated to sunrise and sunset parades of elk, each winding column typically led by a practiced matriarch.

Adult bulls arrive at the most distant summer ranges in the Teton Wilderness and southern Yellowstone National Park three to four weeks earlier than cows. This is largely a consequence of adult females, joined by socially bonded subadults, interrupting their spring migrations to give birth in favored habitats along the way. While summer ranges of many females overlap the birthplaces of their calves, about a third resume their migration to more distant summer ranges. Braving snowmelt-swollen streams, mothers lead the new generation to higher summer pastures. By mid-July large nursery groups grace the greened landscape from seven to ten thousand feet elevation. Surrounded by a surfeit of grazing, life is good for the next four months.

As in other long-lived species, including humans, tradition as well as short-term needs shape daily behavior of elk. Whereas female elk seek traditional areas in and around GTNP to calve each spring, variations in weather conditions control the timing of spring migrations and thus alter where some give birth. For example, both bulls and cows arrived on summer ranges far earlier in 1981 when what little snow fell in winter melted early that spring.

Many of our radio-collared cows calved on or very near summer ranges that in years of more typical snowpack would have provided poor foraging.

Ultimately, the phenomenon of animal migration improves long-term reproductive success by optimizing food available to parents prior to giving birth or laying eggs. Among mammals, the better the food resources during the prebirth period, the more successful mothers are in providing milk and conceiving again. Milk production is highly correlated with growth of offspring, which positively influences survival in temperate latitudes, as we've seen with the Jackson elk.

Elk are a complex social species. Their physical adaptations and behavioral repertoire dictate how they live. Yet in the modern world, their behavior can be condensed into terms of elemental biochemistry. "Elk are attracted to nitrogen and avoid lead," wildlife ecologist Tom Hobbs has succinctly noted. On the nitrogen side of the ledger, it works like this.

Nitrogen is the elemental building block of proteins, which are the fundamental requirements of animal growth and reproduction. Elk spend half their lives eating—consuming ten to fifteen pounds of grasses and other plants daily—to obtain sufficient nitrogen and other nutrients. As a general rule, actively photosynthesizing and growing plants are more digestible and nutrient-dense than plants that are dormant. Thus, elk are forever on the prowl for green vegetation to maximize return on the time they spend feeding. However, the northern latitudes frequented by elk are characterized by several months without significant vascular plant growth. Leaves senesce. Nutrients are locked away in roots and woody stems. Diets of herbivores become nutrient deficient.

On a macro scale, the downslope migrations of mountain-dwelling elk temper the problem of food availability, but not the deficiency of nitrogen during months when plant growth ceases. November through March is a lean time, a period when a thick coat, accumulated fat reserves, and reduced activity all help elk conserve energy. Elk and other ruminants enjoy the additional benefits of a digestive system that generates heat and extracts more calories from quiescent plants than species with simple gastrointestinal systems can.

As 7,500 elk and another 1,000 bison (each bison is equal to two-and-a-half elk in forage requirements) gather on the 25,000-acre refuge each winter, only two-and-a-half acres are available to sustain each animal. Both species spend most of their time on the southern half of the refuge where snow depths are shallower, natural forage is more available, and winter feeding occurs. Thus, a gradient of elk densities ranges from ground zero at feedgrounds to scattered use along the northeastern fringe of the refuge. As we shall see, impacts on habitats from all these hooves and hungry mouths mirror that spatial pattern.

On smaller scales too, the elk exploit nature's gradients and heterogeneity. Across the refuge their feeding patterns are carved in snow as if etched in stone. Besides moving among habitats, elk select certain plants, because some have greater nutrient density than others. Sensory systems hard-wired by generations of trial and error have honed their foraging skills to select the best forage first. Thus, as winter progresses, the quality of their diets declines.

Although plants have evolved with native herbivores, they can withstand only so much damage to tissues. Besides the diminishing returns attendant to repeated grazing and browsing (because older plant tissues yield increasingly lower nutrient returns), many plants have developed defenses to discourage hungry herbivores. These defenses are both chemical and physical (a bad taste or impaired feeding and digestion). In turn, would-be herbivores must develop ways around these defenses. Species try to outmaneuver those they eat and those that eat them. The behavioral response of refuge elk to the recolonization of wolves shows how rapidly prey can behaviorally respond. But plants can't outrun or hide from hungry elk, and novel physiological and anatomical adaptations take much longer to arise. Consequently, intense foraging pressure selects against the most palatable and nutritious species and changes plant composition and growth forms to ones better adapted to herbivory.

Like a successful rancher whose livelihood depends on being a good grass farmer, a successful wildlife program is largely predicated on good management of diverse and productive habitats. The NER's authorizing legislation in 1912 set aside lands "for the establishment of a winter game (elk) reserve in the State of Wyoming lying south of Yellowstone Park. . . ." No mention was made of feeding the elk. Subsequent executive orders broadened the purposes of the refuge to include the conservation of habitat for other big game animals and for birds. Legislation such as the Migratory Bird Treaty and the Endangered Species Act expanded management emphasis to a host of federally protected and managed species.

Most recently the National Wildlife Refuge System Improvement Act of 1997 brought all national wildlife refuges under a legislative umbrella with a shared conservation mission. In administering the system, Congress directed the secretary of interior to "ensure that the biological integrity, diversity, and environmental health of the System are maintained. . . ."[1] This organic act didn't change the NER's main purpose of conservation of elk and their habitat, but it did clarify how this was to be achieved in relation to all refuge resources.

Long before quantitative monitoring of refuge plant communities began, negative changes in NER flora became evident, prompting Buzz Robbins in 1973 to begin monitoring herbaceous plants (grasses, sedges, and forbs). His purposes were to measure annual forage production (the food supply entering winter) and forage utilization (measurements taken in spring of how much forage had been removed), and to track annual trends in these measurements. Although primarily grazers, elk eat a mixed diet, also browsing trees and shrubs. As I continued those surveys each year and updated the methods, I added measurements of woody plants to the data collection.

While total herbaceous production held steady over the years, averaging 17,000 tons, annual fluctuations ranged from 6,710 (a severe drought year) to 27,584 tons in the wettest growing season during the past forty years.[2] But just as too many horses or cows will damage a pasture, overstocking a wildlife range can also prove harmful. By the time they migrated from the refuge each April or May from 1983 to 2003, elk and bison had removed an average 63 percent of all herbaceous vegetation on the south half of the NER. This level of consumption "exceeds the conventional standard for western rangelands of 50 percent (the 'use half–leave half' rule) and significantly exceeds the conventional maximum use of 35 to 40 percent for riparian areas."[3] So how is it that forage production held up on the NER while accommodating so many hungry mouths?

For one, refuge managers had traditionally emphasized producing grasses to sustain several thousand elk each winter. The staff renovated failing fields with more durable and productive grass species, especially those that benefited from flood irrigation. Secondly, most grazing was during the dormant season when aboveground grass tissues were cured (dead). More biomass can be removed after herbaceous plants have cured, and energy stores and meristematic tissues (growth points of plants) are protected underground.

Trees and shrubs, in contrast to grasses and forbs, store significant quantities of nitrogen and carbohydrates above ground in buds, branches, and trunks. This makes them generally more nutritious than the cured, aboveground parts of herbaceous plants. Likewise, meristematic tissues of woody plants are above ground and subject to damage and removal by browsing.

Pawing through snow makes grazing on grasses more costly, whereas palatable woody plants poked above snow and were heavily hedged each winter. As favored plants became rarer over the years, elk found them more desirable. This is what range ecologists call the "ice cream plant effect." Fewer of these plants remained to absorb the repeated browsing by thousands of elk, creating an inexorable downward spiral.

These dynamics provided a competitive advantage to herbaceous species over woody plants. In the vicinity of feedgrounds, woody plants such as sagebrush, snakeweed, and especially Douglas rabbitbrush and willows declined, even disappeared. I attributed this loss to repeated crushing by feed equipment, although willows and rabbitbrush suffered a double blow. They were also shrubs relished by elk.

Despite being fed hay during part of their stay, elk continued to graze and browse standing vegetation on and near the feedgrounds. In large part this was due to elk being elk—occupying their time seeking a balanced diet. As Valerius Geist noted, "Opportunism is the hallmark of adaptability, and elk are opportunistic feeders that shift with good fortune."[4]

Once the bison herd reached several hundred strong, they competed with elk for herbaceous forage and also browsed willow and cottonwood shoots, thus exacerbating the impact. On Yellowstone Park's northern range—where thousands of elk and bison spend winter and spring—biologist Bill Barmore found that 60 percent of aspen suckers were already browsed by mid-January. As a consequence, aspen communities (as well as willow and cottonwood) on the northern range deteriorated during the twentieth century.[5, 6, 7]

Under moderate levels of browsing, woody plants repair damaged tissues, grow, and reproduce. However, in studies ranging from Alaska to Colorado's Rocky Mountain National Park, willows appear poorly defended against browsing, and decline with chronic use. Some plants compensate for tissue lost to browsing by producing more biomass than if they were not eaten at all. But Francis Singer and Linda Zeigenfuss, who studied ungulate-willow relationships in U.S. national parks, found no such compensatory response to heavy browsing in Yellowstone Park.[8] They concluded that willows could tolerate annual removal of only 20 percent of twigs without suffering declines in productivity and suppression of height. Their investigation of willows throughout Jackson Hole showed a startling 57 percent rate of twig removal of refuge willows each year. Similarly, Eric Cole and I measured twig removal from an array of shrub species and found that 40 to 74 percent of twigs were browsed from palatable species while 9 to 52 percent were browsed from species considered of low palatability. More disturbingly, there was no significant improvement in abundance of remaining woody plants up to three kilometers from elk feedgrounds. Still farther from feedgrounds, vegetation was more representative of the native communities that evolved with Jackson's climate, soils, and native grazing regimes.

Shrub Browsing			
Mean percent of previous year's stems browsed on palatable species, less-palatable species, and all species in twelve upland shrub stands, twelve upland woodland stands, ten wetland shrub stands, and nine wetland woodland stands on the National Elk Refuge, as measured in spring 2002 reflecting browsing during winter 2001–02.			
	Mean percent of plants browsed		
Plant community	**Palatable species**	**Less-palatable species**	**All species**
Upland shrub	40	9	22
Upland woodland	41	21	32
Wetland shrub	67	34	52
Wetland woodland	74	52	59

Adapted from Smith, B. L., E. Cole, and D. Dobkin. 2004. *Imperfect Pasture: A Century of Change at the National Elk Refuge in Jackson Hole, Wyoming*. Moose, WY: Grand Teton Natural History Association

Early on, the condition and health of refuge woodlands and shrublands concerned me. Indeed, I was hardly the first. By 1950 Olaus Murie and John Craighead had recorded the heavily hedged condition of what browse plants remained on the refuge. Forty years earlier, Edward Preble noted signs of this in his report to Washington on the condition of the Jackson elk.[9, 10, 11] By 1987 conditions had worsened, so I launched a study of the 1,860 acres of quaking aspen on the refuge. I "hired" Roxane Rogers as a volunteer to help me inventory all 143 aspen stands I'd mapped from aerial photography. With a bustle of blonde hair and an ever-ready smile, Roxane would prove a dedicated and capable field hand who became the refuge's habitat biologist for the next decade.

Aspen communities support the greatest diversity of wildlife species in the Northern Rockies, second only to riparian zones. A successful Pleistocene survivor, aspen thrives on disaster in the sense that fire and other disturbances stimulate root systems to produce new stems, or "suckers." A recent analysis of aspen in the Jackson valley showed that stands regenerate every sixty to eighty years.[12] However, most NER aspen had regenerated after the last wildfire burned refuge lands in 1879. Thus, most mature stems of this short-lived tree had reached their 120- to 150-year life expectancy.[13]

As the most widely distributed, upland, deciduous tree in North America, aspen is an indicator of ecological integrity and landscape health.[14] But across the American West, aspen distribution has declined 49 to 96 percent during post-European settlement, based on comparisons of repeat photography. Among the causes of this decline are wildland fire suppression, subsequent succession to coniferous forest, and excessive browsing of suckers by wild and domestic ungulates.[15]

Based on poor health and lack of recruitment of new stems beyond the browsing reach of elk, Roxane and I rated half of refuge aspen stands in only fair or poor condition. Without fencing ungulates out, new stem growth was unlikely to replace the dwindling overstory trees. Alternatively, we tried to regenerate nine of these failing stands by clear-cutting them—a means of simulating a stand-replacing wildfire. For eight years we monitored these stands and small fenced exclosures erected in four of them. A flurry of sucker production was followed by a flurry of elk browsing. Outside exclosures, sucker mortality was high and 96 percent of stems failed to reach six feet tall, compared to 28 percent inside exclosures. Treating pockets of aspen simply rang the dinner bell.[16, 17]

Elsewhere in Jackson Hole, aspen are also under siege. Despite pre-scribed burning of thousands of acres to regenerate aspen in the Gros Ven-tre drainage (where Wyoming feeds 2,500 elk), Wyoming Game and Fish Department biologist Steve Kilpatrick acknowledged in 1997, "We're not getting the aspen growth we want. An eight-year-old stand is three to four feet high, when it should be ten feet high." Noting the previous winter's record winter count of 16,280 elk in the Jackson herd (including 11,968 on the NER), he added, "One species is dominating the scene."[18]

Kilpatrick and I overlapped for most of my tenure in Jackson. Despite yeoman efforts to conserve and foster these communities, Steve witnessed the decline of aspen, willow, chokecherry, and other palatable browse plants in northwest Wyoming. Even restoring fire to long-protected landscapes could not overcome chronic overbrowsing by elk, as the large-scale fires of 1988 in Yellowstone National Park proved. A short-term pulse of aspen regeneration succumbed to subsequent chronic hedging.[19]

Yet the importance of any given plant community can be a matter of perception or a resource manager's goals. In April 1999 I attended a weeklong workshop in North Dakota that included a field trip to Lostwood National Wildlife Refuge, a rolling landscape of mixed grass prairie interspersed with numerous wetlands. It was established to con-serve breeding habitat for many declining grassland-associated bird species, such as Baird's sparrow. Using prescribed burning and live-stock grazing, refuge staff stifle encroachment by exotic vegetation and woody plant growth.

The woody vegetation clusters in draws and other moist upland sites. Historically, both lightning and American Indian–caused wildfires lim-ited shrubs and aspen to scattered pockets in an ephemeral ebb and flow that dynamically altered those habitats with weather and fire conditions. Following removal of native people and the control of fire to protect pri-vate property, woody communities gained a more permanent foothold. Besides their aesthetic appeal, I suspected these patches added ecological diversity to the prairie. When I questioned the refuge manager and two biologists who led the field trip what upland habitats supported the great-est diversity of birds, they acknowledged their ongoing studies showed that aspen did. Yet managers had chosen the late 1800s—when fires had swept the land and cleared it of most woodlands—as the vignette of his-toric conditions to restore.

It's true that grassland species are among the most threatened birds in the United States.[20] Lostwood's adopted mission focused on those birds endemic to the northern Great Plains. Although I questioned favoring a few chosen species over greater biological diversity, I couldn't escape the irony of this professional dilemma. At the NER, an equivalent management bias played out where it was acceptable to eliminate aspen and other woody communities for the benefit of elk and bison. In the Wyoming scenario, the favored animal species largely proved to be the agents of change. Still, the end result was analogous to the anthropogenic habitat manipulations at Lostwood. This story underscores how contemporary human attitudes now shape most natural systems.

In 1997 Eric Cole was assigned to replace Roxane Rogers. She had taken a position with the USFWS in northwest Montana coordinating habitat enhancement programs on private lands. Eric was a perceptive biologist who had studied habitat use patterns of Oregon elk for his master's degree. Together we embarked in 1999 on what would become a comprehensive analysis of shrub and woodland communities. It began with my hunt for old photographs of the refuge.

Black-and-white images displayed on the walls of Jackson businesses showed a very different town site at the turn of the twentieth century. They inspired me to find historic images that showed how refuge vegetation may have changed. From the University of Wyoming archives and the Jackson Hole Historical Society, to the shoeboxes of photos of one family raised on the refuge, I re-created the past. Of the hundreds of photos I reviewed, two dozen showed high-resolution woodland and tall willow scenes that I could photograph for visual comparison sixty to a hundred years later. The results were an indisputable record of changes in size, abundance, and condition of aspen, cottonwood, and tall willow communities. As complements to our quantitative data, the twenty-five photo pairs made a compelling visual case.[13]

But this was just one of the tools and methods at our disposal. I contracted Ken Dries at the University of Wyoming's Geographic Information Science Center to quantify how tall willows (stands with stems exceeding six feet in height) and cottonwood abundance had changed on the southern refuge. Ken used remote sensing technology to compare a fifty-year time sequence (1954 to 2001) of aerial photographs. His conclusions were astounding. Canopy coverage of vegetation had declined between 59 and 91 percent. Where had those willows and cottonwoods gone? Among a host of abiotic and biotic possibilities, the studies Eric and I conducted concluded what others had reckoned. Among numerous people I interviewed was Virginia Huidekooper, a longtime Jackson Hole resident and author of *The Early Days in Jackson Hole*. In response to my question about what happened to the willows along Flat Creek, she may have said it best: "Well everyone knows, the elk ate them!"

But in another sense, the willows weren't gone at all—at least not below ground. Historic photos showed that tall willows were once widely distributed across broad areas of the Flat Creek marsh. Willow shoots, a foot or more tall, still sprouted resolutely each summer, only to be trimmed back near ground level by elk each winter. To quantify their extant distribution in 2002, Eric and I walked and mapped the perimeter of the remaining patches of plants. We found that willow roots still shot up shoots across 1,457 acres. By comparison, only sixty-two acres of tall willow patches remained on the southern NER—a decline exceeding 95 percent. It was the size and structure of aboveground biomass—the parts of plants we see—that had so radically changed. How radically was fortuitously evidenced by several fenced areas.

Four big-game exclosures built on the NER between 1938 and 1957 showed dramatic fence-line effects of ungulate browsing. As though transported by time machine, dense tangles of willow and aspen filled these protected islands. Our willow mapping, the historic photographic record, and these telltale exclosures testified that willows once lined Flat Creek and adjacent wetlands with thickets seven to ten feet high. On occasion I remarked to field trip participants that the refuge could regrow these communities wherever viable roots persisted. The layout of each fenced exclosure would predetermine each patch's ultimate shape and size.

I wanted to learn the recovery dynamics of refuge woody plants, plants subject to a century of excess. Within the degraded cottonwood corridor of Flat Creek, the damage to both plants and stream banks rivaled any overstocked rangeland I'd seen in the West. Along a reach less than half a mile from two feedgrounds, I chose four matching

Aspen enclosure on the National Elk Refuge, constructed in 1952
(Bruce Smith)

experimental sites—each measuring three hundred by one thousand feet in size. Two were randomly selected and fenced to exclude big game. Years earlier I'd driven Albert Feuz (leader of the Concerned Citizens for the Elk, you'll recall from Chapter 5) to this very place. Albert hadn't visited this interior part of the refuge since the 1940s when he worked as a refuge irrigator. As we approached the streambed, Albert remarked with surprise, "What did you do with all the willows?"

During the first two years of monitoring these experimental sites, differences in browsing and growth were obvious. The amount of annual twig growth removed from young cottonwood, willow, chokecherry, and serviceberry shoots inside the exclosures averaged 17 percent in 2001 and 2002—the work of porcupine and smaller rodents, as evidenced by their incisors' beveled cuttings. Outside the exclosures, browsers removed 72 percent of the beleaguered plants' new growth. After several years of protection, fenced shrubs are reclaiming lost ground and height, and drifts of cottonwood saplings crowd Flat Creek's banks. Outside the exclosures, a zootic disclimax of stunted, bonsai plants persists.[13]

Changes in plant communities are subtle and often escape the untrained eye. Unlike the impression made by a poor hunting season, or songbirds missing from closely watched feeders, vegetation may wane unwitnessed except by the gardener, farmer, or ecologist. And so our Flat Creek experiment also offered visual instruction for touring public groups and government staff.

Our measurements and observations verified that refuge woody plants could recover once browsing pressure was relaxed. Of course, complete exclusion of ungulates is unnatural too. It wasn't browsing per se, but its magnitude that compromised these plant communities. Thus, the occasional moose spied on the southern refuge didn't linger. This consummate browser found little suitable to its needs. Willows comprise 75 percent of moose diets, but barely 10 percent for elk. However, the greater numbers of elk in Jackson Hole (fifteen times greater in 2003) resulted in 37 percent higher daily intake of willow by elk than by moose. Consequently, willow growth, productivity, and size measurements were inversely correlated with densities of elk throughout Jackson Hole.[21] The near elimination of tall willow patches on the southern NER demonstrates the worst-case scenario, yet a science panel that evaluated refuge habitat conditions speculated that relaxed browsing could restore refuge willows. "Height releases and thicket formation of NER willows . . . should occur across large areas of the landscape if percent offtake of willows could be reduced to 13 percent of the annual biomass of shoots."[3]

Besides moose, beaver are common residents of northwest Wyoming stream courses. However, the only one I saw on the south half of the NER was in 1983. Sufficient willows and cottonwoods for food and dam construction were long since gone from the vicinity of Flat Creek. Nothing remains constant in nature, and beaver ponds epitomize this tenet of change. Wetland meadows become willow thickets fit for moose and nesting warblers. Beaver colonize and cut the willows, damming the adjacent stream and flooding the meadow. Chorus frogs and wetland birds take hold. As they exhaust their food and building supplies, the beaver move on, then the pond fills with sediment and is overgrown by sedges and grasses. Eventually willows overtake the new meadow, completing the circle when the moose and warblers return, and inevitably the beaver.

Elk browsing a remnant willow stand on the National Elk Refuge
(Bruce Smith)

Yet on the NER, such progression has ground to a screeching halt. Over the past century, weather cycles, fire, and the ebb and flow of herbivore populations no longer direct successional progressions. Succession has retreated and stagnated in early seral communities—the zootic disclimax noted earlier. As a result, ancient cycles have been arrested and the landscape simplified and homogenized by the overriding weight of overbrowsing.

In his 1938 essay "Conservation Esthetic," Aldo Leopold cautioned, "Damage to plant life usually follows artificialized management of animals." After providing examples of overabundant deer damaging plant life in Europe and North America, he also noted, "The composition of the flora, from wild flowers to forest trees, is gradually impoverished." The overabundance of deer, Leopold identified, arose from destruction of predators that formerly helped limit herds.[22] But as we've seen in Jackson Hole, people can trigger such ecological imbalances through disruption of migration routes, feeding, and creation of artificially high densities of animals—even in the presence of a full suite of predators. The fallout may include lost potential to support some plant and animal species. As we shall see, the constancy of overabundant elk at the NER has produced a trophic cascade of unintended consequences.

A procession of graduate students and professional scientists probed the lives of many of the refuge's residents: songbirds and swans, rodents and raptors, bison and badgers, spotted frogs and boreal toads, coyotes and cutthroat trout, and of course the elk. The NER, and the GYE more broadly, attract scientific investigation like moths to a candle. Presented with the wealth of information generated by these studies, refuge managers and their supervisors in Denver have been well advised of the state of refuge resources. From these investigations, the following picture emerged of a refuge in retreat.

As a group, refuge birds perhaps showed the most obvious alteration in community characteristics. Eric Anderson, a University of Wyoming graduate student, recorded avian composition in Jackson Hole during 2000 and 2001. On the NER, specifically, he found that species of birds were less diverse and less abundant in aspen stands of high elk use. Species such as ruffed grouse and warblers that require well-developed understory vegetation, and other species such as warbling vireo and Swainson's thrush that prefer denser forest canopy, were uncommon.[23] As old and dying aspen stems fell to the ground, numbers of woodpeckers, bluebirds, and other cavity-nesters declined. With few if any young trees being recruited into the overstory, bird communities became impoverished, a pattern repeated elsewhere in declining woodlands.[24,25,26] Likewise in the deteriorating Flat Creek cottonwood corridor, grassland and open habitat species (starlings and western meadowlarks, for example) were doing well, but riparian specialists were scarce or absent.[27]

Anderson also found less diverse bird communities in willow stands within one mile of elk feedgrounds. Tall-shrub specialists—like MacGillivray's warbler, willow flycatcher, and fox sparrow—were uncommon, while ravens, black-billed magpies, and other avian nest predators were more plentiful than in willow habitats with lower elk use. Anderson noted that loss and degradation of aspen and willow are not ecologically equivalent to loss and degradation of other habitat types. He recorded fifty species of birds in aspen and twenty in willow, compared to just ten in sagebrush steppe and grassland combined.[28]

Mountain bluebird at aspen cavity nest
(Bruce Smith)

An independent science panel that evaluated refuge habitat conditions concluded, "Without exception, these studies [of bird populations] found only a small subset of species in cottonwood and aspen habitats of the NER, relative to the potential habitat-appropriate composition for the area. In addition, the relative abundances of habitat-dependent bird species on the NER have been minimal, relative to abundances found for such species in ecologically comparable riparian and aspen habitats elsewhere in the West."[3]

The structurally more complex plant communities of riparian zones typically contain nearly all the small mammal species in neighboring habitats, but the reverse is seldom true.[29] Accordingly, these communities are favored by a variety of terrestrial and avian predators of small mammals. We found low diversity and an abundance of litter-dwelling rodents along Flat Creek, suggesting its decay as an ecologically functioning riparian zone.[13]

Streamside woody vegetation is an important component of fisheries habitats for trout and other salmonids.[30] Refuge feedgrounds, and therefore the highest densities of elk and bison, adjoin Flat Creek and its tributaries (an important cutthroat spawning tributary of the Snake River). While the loss of 95 percent of Flat Creek's streamside tall willows may make fly-casting easier, hydrologist Alan Galbraith also found it makes for less stable stream banks, elevated water temperatures in summer, less terrestrial insect life to nourish fish, and less screening of fish from avian predators.[31] Likewise, herpetologist Debra Patla concluded that the loss of beaver ponds and woody debris along stream courses were limiting factors for amphibian species throughout the Flat Creek marsh.[13]

Other vertebrate species deprived of suitable habitats have suffered declines or even elimination. Dwindling shrub cover offers inadequate winter habitat for Columbian sharp-tailed grouse, which have been missing from the refuge for several decades. In February 2010 a single sharptail was observed and photographed. Ironically, the bird was eating dried berries from chokecherry and serviceberry shrubs thriving inside one of the big-game exclosures along Flat Creek.

The red-tailed hawk provides an example of how habitat erosion insidiously reduces densities of animals. In the 1940s and 1950s, Frank and John Craighead first catalogued nesting pairs in the Jackson valley. John's son Derek and colleagues have repeated those original surveys and identified a number of natural and anthropogenic changes related to waning redtail numbers.

When I arrived at the refuge in 1982, a pair of redtails nested in a small aspen stand adjacent the refuge's McBride feedground. Like other groves near feedgrounds, this stand grew few new stems, and only two dozen live trees remained in the overstory. In May 1993 graduate student Roger Smith and I banded the two nestlings hatched by that pair. Not only was the nest tree no longer living, it was the last stem standing in the grove. At least the redtails picked the right tree! That final aspen soon joined its fallen cohorts, and the redtails were forced to find a new nest tree. Like most bird species, redtails are territorial, so the pair's greater challenge was to establish a territory uncontested by other pairs. Derek Craighead notes that red-tailed hawk territories—and even specific nest trees—are rigidly occupied for decades in Jackson Hole, and a finite number of suitable spaces occur on the land. Birds, like aspen, disappear one pair or grove at a time.

During deep-snow winters, mule deer struggle to survive in Jackson Hole on limited winter ranges that suffer from human encroachment, winter recreational conflicts, and competition with elk for suitable browse. In his 1952 evaluation of the Jackson elk herd, John Craighead observed that "In Jackson Hole, mule deer and elk compete most directly in species of browse preferred and type of country utilized."[10] Numbers of mule deer

Roger Smith banding young red-tailed hawks on the National Elk Refuge
(Bruce Smith)

wintering on the refuge have trended downward in recent years, as have moose.[13] From his studies of Jackson's dwindling moose population, Joel Berger concluded that low pregnancy rates and malnutrition-related mortality during winter indicated deteriorating habitat conditions for moose.[32] In short, the success of Jackson's elk herd has unbalanced its environment for other species.

Like grizzly bears, elephants, and tigers, elk serve as an umbrella species for conservation of communities of other species by virtue of their charisma and need for expansive landscapes. The same cannot be said of chorus frogs, red-tailed hawks, caracals, or gray langurs, despite the distinctiveness of each. Yet all species in a habitat or ecosystem are interdependent, from lowly bacteria to top-rung carnivore. None is dispensable. No more eloquently has this been stated than in Aldo Leopold's *A Sand County Almanac*: "To keep every cog and wheel is the first precaution of intelligent tinkering."

Red-tailed hawk nest in the last remaining tree of this aspen grove

(Bruce Smith)

During the past 550 million years, the planet's biodiversity has suffered five major collapses. Those mass extinctions resulted from increased volcanism, sea level flux associated with climate change, or asteroid impacts. A sixth mass extinction is now underway. Pick a continent, sea, or ecosystem and we find that pollution, invasive species, deforestation, desertification, urban sprawl, excessive exploitation of species for food and other products, and global climate change have conspired to accelerate the background species extinction rate by an estimated hundred- to thousandfold.[33]

Because life and the threats to it are not spread evenly across the planet, places like the GYE are more secure than other ecosystems. It is in the tropical and subtropical regions and certain temperate forests where biodiversity is richest and species losses are out of control. Tropical rain forests, for example, cover just 3 percent of the Earth's surface but support over half of all known species of plants and animals. In a seminal 1988 paper in the *Environmentalist*, Norman Myers identified ten tropical forest "hot spots" characterized both by exceptional levels of plant endemism (species found nowhere else in the world) and by serious levels of habitat loss. The concept of biological hot spots has been widely adopted to focus conservation strategies toward those areas where biodiversity is at greatest risk. To qualify, a region must meet two strict criteria: It must contain at least 1,500 species of vascular plants (more than 0.5 percent of the world's total) as endemics, and it must have lost at least 70 percent of its original habitat.[34] Subsequent reassessments have expanded the list to thirty-four hot spots. Most of the additional twenty-four were added due to rampant fragmentation and destruction of natural plant communities.

Conservation International estimates that the thirty-four hot spots have lost a combined 86 percent of their original habitat and now cover only 2.3 percent of the Earth's surface. Yet they contain more than half the world's plant species and an astounding 77 percent of terrestrial vertebrate species. In biological hot spots like the Guinean Forests of West Africa and the Tropical Andes of South America, catalogued species pale by comparison with scientists' estimates of those still undiscovered. Untold numbers face extinction before they ever become known to science.

Off the eastern coast of Africa, one such biological hot spot is the island of Madagascar. Slash-and-burn agriculture has replaced 90 percent of Madagascar's natural plant communities, largely during the past century. Adaptation and evolution of animal species cannot keep pace with such rapid changes, resulting in ongoing and irretrievable losses of native life-forms. The great tragedy is that 90 percent of the island's animal species are endemic.

Whether a Madagascar rain forest or a Jackson Hole aspen grove, when a natural habitat is degraded or supplanted, more than endemic vegetation is lost. Indri lemurs cannot migrate across a slashed-and-burned landscape to another suitable patch of shrinking forest. Micro-level changes, such as the displaced NER red-tailed hawk, accumulate over space and time. A forest or woodland is more than just trees. This was the scientists' message during the 1990s debate pitting old-growth forest logging against conservation of the Pacific Northwest's northern spotted owls. It's not strictly about the owl, but about the community of life that shares the owl's home. As development fragments and webs of roads slice and dice former wildlands, wildlife become relegated to shrinking and increasingly isolated reserves. Some parcels merely offer transient asylum, bookmarked until chainsaws and dozers turn the page. Others may enjoy formal protection as refuges and parks. Ironically, these safe havens may become victims of their protected wildlife, especially overabundant large herbivores.

CHAPTER 12

Lead

The practice of conservation must spring from a conviction of what is ethically and esthetically right, as well as what is economically expedient. A thing is right only when it tends to preserve the integrity, stability, and beauty of the community.
—ALDO LEOPOLD, 1947, "THE ECOLOGICAL CONSCIENCE" FROM
THE *WISCONSIN CONSERVATION BULLETIN*

The periglacial environment in which North American elk evolved and thrived was harsh, but not particularly rugged. With forests bulldozed and smothered by Pleistocene glaciers, elk were grazers, more so than even now. Their ample, ruminant digestive systems were adapted to feeding on fibrous plants with high cellulose content. Their highly developed social behavior and adaptations for detecting and fleeing predators in open terrain also indicate that elk evolved in grasslands. Their tendency today to use primarily forested and rugged habitats attests to their adaptability in the presence of modern man.

Entire scientific conferences have been devoted to this topic. Study after study throughout North America has documented the vulnerability of elk to hunters, especially where security cover has been reduced by logging, road building, and recreational development. To escape harvest in such modified landscapes, elk have two choices: move "somewhere else" or develop behavioral strategies to thwart contemporary hunters' advantage.

Despite evolutionary honing of sensory organs and survival behaviors, elk are no match for their preeminent predator. Capable of spotting wolves at a mile, smelling a cougar, and outrunning a grizzly bear, elk can't outwit a lead bullet speeding onward at three thousand feet per second. By the time the rifle's report is heard, the quarry is claimed. Roaming tundra and prairie probably helped early Holocene wapiti avoid the primitive weapons of stealthy hunters, but the quarter-mile kill range of rifles favors elk that favor mountainous cover. Hence, from millions that once graced North America's woodlands, valleys, and plains, elk now dwell largely in deep forests and rougher terrain. Harnessed to our twentieth-century conservation efforts, these wildlands saved the last elk from sliding toward oblivion, but couldn't restore long-distance migrations through open country. The casualties include the two-hundred-mile-long historic migrations of the Jackson Hole elk.

Learning about animal migration patterns is vital to conservation. These corridors not only link geographically separate ranges, but provide avenues for outbreeding and gene flow among populations. Yet another reason makes understanding Jackson elk migrations essential. Each September through mid-December, some three thousand elk are harvested from a fall herd numbering fifteen to twenty thousand. As the elk filter south and westward from four summer ranges (Yellowstone, Teton Wilderness, Gros Ventre, and GTNP), they mix during migration and mingle in winter, but are not equally vulnerable to hunters. Their ranges and travel routes vary in escape cover, road access, and hunting opportunity. Therein lies the need for wildlife managers to know when and where elk from various summer ranges, or herd segments, make their fall pilgrimages. Otherwise, as happened during the 1960s and early 1970s, elk from the most exposed summer ranges and migration routes may be disproportionately harvested.

My studies of radioed elk showed that those on national forest lands were most vulnerable (the Gros Ventre and Teton Wilderness herd segments), whereas elk from both national parks were harvested least, and the least of those from GTNP. But knowing this after the fact and not fully understanding why does little to help managers balance the harvest.

Established in 1929, Grand Teton National Park originally included only the Teton Range. Cattle ranches, dude ranches, and hay farming dotted the fifteen-mile-long valley north of the NER. But after a multi-year effort, spearheaded by philanthropist John D. Rockefeller Jr., the lands between the Tetons and mountains to the east—GTNP's central valley—were annexed in 1950, tripling the size of the park.

Park expansion was locally unpopular. Then as now, federal government intrusion was unwelcome by residents, and the State of Wyoming also resisted expansion for fear that elk protected there (including those migrating from Yellowstone through this corridor) would increase without management recourse. Because lands in this migration corridor are administered by the National Park Service, hunting there would have become illegal (by signing the International Treaty for Nature Protection and Wildlife Preservation in the Western Hemisphere, the United States and seventeen other countries had prohibited hunting in national parks in 1942). So to expand GTNP, a compromise was reached.

The enabling legislation (Public Law 81-787) specified that reductions of elk be permitted in those portions of the expanded park east of the Snake River. To circumvent the aforementioned international treaty, the Park Service deputized Wyoming hunters as temporary park rangers, enabling them to shoot elk in the park. Ostensibly to affirm the National Park Service's mission of resource protection, PL 81-787 provided for hunting ". . . when it is found necessary for the purpose of the proper management and protection of the elk." Park Service and Wyoming officials have consulted annually to determine the need for a reduction program (as it's called by agency officials, whereas citizens call it a hunt). In all but 1959 and 1960, such a program has been authorized and conducted each year.

Even before park expansion, the north half of the NER was opened to hunting during World War II. Fewer hunters, a growing summer herd on the refuge (over five hundred elk), and a shortage of hay for winter feeding conspired to threaten a burgeoning herd with starvation. Despite the park and refuge hunting programs, numbers of elk that summered in the expanded area of GTNP increased. Limited to a few hundred prior to 1950, they reached 3,250 by 1968, and as many as 4,500 during the 1980s. Not only had numbers of elk that summered in the park grown, but elk migrations from Yellowstone Park and the Teton Wilderness had also increased through GTNP (two to three thousand animals), while migrations east of the park had shrunk due to greater vulnerability of elk to hunters following logging and roading of national forest lands. As more elk spent summer in and migrated through GTNP, more hunting was focused on the park, and also the NER where almost all those elk wintered. Combined park and refuge harvests rose from 161 annually during 1951–1960 to more than 800 during the 1980s.[1,2,3]

Killing elk in the NER and GTNP (the only national park in the lower forty-eight states hosting big-game hunting) is more than an aberration born of political compromise. Like the culling of deer in suburban Chicago and Minneapolis rose gardens, it attests to the ecological imperfection wrought by human disruption of ancient patterns. Because of the complexity of ecosystems, our attempts to manage them often backfire and/or lead to problems far worse than those we attempted to solve.[4] Once we start tinkering, unforeseen and unintended consequences often follow that require more manipulations.

While some have argued that these park and refuge hunts are needed to save elk from the cruel death of starvation, writer Ted Kerasote has responded, "Of all the arguments for the cull, this is the lamest. Elk have starved with grace and dignity for thousands of years, and don't need Florence Nightingales with rifles to sanitize their deaths." He asserted that as truly responsible stewards of the Earth we would back off from justifying such culls and other subterfuges for their purported good and instead modify our own behaviors that compel such manipulations as obligatory kindnesses.[5]

The Jackson herd increased nearly 20 percent annually during my tenure (the annual birth of three to four thousand calves far exceeds herd losses to natural causes). From our studies, we know that once elk reach one year of age, hunting accounts for 80 to 90 percent of all deaths.[2,6] Humans eat elk, but we are also devouring tracts of wildlife real estate. Despite 97 percent of its land in public ownership, Teton County, Wyoming, experienced explosive growth from 1970 to 2000—more than four times the rate of both Wyoming and the nation. Growth was spurred by quality of life, recreational amenities, the changing national economy, and investment income plowed into second homes. Teton County consistently ranked among the top five of 3,140 U.S. counties in per capita wealth in recent decades, matching the county's wildlife superabundance with an equally anomalous human excess.[7]

An entire industry has arisen on the shoulders of elk, an economic engine the refuge and state feedgrounds help feed. Sporting goods dealers, hunting outfitters, ecotour operators, food and lodging businesses, and the chamber of commerce all benefit from the herd. Elk hunting alone brought between five and six million dollars to the valley in 2000, according to Jonathan Schechter, a Jackson economist. He further described the contribution to Teton County's economy from elk-related tourism as "incalculable."[8]

There's a linear perception among the business community, and maybe the citizenry at large, that the more elk the better for business and hence the county's well-being. Because wildlife feeding breeds the misperception that populations need only be limited by how much hay fits in the barn, concepts of ecological constraints and sustainable stocking rates lose relevance in public forums. For example, at a public meeting during the late 1990s—when the elk herd was trending downward from a forty-year high of eighteen thousand head—a questioner demanded, "So, you tell me where all the elk went!"

The obvious answer to Jackson's elk managers was "into people's freezers." In the questioner's lifetime, hunting may have never been so good.

At another public hearing a decade earlier—when refuge numbers had reached a fifty-year low of 5,300 in 1984—Tom Toman, the Wyoming Game and Fish Department regional supervisor in Jackson, was peppered with accusations about mismanagement of the elk herd. Finally, to one persistent critic who challenged whether his staff knew what they were doing, he responded, "It seems there are ten thousand wildlife experts in Jackson Hole and none are on my staff."

Ironically, the elk herd had purposely been reduced through more-liberal seasons that the public enjoyed each fall (see Appendix B). In 1984, after years of excessive numbers, the Jackson herd had dropped below the state's goal of eleven thousand. As Tom wryly noted after the meeting concluded, "People love the state's population objective whenever there are more elk than that."

In reality, Tom's assertions vex many wildlife managers. But Jackson Hole's unique socioeconomic circumstances, which the elk help feed, amplify public discourse and discord. Wildlife feeding changes everything, but especially public expectations.

At the core of the issue, the state's management objective of eleven thousand wintering elk for the Jackson herd is a contrived number. That target simply mirrors the number of elk that attended the NER and Gros Ventre feedgrounds (plus a grossly conservative estimate of another 1,100 free-ranging elk) in the years prior to 1975, the year when that number was chosen. Targets of 2,400 elk on three feedgrounds in the Gros Ventre and 7,500 on the NER seemed hammered in stone—the latter via a memorandum of understanding signed by Wyoming and USFWS officials in 1974. That MOU revised a 1943 agreement between the agencies specifying that five to seven thousand elk be accommodated on the NER. None of those numbers is rooted in sustainable resource management principles nor ambient habitat or disease conditions on the ground. Obviously, larger populations require larger harvests, but the inverse is also true. This reality accommodates socioeconomic objectives of an artificially large herd, and circularly justifies machinations like unconventional national park and refuge hunts.

But without the GTNP and NER hunts, winter feeding would swiftly lead to out-of-control numbers. More elk would foster more disease and habitat damage than already exists. So are there other ways to limit elk numbers? Rather than hunts in the park and refuge, some have suggested controlling elk numbers with birth-control measures or culls carried out by government agencies. Although some wouldn't object to culling by dispassionate agency officers, in principle, most people who derive food and recreation from harvesting elk would condemn being deprived of their pursuit. Such a cull was conducted in 1935, when elk numbers on the NER swelled to 9,500. Wyoming Game and Fish Department personnel slaughtered 548 elk baited into refuge corrals. The public outcry rendered that a onetime event. Furthermore, the Wyoming Game and Fish Department's budget is largely dependent on hunting license fees to fund and operate wildlife programs. In concert with their primary constituencies—hunters and hunting outfitters—fewer hunting opportunities means fewer elk harvested and fewer dollars earned. Every mention of agency culling that I witnessed died a swift death.

The anti-hunting and animal-rights factions, if they acknowledge the necessity of controlling populations at all, propose nonlethal birth control to limit numbers. Some would argue that this approach is far less intrusive and certainly more humane than killing elk by hunting or culls. Given current technology, lifelong sterilization requires capturing and surgically neutering elk—a costly and invasive procedure. Using darts to deliver immunocontraceptives—like vaccinating elk with biobullets—is disruptive and requires handout-conditioned elk. Significantly, available contraceptives have short-lived effects. Concerted efforts to curb populations of nuisance white-tailed deer in New York and Maryland suburbs achieved reductions of just 20 to 40 percent after four to seven years, and at considerable public expense. Furthermore, the challenge that largely makes the GTNP and NER hunts necessary is the disproportionate number (about three-fourths) of elk on the refuge that summer in national parks. Once elk from the four herd segments arrive at the refuge, they blend like gin and tonic. Contracepting only park elk is impossible, unless carried out on summer ranges. Such a program's immense logistical problems would make it ridiculously costly and potentially conflict with the national parks' mission. As Dr. Jay Kirkpatrick, a conservation biologist who specializes in fertility control of wildlife with vaccines, stated, "The problem in Jackson Hole transcends the science of our vaccine."[9]

An additional argument pitting hunting interests against animal-rights activists is rooted in Darwinism. Beyond condemning the pain inflicted in killing animals, anti-hunting interests assert that trophy hunting—killing the largest-antlered and presumably the fittest bulls—may alter gene pools and therefore the future of populations themselves. (Presumably hunters are less able to discriminate among females and select those that are more fit). Could hunting exert such a selective force? Indeed there are examples.

In the late 1970s and early 1980s, 10 to 20 percent of all the elephants in the wild were being killed each year. At that rate wild elephants would have gone extinct by the end of the century. This was an intense selection event at the hand of man. For poachers, elephants with big tusks were prime targets (as they were for trophy hunters). Elephants with small tusks were more likely to be passed over. Those with no tusks at all were ignored. Elephants were under enormous selective pressure for tusklessness.

Elephant watchers in the most heavily poached areas were noticing an increasing percentage of tuskless elephants. Andrew Dobson, an ecologist at Princeton University, traced this in five African wildlife reserves. In Amboseli, where elephants were relatively safe, the number of tuskless female elephants was small, just a few percent. But in Mikumi, a park where they were heavily poached, tusklessness among females climbed from 10 percent among five- to ten-year-olds to 50 percent of thirty- to thirty-five-year-olds.[10] Tuskless males (males use tusks to fight and establish dominance) became increasingly less disadvantaged in competing for mating services—purveying consequences for mate selection, breeding, and heritable traits of offspring. This same process of selection for tuskless elephants is being repeated in China. The tusk-free gene, which was previously found in 2 to 5 percent of male Asian elephants, has increased to nearly 10 percent of the elephants in China.

Analogous to elephant tusks are changes in antlers grown by European moose. Mature males of this Holarctic species generally sport broad, palmate racks. But sport hunting intensely selected that phenotype in parts of Europe, diminishing the frequency of palmate antlers. Selective harvest favored a cervine-antlered phenotype, the style grown by deer and elk. Conversely, when regulations protected palmate-antlered moose, that phenotype slowly increased again.[11, 12, 13]

Hunting may also foster adaptive behaviors, even curtailing those evolved for mate selection. The bugling of male elk in rut serves to attract potential mates and ward off would-be challengers, presumably those with less forceful calls. It's common knowledge that elk spending the fall on Jackson Hole's national forest lands bugle far less than those in the protected confines of Grand Teton and Yellowstone National Parks. Elk in the parks bugle freely for weeks, delighting tourists at their vocal outbursts of virility. Bugling may serve dominant males to gather and maintain harems, but by attracting hunters such behavior is selected against.

Such anthropogenic selective forces may take generations to express, though it happens more rapidly in small populations and those with highly skewed sex ratios where the sexes experience differential selection. Thus, phenotypic effects within the Jackson elk herd are more likely to appear in the Gros Ventre herd segment where winter counts tally only three branch-antlered bulls per one hundred females. By contrast, male-to-female ratios are ten times that high on the NER, where three-fourths of elk come from the two national parks.

Even if trophy hunting may shape herd genetics, I believe neither hunters nor anti-fertility promoters command the high ground here. Because only some animals need to be contracepted to limit population growth (leaving enough breeders to compensate for annual population turnover from natural mortality), by definition reproduction of some will be permitted while others will not. Who's qualified to make that decision in the best interest of the elk herd? Both methods selectively lead to genetic death of individuals removed from the breeding population.

An alternative solution to the surplus elk problem comes from the Jackson Hole Outfitters and Guides Association, which offered on occasion to truck dozens, even hundreds, of elk calves from the refuge to distant national forest lands. On the surface this sounds like a sensible, humane approach—neither neuter nor kill elk while drawing down refuge numbers. However, experience has shown that hay-habituated elk don't always stay where we desire. There's little assurance they won't hightail it for the nearest rancher's haystack. Furthermore, advocates proposed transferring the elk elsewhere in western Wyoming—country where elk already crowd state-run feedgrounds. Wyoming has a management goal of maintaining eighty-three thousand elk statewide (increased from a goal of sixty-eight thousand elk in the 1980s), yet more than one hundred thousand elk have roamed Wyoming since the late 1990s, despite the Wyoming Game and Fish Department striving to reduce elk numbers to their management goal.[14]

Moving elk near feedgrounds at Dog Creek, or Scab Creek, or anywhere else simply transfers the overpopulation and its associated management costs there. And there the unwilling migrants will eventually fall to hunters, some surely clients of outfitters. Transplanting's utility during the twentieth century was to restore extirpated populations, not to supply put-and-take hunting. Beyond these hitches, Wyoming state government—supported by the U.S. Department of Agriculture—prohibits elk or bison from leaving Teton County alive because of brucellosis, unless shipped to Wyoming's research facilities or consigned to slaughter. Categorically, we can put this proposition to rest.

A more passive option to curb elk numbers is advocated by others: Stop feeding. Stop hunting the refuge and park. Let elk numbers equilibrate without human intervention. This is basically the natural regulation policy implemented in Yellowstone National Park in 1968. Let weather, food, predators, and disease limit elk numbers.

Nothing prevents such a plan from being implemented except an irate hunting community and the inevitable winterkill. Droves of dead and dying elk within sight of thousands of people would be socially, economically, and therefore politically unacceptable (as in the foretaste I described in Chapter 5). The elk bring in millions of dollars of revenue each year as the region's premier big game animal, and arguably its most significant wildlife tourist attraction. Thousands of hunters travel to Jackson Hole each fall, and increasing numbers of tourists come to the valley to observe bugling, migrating, and baby elk. In winter thirty thousand visitors crowd horse-drawn sleighs to watch and photograph elk on the refuge at close range. Letting overabundant herds starve to death, when they have been fed for a century, is simply not going to happen in Jackson Hole.

Practicality, tradition, agency prerogatives, and the economic engine of wildlife recreation make the obvious crystal clear: Hunting is all but certain to remain how Jackson elk numbers are controlled in the future. So wildlife managers and the public must ask: How best can this be done? And why have hunting regulations that hold elk numbers to the herd objective of eleven thousand not been implemented?

My work over two decades showed elk left all summer ranges syn-chronously each fall. Those in the Teton Wilderness and Yellowstone National Park abandoned their high summer ranges as snow accumu-lated in late October and early November, yet GTNP elk oftentimes left when little snow had accumulated in the park's central valley. This

Public sleigh rides at the National Elk Refuge
(Jim Griffin, US Fish and Wildlife Service)

inconsistency brings to mind a quote about animal behavior I once read. To paraphrase: "What they do reflects what they are and what's happening in their environment. That doesn't mean the answer is clear, but it means there is an answer, which is nice to know." Heartening words for any scientist's work.

With a new batch of elk captured and radio-collared as newborns during my doctoral research, I set out to learn the migration dynamics of GTNP elk—that problematic 2,500 to 4,500 head that had been foiling wildlife managers' and hunters' efforts over the years. From 1992 to 1998 I intensively monitored fall migrations. In addition I measured production and utilization of herbaceous forage in GTNP's central valley. Randomly assigning these sampling sites within zones of high and low elk density (based on previous telemetry data and the accumulated knowledge of state and park biologists), I proposed to test two hypotheses. I suspected the timing of migrations of GTNP elk to the NER might correlate with forage production and/or utilization on park lands during summer and fall, and I postulated that survival during hunting season of early migrants from GTNP would equal or exceed survival rates of elk that migrated after the median migration date. If early migration enhanced survival, it could be considered adaptive behavior and favored through selection— not necessarily as a heritable trait, but because increased numbers of early migrants would survive to teach future offspring this behavior.

I found that forage production varied with annual growing conditions, and in years of high production elk migrated later in the fall. Like calf survival, this behavior was governed by annual weather conditions. Because of their greater numbers, elk grazed forage three-and-a-half times more heavily in areas of high versus low elk densities. On average, when GTNP elk left these areas for the refuge, 62 percent of all herbaceous vegetation—both preferred and less desirable species combined— had been removed. I could account for 82 percent of the annual variation in when elk abandoned the park by how little forage remained. The numbers of elk grazing that forage explained nearly half of the remaining year-to-year variation.[2]

In general, the availability of suitable resources across summer/fall ranges was the ultimate factor controlling the timing of Jackson elk migrations. Elk inhabiting the most distant, high-elevation summer ranges migrated as snow limited their access to plentiful food. In contrast, depletion of sufficiently high-quality forage was the proximate factor cue-ing migration from GTNP. Those elk were "food production limited."

Ostensibly, migration appears maladaptive during October and early November from GTNP's hunter-free sanctuary into areas where elk could see, hear, and smell hunters east of the Snake River. What we might construe as reckless behavior instead selectively advanced early migrants' genes. Throughout the decade of the 1990s, I monitored 376 migrations of GTNP radioed elk. Only 4.8 percent of those arriving at the NER before the median migration date were harvested compared to 11.3 per-cent of later migrants. This occurred even though annual opening dates of hunting preceded migrations of elk.[2]

Some mechanisms by which 95 percent of early migrants were able to escape harvest were evident. Elk commonly migrated at night and some-times en masse, diluting the chance of any one individual being killed, like the seventeen-year cicada emerging in swarms or wildebeest over-whelming predators' appetites with synchronized production of calves. Elk were also more difficult to harvest during early stages of migration because of low hunter participation, due to mild weather conditions and hunter perceptions that migrations were yet to begin. Elsewhere that elk occupy similar sanctuaries, they sometimes *delay* fall migrations to avoid enter-ing hunted areas, but in the GTNP case, elk employ strategies that evade hunters and concurrently optimize their diets. As vegetation cured west of the Snake River—where 87 percent of GTNP elk spent summer—both the quantity and quality of forage waned. While elsewhere in the Rockies resources are typically scarce in winter and early spring, due to supplemen-tal feeding at the NER, fall may be the limiting season for GTNP elk. At the end of a trek from the park to the refuge—a jaunt elk can complete in a few hours—a surfeit of ungrazed, irrigated forage rewards them.

Not just GTNP inhabitants found ways to avoid hunters' bullets. Some left the Teton Wilderness for the protected confines of Yellowstone when September hunting began. Others punctuated southward migrations by hop-scotching from relatively secure patches of habitat on national forest lands to jurisdictions closed to hunting. Further evidence convinced me that the lure of nitrogen and aversion to lead compelled migratory behavior. Elk from distant ranges in the Teton Wilderness and Yellowstone Park migrated both east and west of the Snake River to reach the refuge. Those that migrated west of the Snake River, through the central valley's already

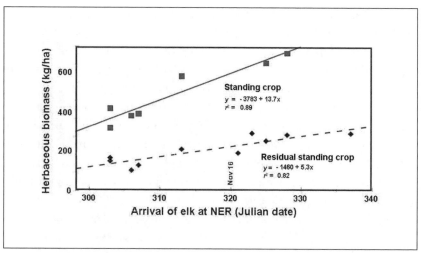

Figure 1. Timing of elk migration (from Grand Teton National Park to the National Elk Refuge) in relation to measurements of the annual standing forage crop and residual standing crop (vegetation remaining after summer-fall grazing) during 1991–2000.

forage-depleted safe haven, arrived at the NER two weeks earlier than migrants to the east who navigated lands completely open to hunting, but where elk densities were lower and forage more generous.

Managers often find themselves playing games of catch-up, learning from failures, and defining problems more clearly in order to solve them. Because the earliest migrants were harvested least, some efforts to reduce the GTNP herd segment as a proportion of the Jackson herd proved counterproductive. By extending hunting into mid-December, increased harvests fell disproportionately on late migrants, primarily herd segments other than GTNP. Here again science was an incomparable instructor. Not that the policy solution to this problem was patent, but the path to a solution was clearer.

In addition to managing for a target population size (or range), wildlife managers in Wyoming and elsewhere often prescribe desired adult male-to-female ratios, calf productivity, seasonal distributions, annual harvests, and other metrics—parameters for which nature has no use. In truth, the managers never succeed, save maybe a lucky year or two when the forces of nature all cooperate. Weather is the great equalizer that recognizes no monthly averages or seasonal norms. Local conditions are dictated by phenomena that defy our prediction and our control. So despite low winter mortality, the Jackson herd has cycled; it's risen and fallen in size over the decades. Some of this had to do, I now suspect, with changes in neonatal survival. But far more influential were harvest levels, or more precisely, the inconsistency of harvesting enough cow elk. Two intractable factors are responsible: the relative invulnerability of elk that summer in national parks, and the vagaries of weather effects on migration behavior.[6]

Finally, lag effects contributed to the amplitude of population peaks and troughs. Demographic lags, due to changes in population structure and consequent reproductive output, were exacerbated by delays in the State of Wyoming responding with sufficiently adjusted hunting regulations to the ups and downs of population trends. As in all public processes, citizen opinion influenced Wyoming's response, and generally to the detriment of reducing excess numbers. And even when all the stars of politics aligned, that pesky issue of harvesting the "right elk" bedeviled the best-laid plans. The right elk are those protected in the two national parks (more so GTNP than Yellowstone, I'd argue, given the vanishing majesty of long-distance mammal migrations[15]). Furthermore, elk migrating from Yellowstone join those that summer on Bridger-Teton's expansive forested lands, which offer the highest-quality opportunities for hunters and the outfitting industry. Recent radiotelemetry data indicate that the size of elk migrations from Yellowstone Park may be declining, according to NER biologist Eric Cole.

Like parks, national forests are also the people's lands. Forest plans and legal authorities direct conservation of resident wildlife species but defer to states to actually manage them. To the credit of both (and to vigilant user groups, as well), Bridger-Teton hosts bountiful elk and other game. So, caught between the granite of not overharvesting national forest elk and the hard reality of less vulnerable national park elk, the Jackson herd has exceeded eleven thousand wintering animals in every year but one since 1975.

I'm among the first to contend that the park and refuge hunts serve a purpose—to harvest elk that seldom venture beyond GTNP and NER boundaries. Yet during twenty-two hunting seasons in Jackson, I chose not to hunt in GTNP or the NER, mainly because I saw those hunts as largely by-products of the refuge's feeding program, and an artificial overstocking of elk. In that regard I'm guilty of working both sides of the street. I fed and provided surplus elk for hunters even as I advocated increased harvests and lower refuge numbers to limit their impacts on habitats. Other conservationists' appeals for more than lip service to the refuge's other 47 mammal and 175 bird species often fell on deaf ears.

"It wouldn't have been named the National Elk Refuge if the place was for dickey birds," one avid hunting guide scolded during a workshop on refuge management.

On many others the irony was not lost of hunting elk on lands designated an elk refuge. Certainly *60 Minutes* scored high ratings on the situation—even if it embellished the circumstances for effect. In its 1984 segment titled "A Sporting Chance," Harry Reasoner introduced the segment as follows:

> *This is a story we had trouble believing when we first heard it. It's about an elk refuge near Grand Teton National Park where food is put out every day so the elk won't starve during those long, hard, Wyoming winters. That's not the part that's hard to believe. What's hard to believe is that the people who run our national parks issue permits for hunters to come into the park and pick off the elk one by one as they make their way into the refuge. They call it thinning out the herd. But it hardly seems sporting to put out food to lure an elk to a refuge and then pick him off on his way to the feeding grounds.*

It's easy to see how an otherwise uninformed audience would be revolted by the storyline, complete with blood-splattered carcasses and the pretext that hunters blasted elk from pickup trucks. Even locals find the Jackson Hole circumstances confusing, as in this e-mail sent to the NER on November 17, 2003:

> *Subject: elk hunt*
> *Hello my name is Anthony ———— for years my dad and I has hunted on the elk refuge every Saturday and Sunday from opening day to closeing day and we nener haved got a elk be for all we see is deer and one or two moose all I am saying can you drive more elk on the refuge.*
> *Please and Thank you*
> *Anthony*

Both scenarios miss the point. The elk come to the refuge on their own and because they have no other choice. Ancient winter ranges are long lost from the herd memory. Food conditioning at the refuge reinforces their fall assemblage. Most importantly, feeding begins long after the hunting has ended. But including those details makes for less rousing TV entertainment and ratings, I suppose.

The reduction program is a messy way of dealing with too many elk. But like many of our imperfect compromises and their unanticipated by-products, the NER and GTNP hunts have been difficult to replace by anything better. This conundrum is underscored by positions at the extremes. For example, one camp advocates doing even more of the same: Open more of GTNP to hunting to kill more elk west of the Snake River. But with participation in hunting on a national decline, congressional action to expand Public Law 787's scope is unlikely. Just thirteen million Americans age sixteen and older consider themselves hunters out of the eighty-eight million (39 percent of the U.S. population) that participate in recreational activities relating to fish and wildlife.[16] And only eleven million of those hunters hunt large mammals, such as elk and deer, while a growing percentage of Americans disapprove of the practice.

But resource management policy is not, and I'd argue should not, be an exercise in democracy. Certainly wildlife is a communal resource held in trust for the people by federal and state governments—but just as directives to the U.S. Defense or Treasury departments should not be voting matters (subject to public whims and mood), wildlife policy formulation must consider many factors. Habitat capacities, landowner tolerance, disease concerns, and the science and art that balance biology, social constraints, and applicable law must all be integrated when crafting objectives and strategies that serve the greater public good.

The wildlife profession's mandate is to sustain all wildlife for the benefit of people in present and future generations. In the American tradition of using the resource, hunting is a legitimate and necessary aspect of wildlife conservation. Hunting animals for food in the modern world provides wholesome protein from a renewable product of the land. And hunters are an engaged constituency for maintaining wild and undeveloped habitats in both public and private ownership. These open spaces support wildlife and simultaneously a host of other environmental services to hunters and nonhunters alike.

I support hunting and hunt myself. But beyond the practical purposes of removing surplus animals and harvesting protein, I believe that hunting should promote balanced communities of animal populations; sustain elk, their habitats, and their genetic diversity; and be compatible with and respectful of all life. The pursuit and experience of hunting should be measured by more than the endpoint achieved by the squeeze of the trigger. About that preoccupation with conquest, conservation writer Dale Burk cautions, "This approach unwittingly separates, even alienates, the elk hunter from the very environment that allows elk populations to flourish. The end results are less concern about what it takes to sustain elk and, ultimately, fewer elk." Marketing the experience of time afield might better serve to connect hunters to the resource that sustains all wildlife, Burk adds. Ultimately, the memories of the experience and the place itself are what make us long to return and renew our spirits amid the bustle of lives otherwise spent separate from nature.[17]

CHAPTER 13

Prescription for Progress

Like the resource it seeks to protect, wildlife conservation must be dynamic, changing as conditions change, seeking always to become more effective.
—RACHEL CARSON, 1948, GUARDING OUR WILDLIFE RESOURCES

It was near quitting time when the phone rang. "Bruce, this is Len Carlman."

Len is a Jackson attorney. When I arrived in Jackson and we became friends, Len was the executive director of the nonprofit Jackson Hole Conservation Alliance before heading to the University of Wyoming for a law degree. We hadn't spoken for a while, so we caught up on each others' lives before I asked, "What can I do for you?"

"Do you know Shirley Cheramy and Marian Meyers?"

"Shirley, yes. Marian, I don't believe so."

"Marian lives in the Solitude subdivision. She approached Shirley and me about the problem of residents feeding wildlife in Solitude. The three of us are meeting to discuss a county regulation to prohibit feeding. We'd like you to join us."

Len explained that they were concerned about what effects feeding by private citizens in Solitude and other county locations might have on the health of deer, moose, and elk. Their primary concerns, however, had to do with threats to people by aggressive moose and food-conditioned black bears. This subdivision north of Jackson and adjacent to GTNP lies three feet deep in snow in midwinter. It's not winter range. Rather, animals were being shortstopped there by bales of hay and barrels of deer chow.

Traveling plowed roadways from one feedsite to another brought eight-hundred-pound moose far too close to schoolchildren. Recent incidents of mountain lions prowling Solitude and other neighborhoods and bears casing houses for garbage and pet food raised concerns about residents' safety. No attacks on humans had occurred, but this dangerous pattern was a brewing crisis—a pattern emerging elsewhere in the West. From California to Colorado, mountain lion attacks on humans had increased in recent years, where subdivisions sprawled into wildlife range, ungulates and bears became food-conditioned to handouts or tasty landscaping, and large carnivores followed their prey. Of course, I told Len, I'd join him and the others. Our evening meeting at the Teton County Library in March 2002 began a two-year odyssey.

From his contacts with local and state officials, Len learned that despite complaints from residents of Casper, Lander, and other communities of deer damage to landscaping and vehicle collisions with wildlife, the Wyoming state legislature had failed to remedy the issue. While Colorado and Montana forbade private feeding of large animals, could it be that Wyoming's own provisioning of thousands of elk made banning private feeding awkward, even hypocritical?

Private wildlife feeding of deer and moose in Jackson Hole
(Mark Gocke, Wyoming Game and Fish Department)

Neither the Teton County nor Jackson governments could preempt state authority over wildlife with local ordinances. But Len had discovered another way to address the problem. The county's subdivision laws included land development regulations (LDRs) that promote human health and safety and other social protections. As a condition of development, feeding of ungulates and large carnivores could be prohibited. With the assistance of the Teton County planner, Len began drafting such an LDR.

Following readings at three county planning board meetings—the last in February 2003—the Teton County commissioners passed the LDR five to zero in April 2003. A four-to-one vote of acceptance by the Jackson Town Council followed a week later. But it wasn't all smooth sailing. The planning board voted three to two in favor at the first and second readings, then under duress the chair switched his vote at the third public meeting, sending the proposal with a not-to-adopt recommendation to the county commission. A locally organized pro-feeding group (comprised largely of Solitude subdivision deer and moose feeders) was bolstered by a group from Fremont County (east of the Continental Divide) that vociferously opposed infringement on feeding.

Some of us who advocated the ban were targeted in a series of paid advertisements in the *Jackson Hole News and Guide*. My testimony as a private citizen at county meetings and my advocacy at other venues prompted charges that I was leading a "stealth agenda" to end all wildlife feeding—not only on private lands, but also on the NER and state elk feedgrounds. I found it flattering yet utterly foolish that anyone considered me to be that influential. For the second time in my tenure at the NER, the pro-feeding lobby called for my transfer from the NER—this time in a letter to the director of the USFWS.

Despite the pro-feeding contingent's determined efforts, as citizens learned of the hazards to people and to wildlife (harassment by dogs, vehicle collisions, digestive disorders, and disease), many others supported the campaign. A truly grassroots effort started by three Jackson residents demonstrated the power of commitment to a civic cause. Moreover, language in the final regulation adopted by the Board of Commissioners applied to all private property within Teton County, whether newly developed or dating back to homestead times.

The NER has persevered on the outskirts of the booming resort town of Jackson despite pressures to transfer and develop portions of the federal refuge for hospital expansion, subdivision sprawl, baseball diamonds, stormwater drainage, and a county landfill. These threats and requests for special uses ranging from dogsled races to duck-hunting blinds have largely been fought off as incompatible with the refuge's mission. In that respect the NER is typical of the National Wildlife Refuge System as a whole. Each of these 553 refuges spanning the nation from Maine to Hawaii, Florida to Alaska makes a unique contribution to America's tapestry of life. All are bound by one commonality: habitats that support wildlife within and beyond our country's borders. Yet many refuges face conflicts with their primary purpose.

The National Elk Refuge beyond the town of Jackson
(Franz Camenzind)

Besides external demands, the NER's mission has been construed by many in Wyoming as a de facto production facility to fill vast summer ranges with elk. With the growth of an alfalfa-addicted bison herd after 1980, demands on beleaguered habitats compelled NER and GTNP managers to propose hunting them on the refuge. Against this backdrop the animal rights organization Fund for Animals sued the USFWS in 1998, challenging the environmental assessment and management plan that proposed the bison reductions. The plaintiffs contended that if the bison were not fed in winter, natural mortality would be higher and negate the need for hunting. The lawsuit cleverly drew elk management of Jackson Hole elk, via the practice of winter feeding, into the judge's ruling in 1998. The U.S. District Court for the District of Columbia ordered the federal government to prepare an environmental impact statement (EIS) to comprehensively address management of bison, including winter feeding (which of course was an elk feeding program in which the bison inexorably participated). This seven-year, two-million-dollar process refueled the divisive debate over winter feeding. Crafting the 2005 draft EIS fostered numerous public meetings and 11,900 written comments on a menu of six management alternatives. Although 65 percent of comments favored phasing out feeding and reducing elk and bison numbers to the refuge's habitat carrying capacity, other, more powerful interests (including the State of Wyoming) argued for something nearer the status quo.

After issuing a final EIS in 2007, the federal government opted to winter five thousand elk and five hundred bison on the NER (numbers still exceeded by more than 50 percent in 2011; see Appendix A), with no firm commitment to ending winter feeding of either. Other significant management actions included expanding the refuge irrigation system, fencing elk (and thereby other large mammals) out of beleaguered willow and aspen communities, and continuing to vaccinate elk with Strain 19 brucellosis vaccine. To partially subsidize the effort, the NER received $4.3 million from the American Recovery and Reinvestment Act of 2009 plus an additional $800,000 of federal money to expand sprinkler irrigation by 1,100 acres.

These two concurrent public processes—the federal EIS to chart long-term management of Jackson elk and bison, and the citizen initiative to ban wildlife feeding in Teton County—achieved dramatically different results. The former institutionalized a century-old paradigm of wildlife management rooted in principles of agricultural production of preferred species. The latter chose a more enlightened direction to limit human intervention and dependence of wildlife on people.

Too often the feeding issue is painted in either-or colors: Either we feed and have a bountiful herd, or we stop feeding and starve the elk. The crux of the matter is that the public is accustomed to tens of thousands of elk, but this comes at significant cost. The price tag for Wyoming's management of elk west of the Continental Divide was $2,758,000 in 1998 compared to elk hunting license revenues of $1,846,000—a $900,000 shortfall. That annual deficit predated the advent of Wyoming's pricey test-and-slaughter program. The red ink would run far higher were it not for federal taxpayers purchasing half the feed and paying all other management expenses at the NER.[1]

As many elk may now roam the GYE as ever. However, dwindling winter range—a consequence of human encroachment and intolerance—is a fact of life there and throughout the West. If the rationale for feeding elk is to fully stock summer ranges, then increasingly few places remain in North America where winter feeding is not justified.

Past migrations from Jackson Hole environs to vast winter pastures in southwest Wyoming ended by 1917.[2, 3, 4] Rather than crowding elk onto feedgrounds, might the size of America's largest elk herd be maintained by restoring those spectacular migrations? Even today, semblances of those migrations persist. Some mule deer that summer in mountains surrounding Jackson Hole still migrate to the Green River basin, and a tenacious herd of two to three hundred pronghorn remember the way from Jackson Hole to windblown winter pastures of the Little Colorado Desert.[5] They follow the same winding route across the Gros Ventre–Green River hydrographic divide that Ira Dodge recorded twenty thousand elk navigating in the late 1800s. Such observations by Dodge and others prompted the first formal pitch in 1898 for a national "winter game preserve" in Wyoming's Red Desert, including a designated migration corridor linking those lands to Jackson Hole.[6] A decade later Wyoming game warden D. C. Nowlin crafted a proposal requesting that Congress donate six townships of public land in the Gros Ventre and Green River drainages to be designated as a "winter game refuge" for the elk.[7] Opposition by stockmen apparently compelled state and federal governments to abandon both propositions.

This brings us back to the Jackson pronghorn migration, which lingers as a long-distance relic. After scouring available reports, records, and trappers' journals to assess historic large-mammal migrations in the GYE, wildlife ecologist Joel Berger compared those findings with the existing situation. He concluded that 58 percent of the elk migratory routes and 78 percent of the pronghorn routes no longer exist due to human hindrance.[8] Of course, tens of millions of American bison made the grandest migrations the land has ever known—wide-ranging journeys that have all long since passed. Migratory land mammals worldwide are increasingly restricted to remnants of former ranges, leaving the Jackson herd's abridged, sixty-mile semiannual trek the longest among North American elk.

Large-mammal migrations, whether elk or pronghorn, caribou or wildebeest, follow traditional, learned routes, passed from mother to offspring. If you've never migrated, why start? And where would you go, especially when conditioned to free lunches at feedgrounds? Restoring the lost knowledge of distant winter pastures would require resurrecting forgotten elk behavior. During the 1940s Wyoming Game and Fish Department biologist Warren Allred coordinated such an experiment. With some coaxing, elk transplanted on the desert margins resumed former migrations, although others already conditioned to hay ended up at ranchers' haystacks. By 1950 Wyoming had abandoned that effort.[2] Still, a coalition of public and private interests formally established a national migratory pathway for the Jackson pronghorn in 2008.[9, 10]

Designating a corridor for two to three hundred migratory pronghorn across lands largely in public ownership, however, is far different than establishing one or more pathways for thousands of Jackson Hole elk. Hundreds of square miles of desert habitat could still host elk from mountainous northwest Wyoming, but to reach these lands elk must bypass haystacks and cattle feedlines on private ranchlands in the Green River basin. Financial incentives and restructured property taxes might encourage some landowners to replace livestock with free-ranging wildlife, although this would certainly be a challenging process. Such an initiative, pursued parcel by parcel, could cumulatively link summer ranges to historic winter ranges in the Little Colorado and Red Deserts. Rather than spending three million dollars annually on feeding, vaccinating, and crop depredations, the USFWS and Wyoming could redirect those dollars to partner with landowners in resolving conflicts that have fostered animosity toward Wyoming's wildlife for years. Such an effort could net thousands more acres of habitat where elk are now unwelcome. Fee title purchase of private parcels may be beyond fiscal reach, but acquiring large-tract conservation easements—from those open to the precepts of keeping rangelands undeveloped for wildlife's sake—could conceivably foster a new conservation direction.

Contrary to game ranching, landowners would neither own the animals nor restrict their movements with feed or fencing in this scenario. Forage and habitats valued by wildlife could be enhanced with state, federal, NGO, and other private dollars, all of which could also pay to fence elk out of livestock feedlines and stackyards on nearby ranchlands. Comparable programs in surrounding states and east of the Continental Divide in Wyoming have proven successful for sustaining large mammals. An example of this concept was achieved in Montana during the 1990s to benefit Yellowstone National Park's northern elk herd.

Nevertheless, resurrecting a century-past migration would pose much greater public relations and logistical problems in western Wyoming than in most places. Teaching elk to migrate as much as two hundred miles would require baiting animals to entice them southward. Negotiating landowner agreements and forage concessions by the Bureau of Land Management and livestock industry poses additional hurdles. Finally, state elk feedgrounds would prove powerful attractants and almost certainly would require dismantling for Jackson's hay-conditioned wapiti to complete their migration.

The window to re-create this grand procession is closing fast as CWD marches west. In a state where the livestock industry and out-of-state energy interests shape land management policies,[11] wildlife concerns are often secondary. As noted previously, ranchers seem to prefer feedgrounds with brucellosis to no feedgrounds at all as a means of reducing elk competition with livestock on both private and public lands. The severance taxes Wyoming levies on energy and minerals, among the highest of any state, have financed state programs and budget surpluses. In concert with obliging federal energy policies, vast tracts of public lands have become increasingly populated with drill pads, storage facilities, and spiderwebs of haul roads, while numbers of sage-grouse, mule deer, and other wildlife decline.[12, 13] Federal land management agencies have tacitly promoted a backward model of leasing important wildlife habitats for development while licensing the crowding and feeding of elk. (Six feedgrounds are on Bureau of Land Management lands; seven are on the Bridger-Teton National Forest; and state lands accommodate another seven feedgrounds.) In the nation's least populous state, where pronghorn numbers rival those of humans, is there neither the room nor the will for mending wild landscapes? If this is an option whose time has already passed, can wildlife feeding be discontinued *without* restoring migrations?

Over the years we have busied ourselves with the details of maintaining an overstocked range (and mitigating the consequences) rather than asking whether we should overstock it. In essence the question is this: Given the ecologically inadequate range to which the Jackson herd is confined, how many elk can we justify without jeopardizing these animals and the wildlife community that shares their habitat?

The EIS process that produced the Jackson Bison and Elk Management Plan in 2007 offered a unique opportunity to implement proactive, sustainable resource policy. Alternative 6 prescribed managing the refuge for healthy elk and bison populations, habitats, and biodiversity by wintering no more than 2,700 elk and 500 bison, phasing out winter feeding in five years, and repairing deteriorated habitats.[14] Without the lure of wapiti welfare at the NER, elk would range more widely across adjacent public lands in winter and spring, taking pressure off beleaguered habitats and reducing the transmission of diseases. Most importantly, when CWD inevitably arrives in Jackson Hole, its impact would be diminished. A coordinated phaseout of feeding in the Gros Ventre (where 2,500 to 9,000 elk wintered before three feedgrounds were established[3]) would transition the Jackson elk to a completely free-ranging herd. Purposeful habitat enhancements on public lands could promote adjustments in elk numbers as habitat conditions allow.[15] With a smaller population, elk hunting on the NER and GTNP could be scaled back. Elk distribution on summer ranges would shift, as the GTNP herd segment would no longer enjoy the advantage of wholesale winter feeding relative to other herd segments. Severe winters would cull less fit elk and bison, but Jackson Hole would sustain viable populations at less risk of epizootic disease.

The Department of Interior did not select Alternative 6, instead opting for a compromise position unlikely to resolve most management issues. Because all politics are local, as the saying goes, it's surprising that the citizens of western Wyoming have not risen up in opposition to an unending cycle of biological tinkering, unrelenting wildlife disease, unflattering national press, and chronic disservice to the most celebrated and treasured elk herd in the world. Instead, cultural traditionalism and political expediency have trumped science and logic. Philosopher and writer George Santayana may have put it best: "Habit is stronger than reason."

Ironically, it was a long lineage of scientists and wildlife managers (many from within the agencies that administer the policy) who argued against crowding elk onto feedgrounds in the past.[16] Nowadays, few speak out. Agency biologists are increasingly resigned to the situation or pressed to support entrenched management policy. Conservation activists are thwarted at every turn by a recalcitrant Wyoming government and a politics of the sort that Wyoming outfitter and conservationist Tory Taylor dubbed "one cow, one vote."

While state and federal resource agencies are entrusted to manage wildlife and their habitats for the public benefit, how "benefit" is defined can be nebulous and controversial. In this regard science can serve as an arbiter to inform more objective policy-making, yet there are always those with something to gain or lose—and so the battle is often joined over the virtues of short-term gain versus long-term value. It's not that current law lacks the teeth to advance conservation's cause. Rather, opposing interests find ways around such inconveniences. Unfortunately, this leaves but one option to advocates of sustainable resource management: litigation. By default, federal judges have become the de facto overlords of land management policy.

Under their respective legislative mandates, the U.S. Forest Service, Bureau of Land Management, and USFWS have resource stewardship responsibilities with which elk feedgrounds may conflict.[17] For failing to analyze the consequences of disease, the reauthorization of elk feeding at six sites in the Bridger-Teton National Forest was unsuccessfully challenged in 2009. A consortium of conservation organizations had already challenged the Jackson Bison and Elk Management Plan, and specifically winter feeding on the NER. Among other claims, the groups argued that the USFWS is obligated legally to maintain the "biological integrity, diversity, and environmental health of the [National Wildlife Refuge] System . . . for the benefit of present and future generations of Americans."[18] An unfavorable court ruling is under appeal.

University of Wyoming law professor Debra Donahue asserts that Wyoming has a legal duty to close feedgrounds under its trust responsibilities to the citizens of the state. She argues, "Can a practice, which the agency [Wyoming Game and Fish Department] itself concedes increases the prevalence of diseases and parasites in elk, seriously be defended as a measure designed to 'preserve, protect, and nurture' populations?" Indeed, Wyoming's chief motivations for feeding are to protect private property—especially to protect livestock from disease carried by elk—and secondarily to maintain larger numbers of animals for hunting than available winter range can support. Neither of these objectives is specifically authorized, much less required, by state law.[17]

Authorizing the feeding of wildlife on public lands is a discretionary call by state and federal agencies. Since nothing in law requires feeding, the public is free to demand an end to this practice. Moving to a more ecologically grounded model of elk management, one that emphasizes environmental health and resource sustainability, will require either a paradigm shift—a change in mindset of state and federal agencies and collaboration with private interests—or a game-changing court challenge to existing policies. Thus far, legal action has proven unsuccessful and has only sharpened divisions between wildlife interests and those opposed to change. Even among wildlife advocates, the feeding issue has pitted those favoring no reductions in elk numbers against others more ecologically minded.

Despite past resistance, I remain optimistic that a collaborative solution can be achieved. I'm optimistic because the stakes of not changing grow steadily each day. Scientists, health experts, and even Montana's governor have called for Wyoming to close its feedgrounds, a necessary step in addressing the maintenance of brucellosis in elk. If the worst should happen, chronic wasting disease would create twenty-three hot spots for infection of cervids throughout the GYE. Wyoming's obduracy would earn national media attention as diseased animals are euthanized to stem the spread of disease. To those who pooh-pooh this scenario and trumpet the benefits of artificially maintaining elk, the rejoinder is simple: better a smaller elk herd than an overstocked range riddled with disease.

I've come to see the Jackson elk herd as a microcosm of the growing environmental challenges that confront humans and wildlife in the modern world. Many national parks and reserves have become ecological islands surrounded by seas of development and natural resource exploitation. Inside parks and other conservation areas, large mammal populations grow increasingly sedentary and isolated. Mountain gorillas cling to their volcano islands and giant pandas retreat to increasingly fragmented bamboo forests. Wild populations on every continent are exiled to parks too small or too homogenous to provide for their year-round needs. The currency of wildlife, its habitat, is under siege. It's merely the pace and cause of alteration that makes Wyoming any different.

The search for solutions begs for scientific guidance to conserve wildlife communities from threats to animals and their habitats. Rebounding bald eagle, whooping crane, and grizzly bear populations attest that wildlife are resilient, environmental legislation works, and human benevolence can prevail over our anthropocentric misdeeds.

In Wyoming I spent more than two decades recording and treating symptoms of a broken ecology, without achieving remedies to the underlying ills. Maybe the single greatest hurdle is the long history of managing the elk herd the same way. People have a hard time envisioning it any other way. If hunters, businesspeople, and the community at large can't picture elk ranging the hillsides all winter, and an economy supported by a smaller but healthier herd, then it won't happen. But now it's time—and indeed, the time is almost past—to imagine and finally set ourselves to the task that needs to be done.

Epilogue

Ah, Montana, with its big rivers, big trout, log taverns, lonely cowboys, boyish fishing guides, pickup trucks, cats sleeping on pool tables, grizzly bears, straightforward sense of humor, and late snowstorms; where they watch the stream flows more closely than the stock market. As a place to drink coffee and figure out what to do next, it's better than most.

—John Geirach, 1989, *The View from Rat Lake*

November 2005

As I jog the two-track lane from the house to the county road, white-tailed deer scatter left and right, their raised tails pumping sidewise in warning to others. The lane bisects the forty acres that Diana and I settled in southwest Montana. It's a mere postage stamp on an alluvial fan that washes west from the Tobacco Root Mountains, rimming the foothills where elk suddenly materialize when snows blanket the high country. The slopes of the Ruby Mountains four miles south offer the best chance to spot elk through a spotting scope from our dining room window.

A year and a half earlier at my retirement party, someone asked me why I had decided to leave the National Elk Refuge. That was a decision I had not come to lightly, so the answer came easily. "I can't think of one more study that I can design, conduct, and publish that will make any clearer what needs to be done in Jackson Hole." What I didn't add was that I hoped in the coming years to reach a broader audience about the change needed to sustain Jackson Hole's elk and other wildlife.

From Jackson I carried fond memories of my work with colleagues, and especially of the animals: capturing and following newborn calves, herds flooding northward in spring migration, and tranquil mornings spent surrounded by the high society and conversation of the refuge's star boarders. It seems so fitting that the elk also brought Diana and me together in my last year at the refuge. As a naturalist educating the public on sleigh rides through the elk herd, she had shared my love of the animals and their environment, which in turn sparked our own love and life together.

On my return from the run, I'm treated to a pair of belted kingfishers making a late fall appearance. They zoom, first upstream then down, through low-hanging branches of willows and river birch that crowd the creek beside our little house. Their raucous croaking reminds me of the otherworldly refrain of sandhill cranes that had already abandoned nearby fields for warmer climes. The leader continues his diatribe as he and the other king of fishers disappear into naked cottonwoods. In spring this would be expected, a hard-wired courtship ritual prerequisite to mating, but on this late November day, I choose to believe the performance was staged just for me.

Back at the house, Diana tells me that friends from Jackson called about the annual Jackson Hole Wildlife Symposium where I had presented my research and participated in panel discussions at the inaugural conference in 2003. After receiving an e-mail and telephone invitation from one of the symposium's organizers, I had still not committed to attend. Now our friends had called asking us to come and to stay with them.

Two days before the December symposium, the Weather Channel advised that a major winter storm was barreling into the Rockies. I was contentedly pummeling the keyboard, composing a manuscript, when some seriously smooth talking from Diana changed that. "Won't it be fun to see all your friends in Jackson?" And, "You always enjoy hearing the new information at these conferences, don't you?" And most surprisingly, "I really don't mind helping with the driving."

Yes, I would enjoy seeing friends and colleagues, and Diana's enthusiasm sealed the deal. She seemed eager to go, in retrospect far too eager for someone who dreaded icy roads and ground blizzards. Later I learned that she was in on the plot—whatever it took—to get me to Jackson. She even pilfered my files and secretly faxed my CV to her co-conspirators.

The drive to Jackson is a tour of the GYE's westernmost vistas—an excursion through intoxicating landscapes where grizzly bears, wolves, mountain lions, and wolverines roam freely. An hour into the trip, we encounter the first snow squall in Montana's expansive Madison Valley with its ubiquitous wintering herds of pronghorn, mule deer, and elk, plus hosts of rough-legged hawks and bald and golden eagles. Diana nervously monitors the sparse traffic, as my eyes dart from the riffles and pools of the Madison River, to grazing pronghorn and elk, and occasionally to the road ahead.

"Look at that bald eagle perched above the river," I gesture to her.

"Honey, you're on the centerline."

"Okay … oh, look! There's another bunch of elk trailing up that ridge."

Diana sighs as the car settles back into the right-hand lane. I give her a winning smile to which she replies, "That was a beautiful eagle. Was he eating something?"

"Fish for brunch. No catch-and-release here."

The highway climbs gently to the top of Raynolds Pass, where the Madison and Gravelly Mountain Ranges fall away to the east and west. Beyond lies Idaho's famous Henrys Fork River and fifty miles farther loom Les Trois Tetons, those towering pillars of granite that beguiled the French fur trappers who so named them. The advancing cloudbank has not yet swallowed the snow-flocked Teton summits, as we wind through the grain fields and potato pastures south of Ashton, Idaho, into the valley the trappers dubbed Pierre's Hole. The final barrier concealing Jackson Hole is 8,400-foot Teton Pass. Highway 22 twists skyward through spruce-fir forests, across avalanche chutes, and past bowls bearing the serpentine carvings of backcountry skiers and snowboarders. Cresting the pass, the Gros Ventre and Snake River Ranges frame the Snake River's cottonwood galleries that bisect Jackson Hole. If you've never seen this piece of paradise, it's a memory to be carried to the afterlife.

From our home in the Ruby Valley, the drive to Jackson Hole during fair weather takes four hours. On this trip we outran the worst of the storm's fury and make Jackson in five hours, including a lunch break beside the Henrys Fork where trumpeter swans float like drifts of snow above the big rainbows.

On the second day of the symposium, the two hundred attendees return with their buffet-style lunches to the main auditorium. Following the luncheon speaker is a special presentation of the prestigious Craighead Wildlife Conservation Award, which had been established two years earlier. As Derek and Charlie Craighead (sons of famed conservationist brothers, John and Frank Craighead) conclude their remarks and are about to announce the 2005 recipient, I turn to my friend Tom Segerstrom. "You have the pulse of the science community. Who do you think will receive the award?"

"Maybe you," he whispers.

Tom is one of the legion of wildlife professionals and citizen conservationists inspired by the Craighead brothers. As professional field biologists who popularized their passion and achievements through written word and television, the Craigheads are among a special breed that have moved citizens to conservation engagement. As I cast Tom a curious glance, Derek Craighead announces my name through the microphone.

On the stage, listening to Derek and Charlie Craighead list my qualifications for receiving the award, I recall the 1960s *National Geographic* TV special that first introduced me to the Craigheads, and to grizzly bears and elk. Life had come full circle for me. I'd received other awards, but when I see the names Craighead and Bruce Smith on the same plaque, I am deeply moved.

Sir David Attenborough, the eminent British natural historian, has observed, "We'll only get people to care for the environment if they know something about it." With the benefit of my years of experience as a scientist and resource manager—most of those in Jackson Hole—I felt obligated to share my perspectives. Since Olaus Murie's *Elk of North America*, the story and challenges of the Jackson Hole elk, and the natural wonderland they inhabit, had not been compiled in a comprehensive writing for the general public. My purpose was to tell that story so that others might care about it too.

Beyond the rewards of my conservation work, I share with millions of others the joy of stalking wildlife with camera or gun, or with only a child's curiosity and wonder. Give me a buzzing, three-gram hummingbird or a majestic elk or a miniature tree frog, if only for a fleeting moment, or the song of a wren or howl of a coyote to heighten my spirits and forget any troubles I may have.

ACKNOWLEDGMENTS

DURING MY TWENTY-TWO YEARS AS THE NATIONAL ELK REFUGE biologist, I worked with many people, both in government and in the private sector, who shared my love and commitment to stewardship of western Wyoming's wildlife. The list is long. But among them, the following were of help in my conservation work and therefore to my inspiration to write this book.

I worked for three refuge managers: John Wilbrecht, Mike Hedrick, and Barry Reiswig. Although we did not always agree on policy matters, each provided me the freedom to pursue my varied research endeavors. Without their forbearance, my time at the NER would have been far less scientifically productive and stimulating. The NER was supervised by the USFWS Regional Office in Denver. Three individuals there were reliable sources of support: Wayne King, Ralph Morgenweck, and Barney Schranck. Among my refuge coworkers, Eric Cole, Marjean Heisler, and Roxane Rogers were stalwart conservation partners, ready to do what was needed to carry out the wide-ranging duties of field biologists.

With many other federal and state resource specialists I conducted resource inventories, carried out management programs, and debated how best to sustain the public's resources. Among them, Steve Cain, Steve Kilpatrick, Bob Schiller, Tom Toman, and Bob Woods stand out as exemplary professionals and friends whose efforts contributed also to my motivation to share the stories, issues, and conservation imperatives I've raised here. The imprint of many citizen conservationists can also be found in this book. For fear of overlooking the names of a very long list of individuals, let me just say they include many members and staff of the Jackson Hole Conservation Alliance, Greater Yellowstone Coalition, Wyoming Wildlife Federation, and Jackson Hole Wildlife Foundation.

During some 2,500 hours of fixed-wing flights and another 600 hours of helicopter missions, I was safely and professionally piloted by Ray Austin, Jerry Ewen, Merlin Hare, Bob Hawkins, Dan Hawkins, Gary Lust, Paul Matero, John Moberly, and Fred Reed. My efforts were dependent on their skills and shared commitment to the work.

A number of people provided data and discussions about the book's topics. Chiefly among them I thank Doug Brimeyer, Steve Cain, Eric

Cole, Lloyd Dorsey, Harry Harju, and Meredith and Tory Taylor. For reviewing some or all of the draft chapters I thank Ed Bangs, Don Burgess, Steve Cain, Franz Camenzind, Eric Cole, Lynn Creekmore, Peyton Curlee, Deborah Donahue, Mike Miller, Tom Roffe, Carol Statkus, and Margaret Wild. Their comments and discussions of the material strengthened the final product.

My publisher, Lyons/Globe Pequot Press, brought to life this story of the Jackson elk. For that I thank my editors, Erin Turner and Kristen Mellitt.

When I wondered if what spilled onto paper would ever see the light of day, my wife Diana was always willing to endure reading another draft of another chapter. For that and your patience, I thank you, my dear.

Finally, there are few places in the world's temperate climatic zone with the dazzling diversity and abundance of wildlife found in and around Jackson Hole. It is a special place with breathtaking landscapes filled with all the extant Holocene species of large mammals. Because few places like this remain, safeguarding this ecosystem is all the more important. As a model for resource conservation and as a sacred trust to future generations, we owe the elk and other animals our best efforts to pursue science-guided sustainable management.

Appendix A:
Elk and Bison Numbers and Elk Harvests

Year	Elk on or adjacent the NER			Total Elk in the Jackson Herd		Elk Harvest [d]	Bison on the NER [e]
	On feed	Off feed [a]	Total	Number Counted	Population Estimate		
1912			7,250				
1913			4,000				
1914			6,150				
1915 [b]							
1916			8,000				
1917			6,000				
1918			10,000				
1919			3,000				
1920			8,000				
1921			3,500				
1922			4,300				
1923			3,400				
1924			4,800				
1925			5,500				
1926 [b]							
1927	5,521	1,104	6,625				
1928			7,500				
1929			6,000				
1930			7,000				
1931 [b]	3,110		3,110				
1932	6,873	1,527	8,400				
1933			7,460				

Year	Elk on or adjacent the NER			Total Elk in the Jackson Herd		Elk Harvest [d]	Bison on the NER [e]
	On feed	Off feed [a]	Total	Number Counted	Population Estimate		
1934 [b]							
1935	8,961	539	9,500				
1936	4,083	117	4,200				
1937			4,000				
1938	6,655		6,655				
1939	7,637		7,637				
1940 [b]			9,500				
1941	10,324	676	11,000				
1942	9,841	1,344	11,185				
1943	9,779	1,921	11,700				
1944 [b]							
1945	5,226	1,217	6,443				
1946	6,241	1,759	8,000				
1947			7,000				
1948 [b]			6,750				
1949	8,059	1,364	9,423				
1950	8,700	1,000	9,700			3,638	
1951	9,500		9,500			4,810	
1952	7,351	1,196	8,547			2,108	
1953	9,000	200	9,200			2,823	
1954	8,115	1,415	9,530			2,594	
1955			8,000			3,207	
1956	11,612		11,612			3,106	
1957	6,800	1,200	8,000			2,252	
1958	5,695	1,305	7,000			3,057	

Year	Elk on or adjacent the NER			Total Elk in the Jackson Herd		Elk Harvest [d]	Bison on the NER [e]
	On feed	Off feed [a]	Total	Number Counted	Population Estimate		
1959	6,047	496	6,543			1,542	
1960	4,746	1,030	5,776			2,074	
1961	5,591	1,114	6,705			2,639	
1962	7,666	556	8,222			1,320	
1963	5,827					2,996	
1964	7,916					2,975	
1965	7,946					3,250	
1966	6,556					3,226	
1967	7,369	296	7,665			2,974	
1968	6,659	150	6,809			3,090	
1969	9,205		9,205			3,444	
1970	8,421	775	9,196			5,680	
1971	8,054	823	8,877			4,245	
1972	7,615	835	8,450			4,086	
1973	7,194	286	7,480			4,684	
1974	7,878	678	8,556			2,774	
1975	7,450		7,450			3,526	
1976	7,858	515	8,373			1,429	15
1977 [b]		5,732	5,732			3,756	0
1978	8,495	396	8,891			2,880	35
1979	7,958	594	8,552			3,321	33
1980	7,774	206	7,980	11245		3,748	37
1981 [b]		6,300	6,300		14,000	4,248	38
1982	6,746	489	7,235	10851	11,350	3,548	49
1983	5,923	346	6,269	8396	9,600	2,355	55

Year	Elk on or adjacent the NER			Total Elk in the Jackson Herd		Elk Harvest [d]	Bison on the NER [e]
	On feed	Off feed [a]	Total	Number Counted	Population Estimate		
1984	5,055	311	5,366	7,665	8,000	1,561	63
1985	5,758	408	6,166	8,500	9,300	1,368	75
1986	6,430	296	6,726	9,593	10,180	1,254	87
1987	7,820	528	8,348	11,276	11,800	1,657	107
1988	7,753	1,106	8,859	12,497	13,000	2,756	116
1989	9,486	604	10,090	14,919	16,500	3,778	119
1990	8,131	1,251	9,382	13,991	15,212	3,401	122
1991	8,314	1,155	9,239	12,906	13,550	4,016	137
1992	8,800	1,069	9,869	13,457	14,400	3,492	149
1993	8,295	1,634	9,929	14,220	15,300	2,648	171
1994	8,500	1,715	10,215	15,248	16,523	4,322	186
1995	9,436	855	10,291	14,986	17,600	3,079	212
1996	10,004	385	10,389	14,721	18,000	3,029	255
1997	10,736	1,232	11,968	16,236	18,825	3,290	321
1998	8,494	1,015	9,509	13,359	16,463	3,159	377
1999	7,300	1,151	8451	13,060	14,970	2,375	438
2000 [c]	5,054	2,526	7,580	12,621	14,178	2,350	489
2001	6,128	1,396	7,524	12,584	14,277	2,485	552
2002	6,366	1,199	7,565	12,132	13,318	2,253	627
2003	6,992	1,519	8,511	12,960	13,457	2,498	670
2004	5,876	1,032	6,908	12,095	13,730	1,818	716
2005	4,969	2,392	7,361	10,858	12,610	1,776	696
2006	6,730	609	7,339	11,853	12,855	1,806	919
2007	7,279	735	8,014	11,786	12,777	1,833	974
2008	7,947	960	8,907	12,370	12,582	1,464	920

Year	Elk on or adjacent the NER			Total Elk in the Jackson Herd		Elk Harvest [d]	Bison on the NER [e]
	On feed	Off feed [a]	Total	Number Counted	Population Estimate		
2009	7,269	655	7,924	10,794	12,881	1,486	806
2010 [c]	4,348	1,093	5,441	9,136	11,691	1,412	762
2011	7,746	313	8,059	11,503	11,978		833
Average	7,402	1,090	7,726	12,188	13,567	2,589	338

[a] Numbers of elk counted from aircraft that were on the NER away from feedgrounds or on national forest lands immediately adjacent the NER to the east. These elk were not counted many years, especially prior to 1970. Animals off-feed were counted from fixed-wing aircraft before 1987 and from helicopter thereafter.

[b] Years in which there was no feeding.

[c] Elk were widely dispersed and counted before feeding began, due to mild winter conditions.

[d] Elk harvest the fall following each winter count.

[e] Does not include Jackson bison that winter beyond the refuge.

Appendix B:
Elk Hunting Seasons, 1978–1986

Hunting season dates and permit levels for elk hunting on the National Elk Refuge (one hunting unit), Grand Teton National Park (three units combined), and Bridger-Teton National Forest (eight units combined) during 1978 to 1986. After 1986, hunting seasons gradually lengthened into December most years; after 2006, hunting seasons generally ended during November and permit levels declined.

Year	NER		GTNP		BTNF	
	Season Dates	Total Permits	Season Dates	Total Permits	Season Dates [1]	Total Permits [2]
1978	28 Oct–8 Dec	639	28 Oct–3 Dec	2,923	10 Sep–31 Dec	
1979	20 Oct–9 Dec	1,024	27 Oct–9 Dec	3,254	10 Sep–31 Dec	
1980	25 Oct–7 Dec	1,549	25 Oct–7 Dec	4,387	10 Sep–31 Dec	
1981	31 Oct–6 Dec	1,126	31 Oct–6 Dec	4,213	10 Sep–31Dec	
1982	30 Oct–5 Dec	1,031	30 Oct–5 Dec	6,012	10 Sep–31 Dec	
1983	29 Oct–30 Nov	767	29 Oct–30 Nov	3,137	10 Sep–30 Nov	
1984	27 Oct–16 Nov	360	27 Oct–11 Nov	2,550	10 Sep–11 Nov	
1985	26 Oct–15 Nov	360	26 Oct–15 Nov	1,750	10 Sep–31 Oct	
1986	25 Oct–14 Nov	360	25 Oct–14 Nov	2,250	10 Sep–14 Nov	

[1] Varies by hunting unit; dates shown represent the maximum
[2] Permit numbers were not limited for Wyoming residents, although after 1983 the number of permits to harvest antlerless elk declined

References

Chapter 1: Mad Elk

[1] Cowley, G. 2001. "Cannibals to cows: The path of a deadly disease." *Newsweek*, March 12.

[2] Samuel, M. D., D. O. Joly, M. A. Wild, S. D. Wright, D. L. Otis, R. W. Werge, and M. W. Miller. 2003. *Surveillance Strategies for Detecting Chronic Wasting Disease in Free-Ranging Deer and Elk: Results of a CWD Surveillance Workshop, December 10–12, 2002.* Madison, WI: USGS–National Wildlife Health Center.

[3] Smith, B. L. 2005. *Disease and Winter Feeding of Elk and Bison: A Review and Recommendations Pertinent to the Jackson Bison and Elk Management Plan and Environmental Impact Statement.* Report to the Greater Yellowstone Coalition. www.greateryellowstonecoalition.org/media/.

Chapter 2: A New Land

[1] Smith, B. L. 2010. *Wildlife on the Wind: A Field Biologist's Journey and an Indian Reservation's Renewal.* Logan, UT: Utah State University Press.

[2] Geist, V. 1998. *Deer of the World: Their Evolution, Behavior, and Ecology.* Mechanicsburg, PA: Stackpole Books.

[3] O'Gara, B. W., and R. G. Dundas. 2002. "Distribution: Past and present." In *North American Elk: Ecology and Management,* ed. D. E. Toweill and J. W. Thomas, 67–120. Washington, DC: Smithsonian Institution Press.

[4] Guthrie, R. D. 1966. "The extinct wapiti of Alaska and the Yukon Territory." *Canadian Journal of Zoology* 44(1):47–57.

[5] Geist, V., and M. H. Francis. 1991. *Elk Country.* Minoqua, Minnesota: Northwood Press.

[6] Faunmap Working Group. 1994. *FAUNMAP—A Database Documenting Late Quarternary Distributions of Mammal Species in the United States.* Illinois State Museum of Science Paper 25, volumes 1 and 2.

[7] Baker, R. 1985. *The American Hunting Myth.* New York, NY: Vantage Press.

[8] Hornaday, W. T. 1931. *Thirty Years War for Wildlife.* New York, NY: Charles Scribner's Sons.

[9] Trefethen, J. B. 1961. *Crusade for Wildlife: Highlights in Conservation Progress.* Harrisburg, PA: Stackpole Books, and New York, NY: Boone and Crockett Club.

[10] Morrison, J. C., W. Sechrest, E. Dinerstein, D. S. Wilcove, and J. F. Lamoreux. 2007. "Persistence of large mammal faunas as indicators of global human impacts." *Journal of Mammalogy* 88:1363–80.

[11] Seton, E. T. 1927. *Lives of Game Animals*. Volume 3, part 1. Garden City, NY: Doubleday, Page, and Company.

[12] Brown, R. C. 1947. "The Jackson Hole elk herd, its history, range, and management." *Wyoming Wildlife* 11(12):4–11, 29–32.

[13] Cromley, C. M. 2000. "Historic elk migrations around Jackson Hole, Wyoming." In *Developing Sustainable Management Policy for the National Elk Refuge, Wyoming*, ed. T. W. Clark, D. Casey, and A. Halverson, 53–65. Yale School of Forestry and Environmental Studies Bulletin 104. New Haven, CT.

[14] Allred, W. J. 1950. "Re-establishment of seasonal elk migration through transplanting." *Transactions of the North American Wildlife Conference* 15:597–611.

[15] Casebeer, R. L. 1961. "Habitat of the Jackson Hole elk as part of multiple resource planning, management, and use." *Transactions of the North American Wildlife Conference* 26:436–37.

[16] Craighead, J. J. 1952. *A Biological and Economic Appraisal of the Jackson Hole Elk Herd*. New York, NY: New York Zoological Society and Conservation Foundation.

[17] Anderson, C. C. 1958. *The Elk of Jackson Hole: A Review of Jackson Hole Elk Studies*. Wyoming Game and Fish Commission Bulletin 10. Cheyenne, WY.

[18] Fishbein, S. L., and R. Gehman. 1989. *Yellowstone Country: The Enduring Wonder*. Washington, DC: National Geographic Society.

[19] Preble, E. A. 1911. *Report on Conditions of Elk in Jackson Hole, Wyoming*. USDA Biological Survey Bulletin 40. Washington, DC: U.S. Government Printing Office.

[20] Sheldon, C. 1927. *The Conservation of the Elk of Jackson Hole, Wyoming. A Report to the Chairman of the President's Committee on Outdoor Recreation and to the Governor of Wyoming*. Washington, DC.

[21] Smith, B. L. 2001. "Winter feeding of elk in western North America." *Journal of Wildlife Management* 65:173–90.

[22] Robbins, R. L., D. E. Redfearn, and C. P. Stone. 1982. "Refuges and elk management." In *Elk of North America: Ecology and Management,* ed. J. W. Thomas and D. E. Toweill, 479–507. Harrisburg, PA: Stackpole Books.

[23] Murie, O. J. 1951. *The Elk of North America*. Harrisburg, PA: Stackpole Books.

Chapter 3: Trials and Telemetry

1. Oldemeyer, J. L., R. L. Robbins, and B. L. Smith. 1993. "Effect of feeding level on elk weights and reproductive success at the National Elk Refuge." In *Western States and Provinces Elk Workshop*, ed. R. Callas, D. Koch, and E. Loft, 64–68. Eureka, CA: California Fish and Game Department.

2. Smith, B. L., E. C. Cole, and D. S. Dobkin. 2004. *Imperfect Pasture: A Century of Change at the National Elk Refuge, Jackson Hole, Wyoming*. Moose, WY: Grand Teton Natural History Association.

3. Smith, B. L., and R. L. Robbins. 1984. *Pelleted Alfalfa as Supplemental Winter Feed for Elk at the National Elk Refuge*. Jackson, WY: U.S. Fish and Wildlife Service, National Elk Refuge.

4. Smith, B. L. 2001. "Winter feeding of elk in western North America." *Journal of Wildlife Management* 65:173–90.

5. Nelson, A. P., and O. J. Murie. 1941. *Report on Carrying Capacity of the National Elk Refuge*. Jackson, WY: Unpublished report in National Elk Refuge files.

6. Murie, O. J. 1944. "Our big game in winter." *Transactions of the North American Wildlife Conference* 9:173–76.

7. ———. 1945. "Jackson Hole National Monument and the elk." *National Parks Magazine* 83:13–17.

8. Cole, G. F. 1969. *The Elk of Grand Teton and Southern Yellowstone National Parks*. National Park Service Research Report GRTE-N-1. Washington, DC.

9. Anderson, C. C. 1958. *The Elk of Jackson Hole: A Review of Jackson Hole Elk Studies*. Wyoming Game and Fish Commission Bulletin 10. Cheyenne, WY.

10. Murie, O. J. 1951. *The Elk of North America*. Harrisburg, PA: Stackpole Books.

11. Graetz, R., and A. B. Guthrie, Jr. 1989. *Montana! A Photographic Celebration*. Volume 2. Helena, MT: Rick Graetz Publishing.

12. Smith, B. L., and R. L. Robbins. 1994. *Migrations and Management of the Jackson Elk Herd*. U.S. National Biological Survey Resource Paper No. 199. Washington, DC.

Chapter 4: Wapiti Welfare

1. Smith, B. L., R. L. Robbins, and S. H. Anderson. 1997. "Early development of supplementally fed, free-ranging elk." *Journal of Wildlife Management* 61:27–39.

2. USDI. 2007. Final Bison and Elk Management Plan and Environmental Impact Statement. National Elk Refuge and Grand Teton National Park, Denver, CO. http://www.fws.gov/bisonandelkplan/index.html.

[3] Smith, B. L. 2001. "Winter feeding of elk in western North America." *Journal of Wildlife Management* 65:173–90.

[4] Duda, M. D., and K. C. Young. 1994. *Idaho Residents' Opinions and Attitudes Toward the Idaho Department of Fish and Game.* Unpublished report. Harrisonburg, VA: Responsive Management.

[5] Fraser, C. 2010. *Dewilding the World: Dispatches from the Conservation Revolution.* New York, NY: Picador.

[6] McKibben, B. 1989. *The End of Nature.* New York, NY: Random House.

[7] Leopold, A. 1970. *A Sand County Almanac: With Essays on Conservation from Round River.* San Francisco, CA: Sierra Club/Ballantine.

[8] Organ, J., and S. Mahoney. 2007. "The future of the public trust." *Wildlife Professional* 1(2):18–22.

[9] Smith, B. L., and T. J. Roffe. 1994. "Diseases among elk of the Yellowstone Ecosystem, U.S.A." In *Third International Wildlife Ranching Symposium,* ed. W. van Hoven, J. Ebedes, and A. Conroy, 162–66. Pretoria, South Africa: Centre for Wildlife Management, University of Pretoria Press.

[10] Geist, V. 1985. "Game ranching: Threat to wildlife conservation in North America." *Wildlife Society Bulletin* 13:594–98.

[11] Lanka, R. P., E. T. Thorne, and R. J. Guenzel. 1992. "Game farms, wild ungulates and disease in western North America." *Western Wildlands* 18(1):2–7.

[12] The Wildlife Society. http://joomla.wildlife.org.

[13] Rocky Mountain Elk Foundation. www.rmef.org.

[14] Peek, J. M., K. T. Schmidt, M. J. Dorrance, and B. L. Smith. 2002. "Supplemental feeding and farming elk." In *North American Elk: Ecology and Management,* ed. D. E. Toweill and J. W. Thomas, 617–48. Washington, DC: Smithsonian Institution Press.

Chapter 5: When Elk Die

[1] Samuel, W. M., D. A. Welch, and B. L. Smith. 1991. "Ectoparasites from elk (*Cervus elaphus nelsoni*) from Wyoming." *Journal of Wildlife Diseases* 27:446–51.

[2] Smith, B. L. 1997. "Antler size and winter mortality of elk: effects of environment, birth year, and parasites." *Journal of Mammalogy* 79:1038–44.

[3] Clutton-Brock, T. H., S. D. Albon, and F. E. Guinness. 1988. "Reproductive success in male and female red deer." In *Reproductive Success,* ed. T. H. Clutton-Brock, 325–43. Chicago, IL: University of Chicago Press.

[4] ———, F. E. Guinness, and S. D. Albon. 1982. *Red Deer: Behavior and Ecology of Two Sexes.* Chicago, IL: University of Chicago Press.

[5] Smith, B. L. 1985. "Scabies and elk mortalities on the National Elk Refuge, Wyoming." In *Proceedings of the Western States and Provinces Elk Workshop,* ed. R.W. Nelson, 180–94. Edmonton, Alberta: Alberta Fish and Wildlife Division.

[6] ———, and T. J. Roffe. 1994. "Diseases among elk of the Yellowstone Ecosystem, U.S.A." In *Third International Wildlife Ranching Symposium,* ed. W. van Hoven, J. Ebedes, and A. Conroy, 162–66. Pretoria, South Africa: Centre for Wildlife Management, University of Pretoria Press.

[7] Peterson, M. J. 2003. *Infectious Agents of Concern for the Jackson Hole Elk and Bison Herds: An Ecological Perspective.* College Station, TX: Department of Wildlife and Fisheries Sciences, Texas A&M University.

[8] Smith, B. L. 2001. "Winter feeding of elk in western North America." *Journal of Wildlife Management* 65:173–90.

[9] "Winter took heavy elk toll." 1984. Lander, WY: *Wyoming State Journal,* May 7.

[10] Smith, B. L. 1998. "Juvenile survival and population regulation of the Jackson elk herd." *Journal of Wildlife Management* 62:1036–45.

Chapter 6: Disease Disputes

[1] Murie, O. J. 1951. *The Elk of North America.* Harrisburg, PA: Stackpole Books.

[2] Oldemeyer, J. L., R. L. Robbins, and B. L. Smith. 1993. "Effect of feeding level on elk weights and reproductive success at the National Elk Refuge." In *Western States and Provinces Elk Workshop,* ed. R. Callas, D. Koch, and E. Loft, 64–68. Eureka, CA: California Fish and Game Department.

[3] Thorne, E. T., and J. D. Herriges. 1992. "Brucellosis, wildlife and conflicts in the Greater Yellowstone Ecosystem." *Transactions of the North American Wildlife and Natural Resources Conference* 57:453–65.

[4] Frye, G. H., and R. R. Hillman. 1997. "National cooperative brucellosis eradication program." In *Brucellosis, Bison, Elk, and Cattle in the Greater Yellowstone Area: Defining the Problem, Exploring Solutions,* ed. E. T. Thorne, M. S. Boyce, P. Nicoletti, and T. J. Kreeger, 79–85. Cheyenne, WY: Wyoming Game and Fish Department.

[5] Nicoletti, P., and M. J. Gilsdorf. 1997. "Brucellosis—the disease in cattle." In *Brucellosis, Bison, Elk, and Cattle in the Greater Yellowstone Area: Defining the Problem, Exploring Solutions,* ed. E. T. Thorne, M. S. Boyce, P. Nicoletti, and T. J. Kreeger, 3–6. Cheyenne, WY: Wyoming Game and Fish Department.

[6] Animal and Plant Health Inspection Service. 2008. www.aphis.usda.gov/ animal_health/animal_diseases/brucellosis.

[7] Smith, B. L. 2001. "Winter feeding of elk in western North America." *Journal of Wildlife Management* 65:173–90.

[8] Thorne, E. T. 2001. "Brucellosis." In *Infectious Diseases of Wild Animals*, ed. E. S. Williams and I. K. Barker, 372–95. Ames, IA: Iowa State Press.

[9] Davis, D. S. 1990. "Recent advances on brucellosis in wildlife populations." In *Proceedings of the Student American Veterinary Medical Association Annual Meeting* 194–99. College Station, TX: Texas A&M University.

[10] Williams, E. S., E. T. Thorne, S. L. Anderson, and J. D. Herriges. 1993. "Brucellosis in free-ranging bison (*Bison bison*) from Teton County, Wyoming." *Journal of Wildlife Diseases* 29:118–22.

[11] Thorne, E. T., E. S. Williams, W. M. Samuel, and T. P. Kistner. 2002. "Diseases and parasites." In *North American Elk: Ecology and Management*, ed. D. E. Toweill and J. W. Thomas, 351–88. Washington, DC: Smithsonian Institution Press.

[12] Lubow, B. C., and B. L., Smith. 2004. "Population dynamics of the Jackson elk herd." *Journal of Wildlife Management* 68:810–29.

[13] Smith, B. L. and T. J. Roffe. 1997. *Evaluation of Studies of Strain 19 Brucella Abortus Vaccine in Elk: Clinical Trials and Field Applications*. Final report. Jackson, WY: National Elk Refuge, U.S. Fish and Wildlife Service.

[14] Roffe, T. J., L. C. Jones, K. Coffin, M. L. Drew, S. J. Sweeney, S. D. Hagius, P. H. Elzer, and D. Davis. 2004. "Efficacy of single calfhood vaccination of elk with *Brucella abortus* Strain 19." *Journal of Wildlife Management* 68(4):828–34.

[15] Keiter, R. B., and P. H. Froelicher. 1993. "Bison, brucellosis, and law in the Greater Yellowstone Ecosystem." *Land and Water Law Review* 28:1–75.

[16] Greater Yellowstone Interagency Brucellosis Committee. 1994. *General Position Statement on Winter Feeding of Elk and Other Wild Ungulates*. www.gyibc.com.

[17] Drew, M., R. Greer, K. Ragotzkie, B. Compton, and K. Eyre. 2001. *Brucellosis Task Force: State of Idaho Brucellosis Management Program Report of Progress to the Governor of Idaho*. Unpublished report. Boise, ID: Idaho Fish and Game Department.

[18] Garton, E. O. 1998. *Review: State of Wyoming's Strain 19 Brucellosis Vaccination Work on Elk*. Moscow, ID: University of Idaho.

[19] Brimmer, C. A. 1999. *State of Wyoming versus USA*. Number 98-CV-037B, District Court of Wyoming, Cheyenne.

[20] U.S. Fish and Wildlife Service. 1997. *National Wildlife Refuge System Improvement Act*. Public Law 105-57. Washington, DC.

[21] Prevost, R. 2009. "Few good options against brucellosis." Billings, MT: *Billings Gazette*, May 13.

Chapter 7: Train Wreck

[1] Smith, B. L. 2005. *Disease and Winter Feeding of Elk and Bison: A Review and Recommendations Pertinent to the Jackson Bison and Elk Management Plan and Environmental Impact Statement.* Report to the Greater Yellowstone Coalition. www.greateryellowstonecoalition.org/media/.

[2] Peterson, M. J. 2005. *Chronic Wasting Disease and the Greater Yellowstone Area.* Report to the Greater Yellowstone Coalition. www.greateryellowstonecoalition .org/media/.

[3] U.S. Fish and Wildlife Service and National Park Service. 2005. *Draft Bison and Elk Management Plan and Environmental Impact Statement* (final plan published in 2007). http://www.fws.gov/bisonandelkplan.

[4] Michigan Department of Natural Resources. 2009. www.michigan.gov/dnr.

[5] Herring, H. 2002. "Game farms trucking in CWD." *Denver Post.* June 2.

[6] Peters, J. J., M. Miller, A. L. Jenny, T. L. Peterson, and K. P. Carmichael. 2000. "Immunohistochemical diagnosis of chronic wasting disease in preclinically affected elk from a captive herd." *Journal of Veterinary Diagnostic Investigation* 12:579–82.

[7] Pritchard, R. S. Welch, L. Creekmore, R. Morales, D. Goeldner, and T. Gidlewski. 2005. Chronic wasting disease in farmed/captive cervids. Poster session, Second International Chronic Wasting Disease Symposium. Madison, WI.

[8] Canadian Wildlife Federation, 2002. Policy Resolution 361.01.632. www.cwf-fcf.org/en/learn/issues/isssues-of-concern/game-farming.html.

[9] Argue, C. K., C. Ribble, V. W. Lees, J. McLane, A. Balachandran. 2007. "Epidemiology of an outbreak of chronic wasting disease on elk farms in Saskatchewan." *Canada Veterinary Journal* 48:1241–48.

[10] Tamgüney, G., M. W. Miller, L. L. Wolfe, T. M. Sirochman, D. V. Glidden, C. Palmer, A. Lemus, S. J. DeArmond, and S. B. Prusiner. 2009. "Asymptomatic deer excrete infectious prions in faeces." *Nature* 461:529–32.

[11] Mathiason, C. K., J. G. Powers, S. J. Dahmes, D. A. Osborn, K. V. Miller, R. J. Warren, G. L. Mason, S. A. Hays, J. Hayes-Klug, D. M. Seelig, M. A. Wild, L. L. Wolfe, T. R. Spraker, M. W. Miller, C. J. Sigurdson, G. C. Telling, E. A. Hoover. 2006. "Infectious prions in the saliva and blood of deer with chronic wasting disease." *Science* 314:133–36.

[12] Walter, W. D, D. P. Walsh, M. L. Farnsworth, D. L. Winkelman, and M. W. Miller. 2011. "Soil clay content underlies prion infection odds." *Nature Communications* 2:200.

[13] Haley, N. J., D. M. Seelig, M. D. Zabel, G. C. Telling, and E. A. Hoover. 2009. "Detection of CWD prions in urine and saliva of deer by transgenic mouse bioassay." *PLoS ONE* 4(3):e4848.

[14] Angers, R. C., S. R. Browning, T. S. Seward, C. J. Sigurdson, M. W. Miller, E. A. Hoover, and G. C. Telling. 2006. "Prions in skeletal muscles of deer with chronic wasting disease." *Science* 311(5764):1,117.

[15] Mathiason, C. K., S. A. Hays, J. Powers, J. Hayes-Klug, J. Langenberg, S. J. Dahmes, D. A. Osborn, K. V. Miller, R. J. Warren, G. L. Mason, and E. A. Hoover. 2009. "Infectious prions in pre-clinical deer and transmission of chronic wasting disease solely by environmental exposure." *PLoS ONE* 4(6):e5916. doi:10.1371/journal.pone.0005916.

[16] Georgsson, G., S. Sigurdarson, and P. Brown. 2006. "Infectious agent of sheep scrapie may persist in the environment for at least 16 years." *Journal of General Virology* 87:3,737–40.

[17] Davis, M. 2006. *The Monster at Our Door: The Global Threat of Avian Flu.* New York, NY: Henry Holt and Company.

[18] McNeill, W. 1989. "Control and catastrophe in human affairs." *Daedalus* 118(1):1–12.

[19] Clifton-Hadley, R. S., C. M. Sauter-Louis, I. W. Lugton, R. Jackson, P. A. Durr, and J. W. Wilesmith. 2001. "Mycobacterial diseases." In *Infectious Diseases of Wild Animals*, ed. E. S. Williams and I. K. Barker, 340–71. Ames, IA: Iowa State University Press.

[20] Miller, M. W., and E. T. Thorne. 1993. "Captive cervids as potential sources of disease for North America's wild cervid populations: avenues, implications, and preventive management." *Transactions of the North American Wildlife and Natural Resources Conference* 58:460–67.

[21] Wild, M. 2011. Personal communication. Preliminary results for research on live chronic wasting disease test for elk in Rocky Mountain National Park. http://www.nps.gov/romo/parknews/pr_cwd_elk_research.htm.

[22] Wyoming Game and Fish Department. 2005. *Wyoming Game and Fish Department Chronic Wasting Disease Management Plan.* Cheyenne, WY: http://gf.state.wy.us/downloads/pdf/cwdmgplansignedbycommission2-06 .pdf.

[23] Cook, W., S. Smith, and J. Logan. 2000. "Feeding wildlife: a recipe for disaster." *Wyoming Wildlife News* 9(5):10, 15.

[24] Williams E. S., and M. W. Miller 2002. "Chronic wasting disease in deer and elk in North America." *Revue Scientifique et Technique* 21(2):305–16.

[25] Miller, M. W., N. T. Hobbs, and S. J. Tavener. 2006. "Dynamics of prion disease transmission in mule deer." *Ecological Applications* 16(6):2208–14.

[26] Hatch, C. 2009. "Feces on feedgrounds could spread wasting disease." *Jackson Hole News and Guide*, September 16.

[27] Thompson, A. K., M. D. Samuel, and T. R. Van Deelen. 2008. "Alternative feeding strategies and potential disease transmission in Wisconsin white-tailed deer." *Journal of Wildlife Management* 72(2):416–21.

[28] Patrek, V. E. 2009. *The Effects of Supplemental Feeding on Stress Hormone Concentrations in Elk*. M.S. Thesis, Bozeman, MT: Montana State University.

[29] Sapolsky, R. M. 2002. "Endocrinology of the stress-response." In *Behavioral Endocrinology*, ed. J. Becker, S. M. Breedlove, D. Crews, and M. M. McCarthy, 409–50. Cambridge, MA: The MIT Press.

[30] Samuel, M. D., D. O. Joly, M. A. Wild, S. D. Wright, D. L. Otis, R. W. Werge, and M. W. Miller. 2003. *Surveillance Strategies for Detecting Chronic Wasting Disease in Free-Ranging Deer and Elk: Results of a CWD Surveillance Workshop*. Madison, WI: USGS–National Wildlife Health Center. www.nwhc.usgs.gov/research/chronic_wasting/CWD_Surveillance_Strateies.pdf.

[31] Miller, M. W., H. M. Swanson, L. L. Wolfe, F. G. Quarterone, S. L. Huwre, C. H. Southwick, and P. M. Lukacs. 2008. "Lions and prions and deer demise." *PLoS ONE* 3(12):1–7.

[32] Wild, M. A., N. T. Hobbs, M. S. Graham, and M. W. Miller. 2011. "The role of predation in disease control: A comparison of selective and nonselective removal of prion diseases in deer." *Journal of Wildlife Diseases* 47(1):78–93.

[33] Cook, W. E., E. S. Williams, and S. A. Dubay. 2004. "Disappearance of bovine fetuses in northwestern Wyoming." *Wildlife Society Bulletin* 32(1):254–59.

[34] McKibben, B. 1989. *The End of Nature*. New York, NY: Random House.

[35] Royster, W. 2005. "How big is the threat?" *Casper Star Tribune*, December 19.

Chapter 8: The Right Questions

[1] Boyce, M. S. 1989. *The Jackson Elk Herd: Intensive Wildlife Management in North America*. Cambridge, U.K.: Cambridge University Press.

[2] Smith, B. L., and R. L. Robbins. 1994. *Migrations and Management of the Jackson Elk Herd*. Washington, DC: U.S. National Biological Survey Resource Paper No. 199.

[3] Livesey, K. B. 1990. "Toward the reduction of marking-induced abandonment of newborn ungulates." *Wildlife Society Bulletin* 18:193–203.

[4] Malthus, T. 1999. *An Essay on the Principle of Population*. New York, NY: Oxford University Press.

[5] Darwin, C. 1859. *On the Origin of Species by Means of Natural Selection*. London, U.K.: John Murray Publishers.

6   Darwin, C. 1871. *The Descent of Man and Selection in Relation to Sex*. London, U.K.: John Murray Publishers.

Chapter 9: Who Lives, Who Dies

1   Smith, B. L., and R. L. Robbins. 1994. *Migrations and Management of the Jackson Elk Herd*. Washington, DC: U.S. National Biological Survey Resource Paper No. 199.

2   ——, and S. H. Anderson. 1996. "Patterns of neonatal mortality of elk in northwest Wyoming." *Canadian Journal of Zoology* 74:1229–37.

3   Schlegel, M. 1976. "Factors affecting calf elk survival in northcentral Idaho—a progress report." *Western Association of State Game and Fish Commissioners* 56:342–55.

4   Singer, F. J., A. T. Harting, and K. K. Symonds. 1997. "Density-dependence, compensation, and environmental effects on elk calf mortality in Yellowstone National Park." *Journal of Wildlife Management* 61:12–25.

5   Schwartz, C. C., M. A. Haroldson, K. A. Gunther, and D. Moody. 2003. "Distribution of grizzly bears in the Greater Yellowstone Ecosystem, 1990–2000." *Ursus* 13:203–12.

6   Anderson, C. R., M. A. Ternet, and D. S. Moody. 2002. "Grizzly bear–cattle interactions on two grazing allotments in northwest Wyoming." *Ursus* 13:247–56.

7   Huntington, R. 2003. "Waltons cease grazing Togwotee Pass." *Jackson Hole News and Guide*, August 6.

8   Grand Teton National Park. 2005. *Biological Assessment, Threatened and Endangered Species for Reissuance of Grazing Permits in Grand Teton National Park*. Unpublished report. Grand Teton National Park, Moose, WY.

9   Smith, B. L., E. S. Williams, K. C. McFarland, T. L. McDonald, G. Wang, and T. D. Moore. 2006. *Neonatal Mortality of Elk in Wyoming: Environmental, Population, and Predator Effects*. Washington, DC: U.S. Fish and Wildlife Service Biological Technical Publication BTP-R6007-2006.

10 Lubow, B. C., and B. L. Smith. 2004. "Population dynamics of the Jackson elk herd." *Journal of Wildlife Management* 68:810–27.

11 Smith, B. L., R. L. Robbins, and S. H. Anderson. 1997. "Early development of supplementally fed, free-ranging elk." *Journal of Wildlife Management* 61:27–39.

12 Merrill, E. H., M. K. Bramble-Brodaho, R. W. Marrs, and M. S. Boyce. 1993. "Estimation of green herbaceous phytomass from Landsat MSS data in Yellowstone National Park." *Journal of Range Management* 46:151–57.

[13] Robbins, C. T., C. C. Schwartz, K. A. Gunther, and C. Servheen. 2006. "Grizzly bear nutrition and ecology studies in Yellowstone National Park." *Yellowstone Science* 14(3):19–26.

[14] Souvigney, J-M., K. Lackey, and S. C. Torbit. 1997. "Concerns about wildlife and brucellosis in the Greater Yellowstone Area: A conservation perspective." In *Brucellosis, Bison, Elk, and Cattle in the Greater Yellowstone Area: Defining the Problem, Exploring Solutions,* ed. E. T. Thorne, M. S. Boyce, P. Nicoletti, and T. J. Kreeger, 161–68. Cheyenne, WY: Pioneer Printing.

[15] Kunkel, K. E., and L. D. Mech. 1994. "Wolf and bear predation on white-tailed deer fawns in northeastern Minnesota." *Canadian Journal of Zoology* 72:1,557–65.

[16] Schwartz, C. S., and A. W. Franzmann. 1991. "Interrelationship of black bears to moose and forest succession in the northern coniferous forest." *Wildlife Monograph* 113:1–58.

[17] Craighead, J. J., and J. S. Sumner. 1982. "Evaluation of grizzly bear food plants, food categories, and habitat." In *A Definitive System for Analysis of Grizzly Bear Habitat and Other Wilderness Resources Utilizing Landsat Multispectral Imagery and Computer Technology, Wildlife–Wildlands Institute Monograph 1,* ed. J. J. Craighead, J. S. Sumner, and G. B. Scaggs, 44–84. Missoula, MT: University of Montana.

[18] Weiner, Jonathan. 1995. *The Beak of the Finch.* New York, NY: Alfred A. Knopf.

[19] Schluter, D. 2009. "Evidence for ecological speciation and its alternative." *Science* 323:737–41.

[20] Albon, S. D., T. H. Clutton-Brock, and F. E. Guinness. 1987. "Early development and population dynamics in red deer. II. Density-independent effects and cohort variation." *Journal of Animal Ecology* 56:69–81.

[21] Griffin K. A., M. Hebblewhite, H. S. Robinson, P. Zager, S. M. Barber-Meyer, D. Christianson, S. Creel, N. C. Harris, M. A. Hurley, D. Jackson, B. K. Johnson, L. D. Mech, W. Myers, J. D. Raithel, M. Schlegel, B. L. Smith, C. White, and P. J. White. 2011. "Predator phenology drives patterns of compensatory mortality for neonatal elk survival in the Pacific Northwest." *Journal of Animal Ecology* 80: in press.

[22] Smith, B. L., and S. H. Anderson. 2001. "Does dispersal help regulate the Jackson elk herd?" *Wildlife Society Bulletin* 29:331–41.

[23] Sawyer, H., and F. Lindzey. 2001. *The Sublette Mule Deer Study.* Unpublished report. Wyoming Cooperative Wildlife Research Unit, Laramie, WY: University of Wyoming.

[24] Gaillard, J. M., M. Festa-Bianchet, and N. G. Yoccoz. 1998. "Population dynamics of large herbivores: Variable recruitment with constant adult survival." *Trends in Ecology and Evolution* 13:58–63.

[25] Smith, B. L., and S. H. Anderson. 1998. "Juvenile survival and population regulation of the Jackson elk herd." *Journal of Wildlife Management* 62:1036–45.

Chapter 10: When Wolves Call
[1] Robbins, J. 2004. "Lessons from the wolf." *Scientific American* 290(6):76–91.
[2] Chadwick, D. 2010. "Wolf wars." *National Geographic* 217(3):34–55.
[3] Kellert, S. R. 1997. *Kinship and Mastery: Biophilia in Human Evolution and Development.* Washington, DC: Island Press.
[4] Daugherty, J. 1999. *A Place Called Jackson Hole: The Historical Resource Study of Grand Teton National Park.* Moose, WY: Grand Teton National Park.
[5] Bailey, V. 1907. *Wolves in Relation to Stock, Game, and the National Forest Reserves.* Washington, DC: USDA, Forest Service Bulletin 72.
[6] Berger, J. 2008. *The Better to Eat You With: Fear in the Animal World.* Chicago, IL: University of Chicago Press.
[7] Smith, D. W., and E. E. Bangs. 2009. "Reintroduction of wolves to Yellowstone National Park: History, values, and ecosystem restoration." In *Reintroduction of Top-Order Predators,* ed. M. W. Hayward and M. J. Somers, 92–125. Hoboken, NJ: Wiley-Blackwell.
[8] Bangs, E. 2009. "Wolves, elk, science, and human values." *Bugle* 26(5):79–83.

Chapter 11: Nitrogen
[1] U.S. Fish and Wildlife Service. 1997. *National Wildlife Refuge System Improvement Act.* Public Law 105-57. Washington, DC.
[2] Cole, E. K., and P. E. Farnes. 2007. "Estimating forage production and winter severity on the National Elk Refuge, Jackson, Wyoming." *Proceedings of the Seventy-Fifth Annual Western Snow Conference.* 137–40. Kailua-Kona, HI.
[3] Dobkin, D. S., F. J. Singer, and W. S. Platts. 2002. *Ecological Condition and Avian Response in Willow, Aspen, and Cottonwood Communities of the National Elk Refuge, Jackson, Wyoming.* Bend, OR: High Desert Ecological Research Institute.
[4] Geist, V., and M. H. Francis. 1991. *Elk Country.* Minoqua, MN: Northwood Press.
[5] Barmore, W. J. 2003. *Ecology of Ungulates and Their Winter Range in Northern Yellowstone National Park: Research and Synthesis, 1962–1970.* Mammoth Hot Springs, WY: National Park Service.
[6] Wagner, F. H., R. Foresta, R. B. Gill, D. R. McCullough, M. R. Pelton, W. F. Porter, and H. Salwasser. 1995. *Wildlife Policies in the U.S. National Parks.* Washington, DC: Island Press.

[7] Kauffman, M. J., J. F. Brodie, and E. S. Jules. 2010. "Are wolves saving Yellowstone's aspen? A landscape-level test of a behaviorally mediated cascade." *Ecology* 91(9):2742–55.

[8] Singer, F. J., L. C. Zeigenfuss, R. G. Cates, and D. T. Barnett. 1998. "Elk, multiple factors, and persistence of willows in national parks." *Wildlife Society Bulletin* 26:419–28.

[9] Murie, O. J. 1944. "Our big game in winter." *Transactions of the North American Wildlife Conference* 9:173–76.

[10] Craighead, J. J. 1952. *A Biological and Economic Appraisal of the Jackson Hole Elk Herd.* New York, NY: New York Zoological Society and Conservation Foundation.

[11] Preble, E. A. 1911. *Report on Conditions of Elk in Jackson Hole, Wyoming.* USDA Biological Survey Bulletin 40. Washington, DC: U.S. Government Printing Office.

[12] Hessl, A. E., and L. J. Graumlich. 2002. "Interactive effects of human activities, herbivory, and fire on quaking aspen (*Populus tremuloides*) age structures in western Wyoming." *Journal of Biogeography* 29:889–902.

[13] Smith, B. L., E. Cole, and D. Dobkin. 2004. *Imperfect Pasture: A Century of Change at the National Elk Refuge in Jackson Hole, Wyoming.* Moose, WY: Grand Teton Natural History Association.

[14] Campbell, R. B., and D. B. Bartos. 2001. "Aspen ecosystems: Objectives for sustaining biodiversity." In *Sustaining Aspen in Western Landscapes,* ed. W. Shepard, D. Binkley, D. L. Bartos, T. J. Stohlgren, and L. G. Eskew, 299–308. RMRS-P-18. Fort Collins, CO: USDA Forest Service Rocky Mountain Research Station.

[15] Bartos, D. 2001. "Landscape dynamics of aspen and conifers." In *Sustaining Aspen in Western Landscapes,* ed. W. Shepard, D. Binkley, D. L. Bartos, T. J. Stohlgren, and L. G. Eskew, 5–14. RMRS-P-18. Fort Collins, CO: USDA Forest Service Rocky Mountain Research Station.

[16] Smith, B. L., and R. L. Rogers. 1990. "Aspen management programs on the National Elk Refuge, Wyoming." In *Aspen, Sagebrush, and Wildlife Management: Proceedings of the Seventeenth Wyoming Shrub Ecology Workshop,* ed. H. G. Fisser, 15–18. Laramie, WY: Department of Range Management, University of Wyoming.

[17] Dieni, J. S., B. L. Smith, R. L. Rogers, and S. H. Anderson. 2000. "The effects of ungulate browsing on aspen regeneration in northwestern Wyoming." *Intermountain Journal of Science* 6:49–55.

[18] Adams, M. 1997. "Record elk numbers prove harmful to habitat." *Jackson Hole News,* February 19.

[19] Forester, J. D., D. P. Anderson, and M. G. Turner. 2007. "Do high-density patches of coarse wood and regenerating saplings create browsing refugia for aspen (*Populus tremuloides* Michx.) in Yellowstone National Park (USA)?" *Forest Ecology and Management* 253:211–19.

[20] North American Bird Conservation Initiative, U.S. Committee. 2009. *The State of the Birds, United States of America*. Washington, DC: U.S. Department of Interior.

[21] Singer, F. J., and L. C. Zeigenfuss. 2003. *A Survey of Willow Communities, Willow Stature and Production, and Correlations to Ungulate Consumption and Density in the Jackson Valley and the National Elk Refuge*. Unpublished report. Fort Collins, CO: U.S. Geological Survey, Biological Resources Division.

[22] Leopold, A. 1938. "Conservation Esthetic." *Bird-Lore* 40(2):101–9.

[23] Anderson, E. M. 2002. *Influences of Elk on Upland Aspen, Riparian Willow, and Associated Landbirds in and Near Jackson Hole, Wyoming*. M.S. Thesis, Laramie: University of Wyoming.

[24] Baker, W. L., J. A. Monroe, and A. E. Hessl. 1997. "The effects of elk on aspen in the winter range in Rocky Mountain National Park." *Ecogeography* 20:155–65.

[25] DeCalesta. D. S. 1994. "Effect of white-tailed deer on songbirds within managed forests in Pennsylvania." *Journal of Wildlife Management* 58:711–18.

[26] Dobkin, D. S., A. C. Rich, J. A. Pretare, and W. H. Pyle. 1995. "Nest site relationships among cavity-nesting birds of riparian and snowpocket aspen woodlands in the northwestern Great Basin." *Condor* 97:694–707.

[27] Trabold, V., and B. L. Smith. 2002. *Effects of Excluding Ungulates on Avian Use of Riparian Areas on Flat Creek, National Elk Refuge, Wyoming*. Final report. Jackson, WY: U.S. Fish and Wildlife Service, National Elk Refuge.

[28] Anderson, E. M. 2007. "Changes in bird communities and willow habitats associated with fed elk." *Wilson Journal of Ornithology* 199(3):400–409.

[29] Cross, S. P. 1985. "Responses of small mammals to forest riparian perturbations." In *Riparian Ecosystems and Their Management: Reconciling Continuing Conflicts*, ed. R. R Johnson, C. D. Zeibell, D. R. Patton, P. F. Ffolliott, and R. H. Hamre, 269–75. USDA Forest Service General Technical Report RM-120. Fort Collins, CO: U.S. Forest Service.

[30] Stuber, R. J. 1985. "Trout habitat, abundance, and fishing opportunities in fenced and unfenced riparian habitat along Sheep Creek, Colorado." In *Riparian Ecosystems and Their Management: Reconciling Continuing Conflicts*, ed. R. R Johnson, C. D. Zeibell, D. R. Patton, P. F. Ffolliott, and R. H. Hamre, 310–14. USDA Forest Service General Technical Report RM-120. Fort Collins, CO: U.S. Forest Service.

[31] Galbraith, A. F., T. L. Svalberg, and D. L. Tart. 1998. *The Flat Creek Riparian Survey*. Unpublished report to the National Elk Refuge. Jackson, WY: USDA Forest Service, Bridger-Teton National Forest.

[32] Berger, J., S. L. Montfort, T. Roffe, P. B. Stacey, J. W. Testa. 2003. "Through the eyes of prey: How the extinction and conservation of large carnivores alters prey behavior and biological diversity." In *Animal Behavior and Wildlife Ecology*, ed. M. Festa-Bianchet and M. Appolino, 133–55. Covello, CA: Island Press.

[33] Wilson, E. O. 1988. *Biodiversity*. Washington, DC: National Academy Press.

[34] Myers, N. 1988. "Threatened biotas: 'Hotspots' in tropical forests." *The Environmentalist* 8:187–208

Chapter 12: Lead

[1] Smith, B. L., and R. L. Robbins. 1994. *Migrations and Management of the Jackson Elk Herd*. National Biological Survey Resource Paper No. 199. Washington, DC: U.S. Department of the Interior.

[2] ———. 2007. "Migratory behavior of hunted elk." *Northwest Science* 81:251–64.

[3] Boyce, M. S. 1989. *The Jackson Elk Herd: Intensive Wildlife Management in North America*. Cambridge, U.K.: Cambridge University Press.

[4] Fowler, C. 2010. *Systemic Management: Sustainable Human Interactions with Ecosystems and The Biosphere*. New York, NY: Oxford University Press.

[5] Kerasote, T. 1993. *Bloodties: Nature, Culture, and the Hunt*. New York: Random House.

[6] Lubow, B. C., and B. L. Smith. 2004. "Population dynamics of the Jackson elk herd." *Journal of Wildlife Management* 68:810–27.

[7] Charture Institute. 2003. *The Jackson Hole Almanac: 2003 Facts and Data about Teton County Area*. Jackson, WY: Charture Institute.

[8] Kerasote, T. 2002. "Feeding on good intentions." *Alliance News: The Newsletter of the Jackson Hole Conservation Alliance* 23(1):1, 22–23.

[9] ———. 1998. "Birth control." *Bugle* 15:40–48.

[10] Dobson, A. P., P. J. Hudson, and A. M. Lyle. 1992. "Conservation biology: The ecology and genetics of endangered species." In *Genes in Ecology*, ed. R. J. Berry, 405–30. Oxford, U.K.: Blackwell Scientific Publication.

[11] Voipio, P. 1950. "Evolution at the population level with special reference to game animals and practical game management." *Papers on Game Research* (Helsinki) 5:1–175.

[12] Kramer, H. 1963. *Elchwald—der Elchwald als Quell und Hort Osptpreussischer Jagd*. Munchen, West Germany: BLV Verlagsgesellschaft.

[13] Nygren, T., J. Pusenius, R. Tiilikainen, and J. Korpelainen. 2007. "Moose antler type polymorphism: Age and weight dependent phenotypes and phenotype frequencies in space and time." *Annales Zoologici Fennici* 44:445–61.

[14] Wyoming Game and Fish Department. 2010. *Annual Report 2010.* Wyoming Game and Fish Commission, Laramie, WY.

[15] Wilcove, D. S. 2008. *No Way Home: The Decline of the World's Great Animal Migrations.* Washington, DC: Island Press.

[16] U.S. Fish and Wildlife Service. 2007. *2006 National Survey of Fishing, Hunting, and Wildlife-Associated Recreation.* Washington, DC: U.S. Department of the Interior.

[17] Burk, D. A. 1992. "The pitfalls of elk as a marketing tool." *Western Wildlands* 18(1):12–13.

Chapter 13: Prescription for Progress

[1] Smith, B. L. 2001. "Winter feeding of elk in western North America." *Journal of Wildlife Management* 65:173–90.

[2] Allred, W. J. 1950. "Re-establishment of seasonal elk migration through transplanting." *Transactions of the North American Wildlife Conference* 15:597–611.

[3] Anderson, C. C. 1958. *The Elk of Jackson Hole: A Review of Jackson Hole Elk Studies.* Cheyenne, WY: Wyoming Game and Fish Commission Bulletin 10.

[4] Cromley, C. M. 2000. "Historic elk migrations around Jackson Hole, Wyoming." In *Developing Sustainable Management Policy for the National Elk Refuge, Wyoming,* ed. T. W. Clark, D. Casey, and A. Halverson, 53–65. New Haven, CT: Yale School of Forestry and Environmental Studies Bulletin 104.

[5] Sawyer, H., F. Lindzey, and D. McWhirter. 2005. "Mule deer and pronghorn migration in western Wyoming." *Wildlife Society Bulletin* 33:1266–73.

[6] Dunham, F. 1898. "Proposal for winter game preserve on the Red Desert." *Recreation* 9:271–72.

[7] Sheldon, C. 1927. *The Conservation of the Elk of Jackson Hole, Wyoming. A Report to the Chairman of the President's Committee on Outdoor Recreation and to the Governor of Wyoming.* Washington, DC.

[8] Berger, J. 2004. "The last mile: How to sustain long-distance migration in mammals." *Conservation Biology* 18:320–31.

[9] Berger, J., S. L. Cain, and K. M. Berger. 2006. "Connecting the dots: An invariant migration corridor links the Holocene to the present." *Biological Letters* 2:528–31.

10 Glick, D. 2007. *End of the Road?* www.smithsonianmag.com/science-nature/pronghorn.html.

11 Western, S. 2002. *Pushed Off the Mountain, Sold Down the River*. Moose, WY: Homestead Publishing.

12 Naugle, D. E., K. E. Doherty, B. L. Walker, M. J. Holloran, and H. E. Copeland. 2010. "Energy development and greater sage-grouse." In *Ecology and Conservation of Greater Sage-grouse: A Landscape Species and Its Habitats*, ed. S. T. Knick, and J. W. Connelly. Berkeley, CA: The Cooper Ornithological Society and the University of California Press. http://sagemap.wr.usgs.gov/monograph.aspx.

13 Sawyer, H., R. Neilson, and D. Strickland. 2009. *Sublette Mule Deer Study (Phase II): Final Report 2007—Long-Term Monitoring Plan to Assess Potential Impacts of Energy Development on Mule Deer in the Pinedale Anticline Project Area*. Cheyenne, WY: Western Ecosystems Technology.

14 U.S. Fish and Wildlife Service and National Park Service. 2005. *Draft Bison and Elk Management Plan and Environmental Impact Statement* (final plan published in 2007). www.fws.gov/bisonandelkplan.

15 Hobbs, N. T., G. Wockner, and F. J. Singer. 2003. *Assessing Management Alternatives for Ungulates in the Greater Teton Ecosystem Using Simulation Modeling*. Fort Collins: Natural Resource Ecology Lab, Colorado State University.

16 Nowlin, D. C. 1909. *Annual Report of the Wyoming Game and Fish Commission*. Cheyenne, WY. "If the State of Wyoming wishes to stop hunting, propagate and deal in elk as a financial venture, then they should be cared for as domestic stock; but, if the policy of conserving and hunting them as wild game is to continue, it will not be wise to inaugurate the expensive system of continuous winter feeding. . . ."
Sheldon, C. 1927. *The Conservation of the Elk of Jackson Hole, Wyoming. A Report to Honorable Dwight F. Davis, Secretary of War, Chairman of the President's Committee on Outdoor Recreation, and Honorable Frank C. Emerson, Governor of Wyoming*. Washington, DC. "The conservation of the elk in Jackson Hole has become a problem directly as a result of the development of that section of the State of Wyoming. Formerly herds of elk from the southern part of the Yellowstone National Park and from the high regions along the Continental Divide immediately south of the Park passed Jackson on their autumn migration and wintered in the Green River Basin. The settlement of the country and the introduction of domestic stock deprived the elk of this wintering ground. As a result the migrating herds now winter in Jackson Hole and vicinity, a region of scant summer rainfall and heavy winter snows in which the elk are unable to get sufficient forage." P. 5

Murie, O. J. 1944. "Our big game in winter." *Transactions of the North American Wildlife Conference* 9:175. "There has been too much reliance on feeding of hay as a solution, rather than herd reduction to range carrying capacity. Hay feeding concentrates the animals and is the surest way to destroy the browse of a range where it is practiced."

Brown, R. C. 1947. "The Jackson Hole elk herd." *Wyoming Wildlife* 11(12):4–11, 29–32. "As range conditions become worse each year, with competition for it accelerating, and as the sportsmen's demand for a herd increase becomes greater each year, we find ourselves between the horns of a "Cervid dilemma." I hope that we are not viewing the last stand of America's elk herds: the fact is, I *know* that we are *not* if the emergency measures of the past, dictated by the circumstances of necessity, can be supplanted by well considered, permanent solutions."

Allred, W. J. 1950. "Re-establishment of seasonal elk migration through transplanting." *Proceedings of the North American Wildlife Conference* 15:597–611. "Feeding has been necessary in the past in order to maintain the Jackson elk herd, but game officials have recognized the feeding program as an emergency solution to an acute problem. It has been found that long feeding of artificial food and large concentration of these animals in close proximity promote disease with ultimate heavy losses."

Craighead, J. J. 1952. *A Biological and Economic Appraisal of the Jackson Hole Elk Herd.* New York, NY: New York Zoological Society and Conservation Foundation. "Elk numbers have been maintained but the basic problem of maintaining an elk herd within the carrying capacity of the winter range has been only aggravated through the years—not solved." P. 7

Anderson, C. C. 1958. *The Elk of Jackson Hole: A Review of Jackson Hole Elk Studies.* Cheyenne, WY: Wyoming Game and Fish Commission Bulletin No. 10. "The outstanding problem in the management of these elk concerns the almost total lack of natural winter range brought about many years ago by termination of migration to ancestral wintering grounds on the prairies outside Jackson Hole . . . This greatly reduced ground area is marked by hedging of browse plants and by vegetative departure from ecological climax which show a downward range trend. If continued this trend spells still more trouble for the elk . . ." P. 12

"Nearly fifty years of extensive winter feeding has not proved to be the solution to the "elk problem." . . . Feeding has maintained the population at a high level, but many of the faults blamed directly upon feeding programs in Jackson Hole resulted from the high population density rather than feeding. These faults include the concentration of elk in winter and spring, disease, and at least part of the range deterioration." P. 50–51

Blair, N. 1987. *The History of Wildlife Management in Wyoming*. Cheyenne, WY: Wyoming Game and Fish Department. "The single most acute game management problem [in Wyoming in the 1940s] was considered to be that of supplying winter range for big game. Elk were being fed in several areas but this was considered to be only a temporary measure and in no way a permanent solution to the shortage of wintering areas." P. 46

Platts, W. S. 2002. *Memo from Riparian Ecologist Dr. Platts to Refuge Manager Barry Reiswig Regarding Condition of Woody Plant Communities on the National Elk Refuge*. "To expect that elk herds, blocked from migrating and concentrated through artificial feeding do not cause the same changes in woody plant condition as cattle would under these same conditions is completely inconsistent with the western experience."

[17] Donahue, D. L. 2010. "Trampling the public trust." *Boston College Environmental Affairs Law Review* 37(2):257–316.

[18] U.S. Fish and Wildlife Service. 1997. National Wildlife Refuge System Improvement Act. Public Law 105-57. Washington, DC.

Index